# Scenic Splendor of China

# Scenic Splendor of China

Compiled by
CHINESE NATIONAL GEOGRAPHY

Wanxinda Culture Dissemination Co.,Ltd

This book can be ordered on the line
Website:http://www.cwxd.com
Email Address: Info@cwxd.com
Sales@cwxd.com

ISSN 1009-6337
CN11-4542/P

Published by Wanxinda Culture Dissemination Co.,Ltd

NO.39 Baohua Rd., Xinhua Town, Huadu District
.Guangzhou 510800 China

C & C JOINT PRINTING CO.,(GUANGDONG)LTD

*Printed in the People's Republic of China*

# Presented to You
# China's Most Beautiful Places

I collect precious memories, not precious objects. Indeed I have given away as gifts many objects, including things that went through thick and thin with me on scientific expeditions to the North Pole and the South Pole. But there are two exceptions that I keep and treasure. One is a plaque, the other a woodcut and they have accompanied me throughout my career.

The plaque is made of plastic, and bears the words "Landform Research Office" in red characters on a white background. That was where my professional life began in 1987. In the 10-odd years that followed I worked at that office or away from it conducting scientific surveys on the Qinghai-Tibet Plateau and at the North Pole and South Pole, and it was here that I learned the meaning of geography.

On the woodcut are engraved the words "Geographic Knowledge," the original title of *Chinese National Geography* when the magazine was first published in 1950. It was the calligraphy of Wu Chuanjun, a renowned scientist and one of the magazine's founders. In the early days, the magazine title was printed by hand-rubbing this woodcut block.

The plague and the woodcut encapsulate my career over the past 20 years. In 2000, three years after I moved from the Landform Research Office of the Chinese Academy of Sciences to work at *Geographic Knowledge*, we changed the magazine's name to *Chinese National Geography*. In 2005, the magazine celebrated its 55th birthday.

The motto of the launch issue, 55 years earlier, had been "A modern citizen must have basic geographic knowledge about the world and China." Half a century later, it was changed to "Opening the doors of nature and showing the essence of civilization." These different wordings reflect the magazine's different purposes. It marked a change in our role — from the task of spreading geographical knowledge to a conscious pursuit of and emphasis upon harmony between man and nature. Several years of doing this have shown that *Chinese National Geography*'s many original, authoritative and accurate reports and themes have been well received by readers, creating much public and media attention. For many Chinese it has even changed their understanding of geography.

As we were preparing for the magazine's 55th birthday, we wanted to make a special gift, one to express our good wishes and love for geography, especially for the natural and cultivated landscapes on earth, to salute the soil on which we live, and to present the beauty of China to our readers. So, the

October 2005 issue was a special edition with 400 extra pages — *Chinese National Geography: Scenic Splendor of China.*

It's really hard to tell how many beautiful places there are on China's 9.6 million square kilometers of land and its 3 million square kilometers of seas. Though many similar comparisons have been made, using different criteria, methods and categories, we still believed that we should make our own summary. I am sure you will fully appreciate this, as you browse the pages of this book.

Granted, a single issue of the magazine can by no means cover every beautiful place in China, but I still believe our painstaking work was worthwhile: the October magazines were sold out across China within two days of becoming available and we have had to reprint it time and time again; currently we are on the seventh impression, exceeding one million copies. We have received countless calls, letters and e-mails from readers, voicing one and the same message: China has so many beautiful places, a lifetime is not long enough to see them all.

The enthusiasm of readers and suggestions of overseas friends prompted us to go one step further: to help more people with an interest in China get a better understanding of the country. Hence this English edition of *Scenic Splendor of China.* You may be thinking about visiting China, or just arrived, or perhaps you already know a little; whatever the case, I am confident this book will be a big help in your appreciation of China's natural and cultivated landscapes.

Zhuang Zi, a great Chinese thinker some 2,000 years ago, said that the beauty of nature was beyond description. If reading this book inspires the same feeling in you, we shall feel highly gratified.

I am just reminded that some friends have told me that the October issue is being kept as a collector's item by many people who wish to treasure and cherish the beauty of China. I would like to say, "Me, too." Now, this special issue stands quietly in my bookcase, alongside the woodcut and the plastic plaque.

Li Shuanke
President and Editor-in-Chief
*Chinese National Geography*

# The Distribution of China's Most Beautiful Places

Shan Zhiqiang

We have just completed an unprecedented task — ranking the most beautiful places in China (mainly natural landscapes). We classified China's scenic spots into 17 categories and, with the help of several hundred Chinese experts and after all sorts of difficulties, finally completed the great project of ranking the most beautiful spots in each of the categories. Then we produced a map showing the locations of the top-ranking beauty spots.

I have this map in my hand right now — appreciating it and pondering on it at the same time.

I try to find a law applying to this map of China's most beautiful places, trying to find something instructive — for example, where do these most beautiful places concentrate and why?

The first thing I notice is that the place they concentrate is in southwest China, where Sichuan, Yunnan and Tibet meet, namely, the Hengduan Mountains area. Another area of concentration is the Tianshan Mountains in Xinjiang, and this I did not anticipate.

As we know, China steps down, geologically speaking, in three successive tiers. We discovered the law that China's most beautiful places are mainly located on the boundaries of these steps, in other words, at the "sloping edges" where two steps meet.

There are many beautiful landscapes on the "sloping edges" since they are in the areas where the earth's crust rises and falls sharply as the result of internal force. Here the land breaks and sinks to form valleys or cliffs, or bulges and rises to form mountains or ranges of mountains — a background of "sharp rise, sharp drop." Only with this kind of landform can mountains be angry, and currents swift. Against this "sharp rise" background, the land is nurtured by melted ice flowing down super-high snow mountains against the blue heavens; while "sharp drop" rivers cleave mountains into valleys and break up into waterfalls. Because of "sharp rise, sharp drop" even caves become deep and long.

China's terrain has three steps with two sloping edges, and these are home to many beautiful landscapes.

One such is the rim of the Qinghai-Tibet Plateau, a line whose ends join up to produce the ostrich-shaped outline of the Qinghai-Tibet Plateau. The ostrich's head is outlined by the Karakoram Mountains between China and Pakistan, its back by the Kunlun and Qilian mountains, its abdomen by the Himalayas, its feet and claws by the Hengduan Mountains.

It is height that makes mountains what they are, that makes them beautiful, so it stands to reason that the most beautiful mountains are to be found along the encircling rim of the Qinghai-Tibet Plateau, the highest place on earth. We know that plateau surfaces are rather flat and relatively low, so super-high mountains can be formed only along the edges of plateaus, i.e., at the sloping edge between the first and second steps. Owing to the big difference in elevation, glaciers and rivers scoured and cut their way deep into the earth, and thus high mountains appeared. As a result, this area has China's extremely high (over 4,500 meters above sea level) mountains. Their snow-capped peaks and glaciers make it the soaring ice and snow zone of all China. Each snow-capped peak is like a diamond, glittering and brilliant.

I believe that these snow mountains and glaciers are China's pride and glory. China has no grand waterfalls like the Niagara Falls in North America or the Iguassu Falls in South America. China does not have America and Canada's Great Lakes, nor vast prairies like the Argentine Pampas. But when it comes to snow mountains and glaciers, we take pride in those on the rim of the Qinghai-Tibet Plateau, more beautiful by far than the Alps or the Andes.

If you assume these mountains that fringe the Qinghai-Tibet Plateau comprise a world of nothing but ice and snow, you would be wrong. Totally ice-and-snow areas are neither unusual nor particularly moving; for example, high-latitude areas such as the

Arctic Circle and Antarctic Circle are covered with ice and snow all year round, and in northeast and northwest China winter snows change the color of mountains and rivers, but these things do not constitute beautiful scenery. However, the ice and snow here are different, being sub-tropical and temperate zone ice and snow. The extreme height causes low temperatures, allowing ice and snow to exist. In other areas on the same latitude there are either hot deserts or broadleaf tree zones, but this is a world of ice and snow, unique and beautiful. Hence this ice and snow exists in broiling temperatures, side by side with green trees.

If you could look down on it, you could just make out through the clouds the diamond necklace edge of the Qinghai-Tibet Plateau, like jewelry presented by the land to the sky. This line is undoubtedly the link between the most beautiful places in China. Without going there you cannot know how beautiful nature is, how beautiful China is.

Another law is this: if you draw a line along the boundary of the second and third steps, one end in Kaikukang Township in the northwest of Heilongjiang Province and the other in Dongxing City in Guangxi, you will discover this to be another beautiful landscape belt. On this belt, there are mountains such as the Greater Xing'an Mountains, the Taihang Mountains, Mount Hua, the Wudang Mountains, Shenlongjia, and Zhangjiajie, gorges such as the Shanxi-Shaanxi Yellow River Gorges and the Three Yangtze Gorges, waterfalls such as the Hukou, Huangguoshu and Detian waterfalls; even more noticeable are the beautiful caves, among them Shuanglong (Double-Dragon), Tenlong (Flying-Dragon), Xueyu (Snow Jade), Huanglong (Yellow Dragon) and Zhijin (Gold-Weaving) caves, and karst formations such as Tiankeng (Heavenly Pit), Difeng (Earthly Rift Valley), Shujing (Vertical Shaft) and Tianshengqiao (Natural Bridge).

This line is not only a landscape belt; it is also a boundary line in terms of nature, style and number. It bisects China: east of the line scenic natural landscapes are relatively scarce, while west of it they abound. But in terms of places of cultural interest, the situation is reversed; thus, this line can be seen as the boundary between dense and sparse natural landscapes and places of cultural interest. The line is also a boundary between places of Han cultural interest and ethnic minority cultural interest. East of the line are many places of Han cultural interest while west of it (with the exception of the Central Shaanxi and the Sichuan basins) places of ethnic minority cultural interest predominate. Apart from numbers, the line is also a boundary between different natures and styles of landscape. East of the line, the landscapes are more refined, elaborate, misty and graceful; west of it, they are more imposing, majestic, bold and rugged. In terms of breathtaking beauty, China's three geological steps are also aesthetic steps, rising from east to west, each one more breathtaking than the one before, and reaching its climax on the Qinghai-Tibet Plateau.

But there is one exception — a landscape belt east of this line, namely China's coastline and offshore island chains. Once past the scenically sparse plains and hill areas, another transformation takes place — from continent to sea. If we look at the continental shelf as a continuation of the land, then this constitutes the fourth step. And, as before, the most beautiful landscapes are to be found on the "sloping edge" — at the divide between land and sea. Under the action of such factors as sea waves, marine organisms and river estuaries, its topography is transformed into landscape beauty.

It strikes me from the map that the area that is most densely populated, most developed and richest in cultural heritage is also something of a scenic vacuum. What is the significance of this? I am reminded of the theory raised by a famous scholar who divided human needs into five levels: the first, most basic needs are physiological and include food and clothing; the next are safety needs; then come belongingness and love needs; the fourth are esteem needs; last come self-actualization needs, including aesthetic appreciation. Successive waves of people left gorge and mountain areas where the terrain is beautiful but life is hard, and came to the alluvial plains and basins, which are the least scenically endowed but are the richest and easiest places to live. As a result these became the most densely populated areas.

From this we can arrive at a law of scenic landscape distribution: scenic landscapes are to be found in sparsely populated areas rather than in densely populated ones. Our results — that our most beautiful places are concentrated in the west of China — are in direct contradiction to the fact that China's national-level scenic areas are mostly located in the densely populated east of the country.

This reminds me of the famous Hu Line. The geographer Hu Huanyong plotted a line between Aihui (present-day Heihe) in Heilongjiang and Tengchong in Yunnan, dividing China into two parts — northwest and southeast. Mr. Hu discovered a special relationship between China's population distribution and land area: the area northwest of the Hu Line accounted for 64 per cent of China's total land mass but only 4 per cent of its population; southeast of the line, on the other hand, constituted 36 per cent of the land and a dramatic 96 per cent of the population. Replace the word "population" with "national-level scenic areas" and it still holds true.

Similarly, China's railways, highways and more developed areas are also concentrated southeast of the Hu Line.

Why should it be this way?

One thing strikes me. When we were discussing "China's Most Beautiful Mountains" and "China's Most Beautiful Gorges" we did not know to whom we should present the awards. For example, none of the winners — Namjagbarwa, China's most beautiful mountain, the Yarlung Tsangpo Grand Canyon, our most beautiful gorge, or the Hulun Buir, our most beautiful grasslands — would step up to accept an award, nor could we find people to represent the winners. When you get down to it, "China's Most Beautiful Place" and "National Level Scenic Area" are simply labels that men have attached to them.

In the past we thought of titles, remarks, poems and articles about scenic landscapes as descriptions, pictures and reflections of them ... but with the passage of time, we end up thinking of those symbols as the landscapes themselves.

When we see Lushan, Huangshan mountains and Mount Tai, or appreciate the West Lake, Dongting Lake and Taihu Lake, many words, poems,

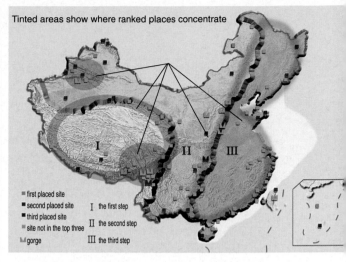

Tinted areas show where ranked places concentrate

- first placed site
- second placed site
- third placed site
- site not in the top three
- gorge

I   the first step
II  the second step
III the third step

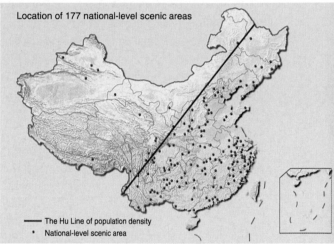

Location of 177 national-level scenic areas

—— The Hu Line of population density
•  National-level scenic area

paintings and legends spring to mind. But when we see snow mountains such as Namjagbarwa, Gongga and Meili and glaciers such as Rongpu, Tomur and Midui, remote from the attentions of literati and artists of the past, we reach out in vain for the vocabulary to describe them.

Our selection of Namjagbarwa as supreme among China's Most Beautiful Mountains will change it not one jot; it will remain silent in the clouds and mists of southeastern Tibet with its luxuriant forests and roaring rivers, just occasionally glancing at the human world. It was there for hundreds of thousands of years before the appearance of man. Totally indifferent to the opinion of mankind, it just keeps silent.

And I know that China has many Namjagbarwas, keeping silent....

# Members of the Review Committee of China's Most Beautiful Places

**Feng Zongwei** member of the Chinese Academy of Engineering. Engaged for years in research on forest environment and ecological environment recovery.

**Lu Yaoru** member of the Chinese Academy of Engineering. Geologist. Engaged for years in research on karst geology.

**Liu Dongsheng** member of the Chinese Academy of Sciences. Quaternary Period geologist, ancient vertebrate zoologist, and environmental geologist. Winner of National Natural Sciences Award. Engaged mainly in loess research.

**Liu Jiaqi** member of the Chinese Academy of Sciences. Volcano geologist and Quaternary Period geologist. Has carried out much systematic research on volcano geology and Quaternary Period environment and geology.

**Ren Jizhou** member of the Chinese Academy of Engineering. Vice-chairman of Chinese Grassland Society. Among the founders of modern Chinese grassland science.

**Sun Honglie** member of the Chinese Academy of Sciences. Soil scientist, geographer and land resources expert. Former vice-president of the Chinese Academy of Sciences and former vice-chairman of the International Council of Scientific Unions. For years directed the comprehensive exploration of Qinghai-Tibet Plateau sponsored by the Chinese Academy of Sciences.

**Shao Dazhen** professor of the Central Academy of Fine Arts. Famous fine arts critic. Editor-in-chief of *Art Research* and *World Art*.

**Li Wenhua** member of the Chinese Academy of Engineering. Former chairman of the Chinese Ecological Society. Mainly engaged in research on forest ecology.

**Wu Chuanjun** member of the Chinese Academy of Sciences. Cultural geographer and economic geographer. Former chairman of International Geographical Union.

**Wu Liangyong** member of the Chinese Academy of Sciences and the Chinese Academy of Engineering. Architect and urban designer. Chairman of World Habitat Society, and director of Research Center for China Human Settlements Environment.

**Chen Shupeng** member of the Chinese Academy of Sciences. Geologist, cartographer, and remote sensing applied scientist. Former chief compiler of the *Atlas of China*.

**Fan Di'an** vice-president of the Central Academy of Fine Arts. Deputy director of the Theoretical Committee of Chinese Artists Association. Engaged for years in research on Chinese fine arts.

**Shi Yafeng** member of the Chinese Academy of Sciences. Geologist and glaciologist. Among the pioneers of China's modern glaciology research.

**Nie Zhenbin** famous aesthetician. Vice-chairman of Chinese Society for Aesthetics. Former deputy director of Aesthetics Office of Institute of Philosophy, Chinese Academy of Social Sciences.

---

## Representatives of Societies

Zhang Guoyou, secretary-general, Geographical Society of China

Wang Mili, secretary-general, Geological Society of China

Yang Xuezhi, secretary-general, Chinese Society of Landscape Architecture

Wang Xingguo, secretary-general, China's Forest Landscape Resources Evaluation Committee

Chen Anze, chairman, Tourism Geography and Geological Parks Society

## Writers

Ai Ping, Bai Tao, Chen Qingchao, Ding Liangfu, Dong Peiqin, Du Hong, Gao Tunzi, Gu Dao, Huang Yi, Jean Bottanzzi, Jiao Husan, Jin Zhiguo, Jing Shi, Kong Shan, Li Bosheng, Li Qingsong, Li Yide, Lin Ruizhu, Liu Jian, Liu Liangcheng, Ma Wenqi, Ma Yi, Ma Zhanfeng, Niu Huang, Peng Hua, Ruo Shui, Shen Wei, Shu Ting, Sun Min, Tie Mu'er, Wang Xufeng, Wei Tiemin, Xiang Hongxing, Xiao Yan, Yang Yang, Yang Yichou, Yang Yong, Yao Feng, Yi Min, Yu Jian, Zai Zai, Zhang Fan, Zhao Mu, Zhu Yong, Zhuang Yanping, Zi Jin

## Photographers

A Chou, Bao Lixia, Chen Hao, Chen Jianxing, Chen Weihai, Chen Xun, Chen Jundong, Dai Songtao, Du Zequan, Dorje Phuntsok, E Bo, Fu Lanke, Galen Rowell/ c, Gao Bing, Gao Tunzi, Gao Dongfeng, Gao Jiang, Ge Yuxiu, Gu Xiaojun, Hao Pei, Hou Heliang, Hou Jianhua, Huang Dingsheng, Hui Huaijie, Jiang Guangshu, Jiang Jiang, Jiang Ping, Jin Long, Ju Jianxin, Lai Yuanhai, Li Bin, Li Bing, Li Bosheng, Li Dan, Li Haijie, Li Guiyun, Li Quanju, Li Xin, Li Xueliang, Liang Feng, Liu Jianming, Liu Shizhao, Long Yunhe, Lu Hailin, Lu Huachun, Lu Suibin, Lu Jiangtao, Lu Shunping, Luo Dinglai, Luo Jiakuan, Lü Linglong, Ma Peihua, Ma Zhanfeng, Macduff Everton, Mark M. Lawrence/c, Mei Zhiqiang, Pan Songgang, Qi Bolin, Qin Hongyu, Qin Yuhai, Qu Limin, Ren Chuncai, Sang Yuzhu, Shan Zhiqiang, Shen Putian, Shen Xuexi, Shen Rui, Shi Huaixun, Shi Ming, Shui Xiaojie, So Hing-Keung/c, Song Shijing, Sun Jianhua, Sun Jun, Sun Youbin, Sun Yuefeng, Sun Zhijun, Teng Bin, Tian Jieyan, Tong Kaijian, Wang Jiafu, Wang Hongwei, Wang Jianjun, Wang Keju, Wang Shuzhou, Wang Shuilin, Wang Tong, Wang Xingguo, Wang Yaoshi, Wang Yue, Wang Zhengming, Warren Morgan/c, Wu Jianguo, Wu Sa, Xiao Yunji, Xian Yunqiang, Xin Xin, Xu Zhaopang, Xu Zheng, Xue Yao, Yao Xichun, Yang Guang, Yang Hua, Yang Jinghua, Yang Shaoquan, Yang Xiao, Yang Xueguang, Yang Yichou, Yang Zhi, Yuan Xuejun, Zeng Linghong, Zhang Chaoyin, Zhang Dehai, Zhang Jiangqi, Zhang Tao, Zhang Xinmin, Zhang Yan, Zhang Zhan, Zhao Cheng'an, Zheng Fuxin, Zheng Yunfeng, Zhong Mingji, Zhu Qingfu, Zhu Xuewen, Zhou Wei, Zhou Xiaolin, Zhou Yong, Zhuang Yanping

## Pictures Provided by

Ding Liangfu, Tong Kaijian, GIMR&PSCJA2005, Penghu County Government, PSCJA TOP PHOTO, Xu Fengxiang, Yu Zhangtao.

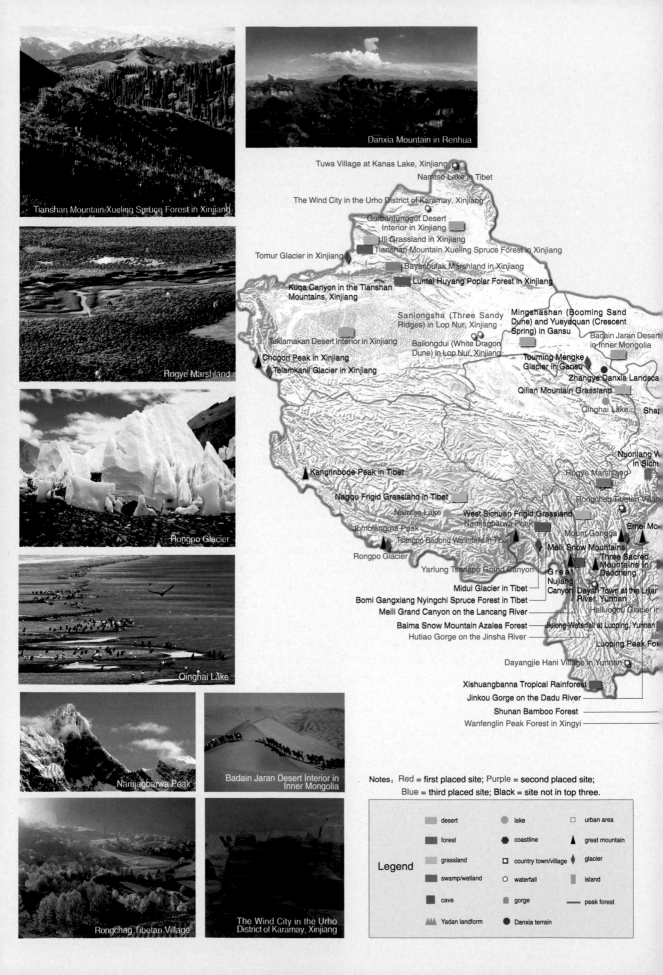

# Location of China's Most Beautiful Places

Xing'an Larch Forest in the northern part of the Greater Xing'an Mountains

East Hulun Buir Grassland in Inner Mongolia

Sanjiang Plain Marshland

Zhalong Marshland

Xilin Gol Grassland in Inner Mongolia

Changbai Mountain Mixed Korean Pine and Broadleaf Forest

Benxi Water Cave in Liaoning

Tianchi Lake on the Changbai Mountain

Liaohe River Delta Marshland

Shichahai District in Beijing

Changli Golden Beach

The Yellow River Delta Marshland

Miaodao Islands

Chengshantou in Rongcheng, Shandong

Shanxi-Shaanxi Gorge on the Yellow River

Taihang Gorges

Badaguan Scenic Area in Qingdao

Mount Tai

Hukou Waterfall on the Yellow River

Suzhou Old City

Putuoshan Island

Huangshan Mountains

West Lake

Three Yangtze Gorges

Ziyuan Village Group in Jiangxi

Tenglong Cave in Hubei

Quartz Sandstone Peak Forest of Wulingyuan

Granite Peak Forest of Sanqingshan Mountain

Huanglong Cave in Hunan

Longhu Mountain at Yingtan

Nanji Islands

Landscape

Wuyi Mountain in Nanping

Dayushan Island

uizhou

Dajin Lake in Taining

uoshu Waterfalls in Guizhou

Chongwu Beach in Fujian

Yeliu in Taiwan

Zijiang River - Baijiaozhai - Langshan Mountain

Danxia Landform

Gulangyu in Xiamen

Tailuge (Taroko) Gorge

Landscape

Danxia Mountain in Renhua

Penghu Islands

o Yangshuo

Dapeng Peninsula Beach in Shenzhen

aterfall in Guangxi

toric Center of Macao

Victoria Bay in Hong Kong

u Island

Hailing Island

Linjin and Nanding Islands in Fujian

ng Dong in Liping, zhou

Dongzhaigang in Qiongshan, Hainan

Jianfeng Ridge Tropical Rainforest in Hainan

ng Bay in Sanya, Hainan

in Guizhou

Xisha Archipelago

Nansha Archipelago

Xisha Archipelago

Yalong Bay in Sanya, Hainan

Lijiang River Landscape from Guilin to Yangshuo

Tsangpo Badong Waterfalls in Tibet

Zhijin Cave in Guizhou

Gulangyu in Xiamen

Yarlung Tsangpo Grand Canyon

East Hulun Buir Grassland in Inner Mongolia

# Contents

## China's Ten Most Beautiful Mountains

## China's Seven Most Beautiful Danxia Landscapes

## China's Five Most Beautiful Lakes

# China's Five Most Beautiful Peak Forests

# China's Five Most Beautiful Deserts

# China's Ten Most Beautiful Gorges

# Contents

## China's Three Most Beautiful Yadan Landforms

## China's Eight Most Beautiful Coastlines

## China's Six Most Beautiful Waterfalls

## China's Six Most Beautiful Glaciers

## China's Ten Most Beautiful Forests

# Contents

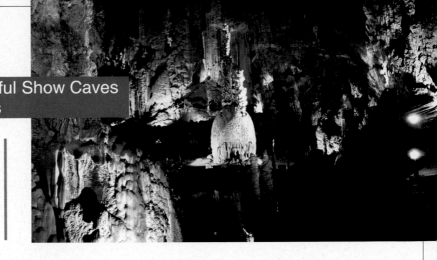

## China's Six Most Beautiful Show Caves Plus the Record-holders

## China's Five Most Beautiful City Districts

## China's Six Most Beautiful Country Towns and Villages

# China's Ten Most
# Beautiful Mountains

Western slope of Mount Gongga

## Ranking

China's Ten Most Beautiful Mountains

Number *1*

# Namjagbarwa Peak
## *Paradise in the Clouds*

Namjagbarwa, seen from the entrance to the Yarlung Tsangpo Grand Canyon.

The first impression of Namjagbarwa started with a glimpse of its beauty during my first visit to Tibet in 1998.

How beautiful is Eastern Tibet at the height of summer?

The blue river water reflects the snow capped peaks, and the crystal-clear glacier winds through the green primal forests. The brightly-colored Tibetan villages, the graceful and healthy girls, herds of cattle and sheep on the pastures, and wild flowers of every color in full bloom form a picturesque landscape unfolding before the eyes of every traveler who, too long fettered by the bustle of city life, yearns for the beauty of a natural paradise.

I stood surrounded by the magnificent Tibetan scenery on the Serkhyim La Mountain, gazing at wave after wave of towering mountains. The white clouds surged like tides, casting down shadow after shadow from the snow-capped mountaintops. A bank of cloud attaching itself to the mountain was carelessly driven off by a gust of wind, and this was the sharply defined triangular peak of the Namjagbarwa exposed to view. I was immediately captivated by its peerless beauty.

But almost immediately, the rolling clouds veiled the mountain once more. When I tried for a second glance, the sky was clouded again and the mountain shyly hidden.

The Namjagbarwa area is a sea of clouds all year round. Some foreign explorers came here via India in the early 20th century in the hope of seeing its scenery and taking pictures, but they waited for a month in vain; the mountain was heavily shrouded in thick cloud, and they had to leave amidst sighs and regrets. Even local people can see its true appearance only on a few days each year.

Tibetans regard Namjagbarwa as the road to Heaven, a holy place which ordinary people

The main peak of the Namjagbarwa pierces the clouds. The legend goes that deities descended from Heaven and burned mulberry leaves on the summit; so the streaming clouds on the high-altitude winds are the smoke from those mulberry fires. The canyon dwellers show matchless reverence for this steep and dangerous peak.

must absolutely not disturb. They describe it as "a burning fire of snow and lightening" and "piercing the blue sky like a long-handled spear." And they have endowed it with many outstanding titles too: god of heroism, the spoiled and beloved son of the extraordinary beauty and valor of the Nyanqentanglha Mountain, the brutal brother who cut off the head of his kinsman in a fight, and the self-respecting husband not allowing others to see

his grief at being separated from his wife.

The Tibetan metaphors originate from unseen, unverifiable traces of the deities, but scientific metaphor has added a bold stroke to the age-old legends.

Geologists have likened Namjagbarwa to a divine needle that pacifies the earth.

The Qinghai-Tibet Plateau and the Himalayas have been hailed as mankind's last land of mystery, and even regarded as the "golden key" that can open the gate of the earth. The most mysterious thing is that at each end of the Himalayas two peaks stand on the mysterious tectonic knots: at the eastern end stands Namjagbarwa (7,782 meters) and at the western end Nanga Parbat (8,125 meters), the world's ninth highest peak. They not only attach the magnificent length of the Himalayan chain to the southern edge of the Qinghai-Tibet Plateau, but also fix the Eurasian plate to the Indian plate.

Lhoba and Monba people live here. Their way of life and religious beliefs are very traditional, and they have a unique morality. Simple people, they live mainly on hunting, and are frank and hospitable. They still preserve the primitive life style of slash-and-burn farming. The children in the photo are from Zhibai Village.

Perhaps it is coincidence, but in the age-old legend of the "Battle at Menling" which is in the vicinity, Namjagbarwa was the divine sword used by King Gesar to rescue the people and safeguard the earth.

In fact, the mystery of the mountain itself is no less interesting than the mystery of these geographical phenomena.

Namjagbarwa has existed for over 700 million years. The first piece of land in the Himalayan region to emerge from the sea, it deserves its title of Number One among the Eastern Himalayan Mountains. The changes it has experienced are beyond the reach of our current knowledge.

Even today, we still know very little about Namjagbarwa. This is not because we do not admire its outstanding beauty; rather, because the mountain has deliberately made a curtain of the clouds and mists, made a protective screen of the canyon and torrents, thus preventing any alien creature from disturbing the solitude and silence that it has enjoyed for hundreds of millions of years.

Those who have been close to it all know that once you have taken the routes to Namjagbarwa, no others really deserve to be called "dangerous." The first human conquest of Namjagbarwa did not happen until 1992, but the great Japanese climber Takei Yoshitaka was killed in the previous attempt in 1991. Over 10 years have passed, and sophisticated mountaineering equipment means "everything is possible" today, but no one else has tackled it again.

A month after seeing the mountain, I personally traveled part of the "routes" — walking through the Yarlung Tsangpo Grand Canyon.

It is a mystical canyon, concentrating every type of fine environment and natural beauty, where you can experience the majesty of the

The complex geology of the Yarlung Tsangpo Grand Canyon area, where Namjagbarwa stands, and strong plate tectonic movements are the origin of many steep mountain cliffs and constant earthquakes and avalanches. The magnificent but dangerous cliffs and unpredictable weather combine to make the ascent of Namjagbarwa extremely difficult. A Chinese team attempted the peak for the first time in 1984, but failed. A joint Sino-Japanese team repeated the challenge in 1991, but to no avail. A third attempt was made on October 30th, 1992 resulting in final success for the Sino-Japanese team. It is still a target for mountaineers everywhere today.

Amazon and the austerity of the Himalayas. Passing through it, you are enshrouded in heavy mist, sometimes winding around your fingertips, sometimes circling over your head, as if you were living in a fantastic wonderland.

But extreme beauty often goes shoulder by shoulder with death.

After the great Medog earthquake in 1950, everything within the 100 kilometers from the village of Gala to the canyon became a no-man's land, haunted almost only by beasts. On the densely wooded mountain ridges, we could walk only on a small path heavily overgrown with overhanging tree branches and bushes.

The road to paradise is never smooth and level. While the body climbed nearly perpendicular rocks, and the hands grabbed for dear life onto weeds and small branches, beneath the feet flowed the guardian of the sacred mountain, the Yarlung Tsangpo, its seething waters roaring

Monba people walking in dense woods at the foot of Namjagbarwa.

From the foot of Namjagbarwa, several hundred meters above sea level, upwards to the 7,782-meter summit, is the following sequence of ecological systems: tropical low mountain evergreen or semi-evergreen monsoon rain forests; sub-tropical mountain evergreen and semi-evergreen broadleaf forests; warm temperate mid-mountain evergreen conifer forests; cold temperate sub-alpine evergreen conifer forests; sub-frigid alpine bushes and grassy marshland; and sub-frigid alpine ice source and frigid ultra-alpine ice and snow. This great abundance of mountain eco-systems, mountain vegetation forms and bio-communities is compressed in one tight area; it can be rated the best in the world, and as a world natural museum of mountain vegetation forms. (right page)

down, water mist rising as the waves hit the rocks of the river's many dangerous shoals.

In the mysterious land of the canyon where the earthquake collapsed glaciers to the ground, Namjagbarwa and Gala Village face each other on opposite banks of the river, forming the entrance of the canyon.

The wind swept past the tattered prayer flags on a high platform. The colorful lichen lay as thick as a wool carpet, the six-character-mantra inscribed on a *mani* stone in earth was faintly visible. The dilapidated walls left after the earthquake reminded us of the mysterious land where Buddhist monks had chanted sutras. But they were a reminder too that Namjagbarwa's violent character originates from the fact that it stands at the heart of the powerful upthrust of the Himalayas.

After making a horseshoe bend, the roaring river turns south, carrying branches and leaves with it. Because of this unusual turn, warm air from the Indian Ocean has an easy passage into the Qinghai-Tibet Plateau, and the canyon has become the warmest and moistest region on the plateau.

Straining to look up at the summit until our necks could bend no further back, we could see only as far as the mountain mid-levels, surrounded by chains of white clouds. Several huge ice falls broke through the clouds, sweeping down the misty body of the mountain into the river below, as if huge jade dragons had been ordered to leave the divine halls on the summit to rush upon the intruder at the foot.

A faint mist rose from the bottom of the valley, a light cascade of cloud slipped smoothly from the top, floating white clouds encircled the mountain, and the sword-like gleaming snow peaks were partly hidden, partly visible.

Then, like passing through the final gateway to Heaven, the cold and lifeless atmosphere suddenly disappeared. There was the white of curling clouds, the green of jade-green leaves, the purple of carving-like grapes, and the red of blossoming flowers. The beauty of a dimly discernible fairyland was there right in front of my eyes.

Looking at the mountain from afar, all you can see are floating clouds. Looking at it from nearby, over 5,000 meters above you, it is almost invisible. It stands in the world, but very few people can see it. It is hidden in the clouds, but connected with the world we all inhabit.

Man has never stopped longing for a distant, unattainable paradise, and Namjagbarwa is precisely that.

Mount Gongga is the Number One peak in the Hengduan Mountains and amongst the most famous peaks in the world. At 7,556 meters, it is the highest peak in Sichuan Province, and called "the King of Sichuan Mountains." Looking up at Gongga's main peak and its sister mountains from Quanhua Beach at its western foot, one is sure to be fascinated by a most beautiful picture of the white snow and the green vegetation.

China's Ten Most Beautiful Mountains

Number 2
# Mount Gongga
*Where the Wind Stops to Rest*

The Hehe (Lotus) Lake is so called because of the lotus flowers that grow in it. The lake lies in the Kuxirong Mountain Valley 3,000 meters above sea level in Pusharong Township, Kangding County, 120 kilometers from Kangding Town and between Mount Gongga and Lake Odkyi scenic area.

The word "*Gong*" in Tibetan means permanent snow cover, and "*ga*" means white, so Gongga means white snow cover. Mount Gongga is located in the Miya Raogang area, a traditional Tibetan Buddhist administrative division. Local people also call it Miya Gongga.

It was nearly dusk when we reached No. 3 camp on Mount Gongga so we went to the viewing platform at dawn the next day. It was a solitary wooden pavilion, conspicuous against the white snow.  Far off in the distance, the morning sun rose in the east, directing an unforgettable "blockbuster" over the main peak and over the tens of other peaks connected with it.

A streak of blood-red light pierced the dark clouds, revealing over 50 steep snow-capped summits, shining, dazzling and thrusting into the clouds like golden swords. On the other side of the valley were pinewoods, dark green in the sunshine, like green flower garlands above the mountain fields girdling the immeasurably high

Quanhua Beach is located at the western foot of Mount Gongga, over 20 kilometers from Liuba Township in Kangding County. A spring rises at the top of the beach, and the stream is 900 meters long and 100 meters wide. There are eight terraces, each with between two and four pools of different shapes and sizes. The surface area of the pools is between a seventh and a third of a hectare and the water is between 40 and 70 centimeters deep. They present a magnificent sight, like a giant dragon about to fly. The pools are clear and clean, adorned with flowers and waterweeds. Picture shows local herdsmen.

The Hehe Lake covers an area of 33 hectares. This picturesque freshwater lake on the high mountain is surrounded by pastures, woods and snow mountains.

golden snow-capped summits.

This "Sunshine over the Golden Mountain" is the most famous scenic view in the Gongga area.

At this tranquil time and place, the mountains and the sky, the sun and the clouds were showing their earliest beauty and brilliance of the day.

The air was quiet and peaceful. Apart from the clicking of camera shutters, there was not another sound. The cold wind that had been blowing when we came out was gone. I felt as if I was standing at the same time and spot as the Indian M.S Kohli who scaled Mount Qomolangma in 1965 and sighed from the bottom of my heart. At this moment, it seemed like even the wind had stopped to rest.

The world's summit reveals its loftiness on occasion.

Number *3*

# Qomolangma Peak
## *The Soul's Sentinel*

The Qomolangma Peak seen from the base camp on the northern slope. (above)

The Qomolangma Peak straddles the border between China and Nepal. The main peak of the Himalayas, it is also the world's highest mountain. It has been called the most revered of all mountains and the world's third pole. The whole mountain looks like a huge pyramid, mighty and imposing. Its surrounding landforms are very steep and dangerous, making its ascent very difficult. (right)

It has been a long-cherished dream of mine to climb the Qomolangma Peak, but when I approached it for the first time in my life, it still took me by surprise.

As we arrived at Rongpu Monastery, and drove up a gentle slope, the driver said in hushed tones, "Now we can see it." We lowered our heads and stretched forward to look, and saw a dark green mountain moving towards us. There was not a great deal of snow — a few snow belts lying up the slopes.

"Majestic and beautiful," someone shouted. I said, "Its beauty takes your breath away." Everyone laughed, saying that my altitude sickness must be very bad. The team leader said, "Qomolangma is sitting, protecting Mount Changzheng, Mount Jianshe and Mount Zhangzi on its right hand, and Mount Guangming on its left. The sash of its skirt is flying toward us. Look, this is the middle Rongpu Glacier...."

## Beautiful Flag Cloud and Soft Knife

Its streaming flag clouds are Qomolangma's most famous sight.

There were no clouds against the backdrop of the azure sky. The rosy glow of morning covered a third of the summit. Called "Sunshine over the Golden Mountain," it is often seen in photographs, but in this tableau, a long thin ribbon of white silk appeared from the summit. It has long been called the "flag cloud" because it looks like a streaming flag.

Looked at from a distance, it always hangs silently on the summit, giving the impression of calmness and beauty. But in fact, it is just the time when the goddess is in a rage: no expert climbers would dare go near it at this time and if they meet it en route, they can only retreat, or they will stay on the mountain for life.

I remember once, when we were attempting an adaptive climb of a 7,790-meter height, the wind gradually grew stronger and the route rope

was blown up into the air in an arc. The snow was whipped up and cut into our faces like a knife. At 7,540 meters, we could no longer stand steady; we looked round only to see the flap cloud appearing on the summit.

Headquarters ordered us to turn back immediately. The overwhelming force of the gale completely put a stop to our advance.

The tent was torn apart and the oxygen cylinders and equipment stored in it were all blown away. I don't know why, but that day I was completely free of fear; on the contrary I was excited; the team struggled on in the teeth of the snowstorm, the flag cloud hanging elegantly from the summit. What a magnificent scene!

I love striking contrasts like this.

## Qomolangma in Mist

Looking at flowers in a mist is an artistic conception. The Qomolangma Peak in the morning or evening mist is another artistic conception, but fumbling in the mist at zero distance from the summit was something else altogether.

When I finally stood on the summit of the mountain, I was encircled by clouds and mist. Had it not been for the long colorful prayer streamers and the cheering climbers, I would not have dared believe I had reached the top.

Standing there, I had no lofty sentiments about the smallness of the mountains below, rather grievance and distress. My eye at the viewfinder misted over, my tears flowing. I could never express this state of mind. Even today I

Since the 18th and 19th centuries, explorers and mountaineers from other countries went to the Qomolangma Peak (aka Mount Everest) to explore its secrets. In the 1920s and 30s seven attempts were made by foreign mountaineering teams to climb Qomolangma via the north face, but all failed. A Chinese mountaineering team conquered the summit from the north face for the first time in 1960. Even today, it is still a cherished goal of countless mountaineers. (right) The above photo shows the Rongpu Monastery below the north face.

Qomolangma is 8,844.43 meters above sea level. Its northern slope is in Tingri County, Tibet, China and its southern slope lies within Nepal. It is surrounded by towering mountains for a radius of 20 kilometers, more than 40 of them over 7,000 meters high. They include the famous Lhotse (the world's 4th highest peak) about three kilometers away to the south and Makalu (the world's 5th highest peak) to the southeast. There are other first-rate peaks beyond. Kangchenjunga (8,586 meters), the world's 3rd highest peak, is to the southeast, and to the west stand Gyachung Kang (7,986 meters), Cho Oyu (8,201 meters) and Gasherbrum (8,027 meters).

cannot answer the questions "Why climb mountains?" and "Why climb Qomolangma?"

Only one thing was clear. When I took off my gloves, my hands could touch the clouds and mist on the top of the world. It was cold, moist and somewhat bleakly beautiful.

## Qomolangma's Beauty Originates from My Heart

There are countless snow-capped mountains in the world. There are also countless snow-capped mountains that have been given special divinity by the people who love, worship and fear them. Indeed almost all those who live near to the snow mountain that they guard believe that mountain to be the most beautiful, the most sacred.

Qomolangma is beautiful to me, because it's part of my very bones. The reason it's the most beautiful is that it originates from my heart.

Number *4*

# Meili Snow Mountains

*Guard of Honor for the Snow God*

Miancim Peak in the Meili Snow Mountains

The Meili Snow Mountains are located on the border between Deqin County in Diqing Tibetan Autonomous Prefecture, Yunnan and Zayu County in Tibet, lying deep in the Hengduan Mountains where the three waters of the Jinsha, the Lancang and the Nujiang rivers converge.

It is a holy place of pilgrimage for Tibetan Buddhists, and the first of the eight great divine mountains in the Tibetan region. They connect with Mount Adongeni to the north, and with Biluo Snow Mountain to the south. Its main peak is Kang Karpo, 6,740 meters above sea level, the highest peak in Yunnan Province.

To local Tibetan people, Mount Kang Karpo is the residence of their guardian deity and they believe that once the mountain is scaled by man, the god will leave, and without the god's blessing, disasters will happen. In the Feilai Temple, Miancim, the wife of Kang Karpo, is worshipped. She is a pretty woman riding a wild deer. In fact, whether Miancim or Kang Karpo, all the 13 high peaks in the Meili Snow Mountains have an enchanting beauty.

The four seasons in the snow-capped Meili are distinctly different. Between the foot and the summit are several systems of plant distribution, transitioning from the tropical zone to the northern frigid zone. Above the snowline, there are steep snow-capped peaks encircled by clouds and mist, but below it are evergreen vegetation and flowers in full bloom.

Glaciers are widely distributed in the Meili. Here low-latitude and high-altitude monsoon modern marine glaciers have developed. They wind down along the valley, their ice tongues stretching down to the 2,700-meter forest area, just over 800 meters away from the waters of the Lancang River. The natural proto-ecology around the glaciers is well preserved, representing the diverse natural and geographical

Kang Karpo, the main peak in the Meili Snow Mountains, means the "God of the Snow Mountains" in Tibetan. Nearby, 13 peaks line up, like a guard of honor for the God.

characteristics of the xerothermic valley of the Lancang River.

The complex geology of the Hengduan Mountains and the changeable climate in the low-latitude snow mountains mean that the Meili are fraught with fatal dangers. Violent glacier movements have aggravated fissures in the mountain body still further, giving rise to suspended glaciers, hidden ice crevices, ice avalanches and snow avalanches. When a joint Sino-Japanese team climbed the mountain, a snow avalanche killed all 17 members and even today, the Meili Snow Mountains still remain unconquered.

In late autumn and early winter every year, pilgrims from Tibet, Sichuan, Qinghai and Gansu travel hundreds of kilometers to pay homage to the sacred mountain. They prostrate their way round the holy mountain for one to two weeks. This is called "circumambulation" by local residents. Each Goat Year in the Tibetan calendar, the number of "circumambulators" increases a hundredfold. Picture shows religious activities at the foot of the Meili Snow Mountains.

The Huangshan Mountains, or Yellow Mountains, renowned worldwide for its "strangeness," is located in southern Anhui Province. It is the central mountain of the mountains in southern Anhui and the watershed between the Yangtze and the Qiantang river systems.

In antiquity it was known as Mount Yi, but its name was changed because, as legend has it, it was here that the Yellow Emperor ascended to Heaven and became immortal. Huangshan covers an area of 250 square kilometers. Its mountain body is extraordinary and magnificent, with dangerous cliffs thrusting skywards, and crisscrossed by quiet gullies. It is a place where strangeness, depth, magnificence, sheerness and mystery concentrate in a single body.

It has 72 named peaks. They are either towering and powerful, or steep and beautiful, laid out in graceful disorder and naturally formed. The Tiandu (Heavenly Capital) Peak, Lianhua (Lotus) Peak and the Guangming (Brightness) Peak stand high in the central area, all 1,800 meters above sea level. The Huangshan Scenic Area radiates from this center, sinking into deep valleys or rising into high peaks, forming classical peak and forest configurations.

Huangshan has four superb characteristics: No rock without a pine tree and no pine without a curious form; range upon range of grotesque peaks and outlandish rocks, seemingly sculpted; flying clouds and moving mists like seas seething into a vast expanse of roaring waves; every spring gushing with crystal clear water, flowing in every season irrespective of droughts. The other attractions are the sunrise, sunset, bright colors, Buddhist light and hoar frost.

The praises of visitors of every age are condensed in the saying, "All famous sights under the sun are found at Huangshan" — the magnificence of Mount Tai, the steep height of Huashan, the smoky clouds of Hengshan, the flying falls of Lushan, the grotesque rocks of Mount Yantang and the pleasant coolness of Emei. The Ming Dynasty (1368-1644) geographer Xu Xiake wrote the following famous lines, "Once you've seen the Five Sacred Mountains, you've no need to visit another mountain. Once you've seen Huangshan, you don't need visit the Five Sacred Mountains."

## Number 5
# Huangshan Mountains
## *God's Miniature Landscape*

The sea of clouds over Huangshan is a unique natural spectacle that also enhances the beauty of the landscape. The grotesque peaks and strange rocks appear fantastic and bewildering and are thrown into relief by the erratic clouds and mists, rendering them even more grotesque, more strange.

# Number *6*

# Three Sacred Mountains in Daocheng

## *Landmark of "Shangri-La"*

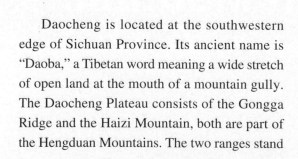

Daocheng is located at the southwestern edge of Sichuan Province. Its ancient name is "Daoba," a Tibetan word meaning a wide stretch of open land at the mouth of a mountain gully. The Daocheng Plateau consists of the Gongga Ridge and the Haizi Mountain, both are part of the Hengduan Mountains. The two ranges stand opposite to each other north and south, accounting for almost a third of the area of Daocheng. From these meandering ranges emerge the three sacred mountains of Daocheng — Xiannari, Yangmaiyong and Xianuoduoji.

Since the ancient times, the three sacred mountains have been a sacred place for Tibetan

Buddhism.

Xiannari (6,032 meters), the main peak of the three sacred mountains, is first among Daocheng's high peaks. According to legend it is the incarnation of the Buddhist Goddess of Mercy Guanyin or Avalokitesvara. Its slopes are vast, its gradient gentle, the mountain looks like Great Buddha sitting in peace, graceful and poised. Yangmaiyong (5,958 meters), the southern peak, means the Bodhisattva Manjusri, dignified and stately, gentle, quiet, noble and impeccable. Xianuoduoji (5,958 meters), the eastern peak, means Buddha with warriors' hands, resembling a young man of strong

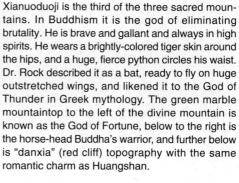

Xianuoduoji is the third of the three sacred mountains. In Buddhism it is the god of eliminating brutality. He is brave and gallant and always in high spirits. He wears a brightly-colored tiger skin around the hips, and a huge, fierce python circles his waist. Dr. Rock described it as a bat, ready to fly on huge outstretched wings, and likened it to the God of Thunder in Greek mythology. The green marble mountaintop to the left of the divine mountain is known as the God of Fortune, below to the right is the horse-head Buddha's warrior, and further below is "danxia" (red cliff) topography with the same romantic charm as Huangshan.

The famous sacred lake Wusehai, or "Five-color Lake," lies between Xianari and Yangmaiyong, 4,800 meters above sea level. The lake is oval-shaped, and covers an area of 0.7 hectare. The snow mountains are reflected in the water and under refracted light, the lake surface produces five different fantastic colors.

character, tall and handsome.

Within a thousand square kilometer range of the three mountains, rise dozens of peaks, like a myriad of stars surrounding the moon. To Tibetan thinking, they represent Buddhist gods performing their role of protecting the three sacred mountains.

At their foot lie wide pasturelands, crisscrossed by brooks and streams flowing gently into lakes. There are woods and bushes too, and waterfalls formed by melting ice and snow creating captivating scenes. Year after year, they have flowed in silence and this land of mystery had remained unknown to the world outside.

In 1928, when the American botanist Dr. Joseph Rock advanced into the Gongga Ridge area, "the clouds suddenly cleared to reveal the true look of the Thunder and Lightning Guardian — a sharply defined pyramid." Stumbling upon this holy place by mistake, he shouted in surprise, thus bursting open the gate of the "garden preserved by God."

Many years later, the name of "Shangri-La" — the imaginary utopia described in James Hilton's novel *Lost Horizon* — was given to this place, a paradise sought by many people troubled by worldly life, and stirred up an unabating tide of "Returning to Nature."

Yangmaiyong has a pyramid-like peak. Joseph Rock described it as the world's most beautiful snow mountain.

China's Ten Most Beautiful Mountains

Number *7*

# Chogori Peak
*Distant Mystic Land*

Carrying supplies up the mountain.

How should we define the "most beautiful" peak?

Another mountain lover Wang Haozheng (author of *Dangerous Footsteps*) said, "The peaks I find safe and reliable are the most beautiful."

By this criterion, even if every other mountain in the world were chosen, the dangerous Chogori (K2) could not perhaps qualify. Even so, I want to look at it with the

140 years later than the Englishman Henry Godwin-Austen in 1856.

Chogori is a transliteration of the Tajik language, meaning "high, great and magnificent." Internationally, it is better known as K2, which is the only major mountain in the world that has surveyor's notation as its common name (K stands for Karakoram, 2 means it was the second peak listed).

Like Qomolangma which was once incomparably remote from us, Chogori still looks very remote from us.

Chogori lies in the middle of the Karakorum Range. Its southern slopes are in Pakistan, and its northern face is part of Yecheng County in Xinjiang Uygur Autonomous Region.

There are six ridges on Mount Chogori: The northwestern-southeastern ridge is the principal ridge line of the Karakorum range, also the dividing line between China and Pakistan. The other five ridges are the northern ridge, the western ridge, the northwestern ridge and the southwestern ridge. It is more difficult to climb the Karakorum Range from the northern slope than from the southern slope. It is even more difficult to climb Chogori.

First of all, the dangerous slope with an average gradient of 45°, as if shaped by knives and axes, are covered with steep cliffs and sliding chutes arising from avalanches. From the base camp on the northern slope to the summit, the

"most beautiful" eyes.

In fact, we should have done so much earlier. Chogori stands on the Chinese-Pakistan border, but the first time China surveyed this absolutely masculine peak at a close distance was nearly

Chogori is a steep and dangerous peak. It is internationally renowned for its challenging climb; of the world's 14 peaks above 8,000 meters, it is the most difficult mountain to climb. (top left)

Because of its special landform and geomorphology, ropes have to be fixed along the whole route from the advance camp to the summit. The gradient is between 80° and 85° in some places, and there is almost nowhere for team members to rest. (above)

The dangerous landform and changeable weather have caused a death rate as high as 30% in attempts on the summit. Climbers have dubbed it "the wild peak." (bottom left)

vertical height difference is 4,700 meters. It is the biggest vertical height difference among the peaks 8,000 meters above sea level in the world. The steep slope makes it extremely difficult to find safe places for setting up high-altitude camps. If too many climbers climb the same route, it is very likely that the later climbers have to climb non-stop for lack of intermediate camps, thus greatly increasing the risks.

Even grimmer than the steep slope is the nasty weather on the Karakorum Range.

Between May and September, none of the lucky mountaineers have ever had one whole week of fine weather for decades, although this is the best season for mountain climbing.

"The peak from which the fewest return" has left the following bloody statistics: Since 1954, only 164 people have scaled the summit, and 49 others have been killed; of all the 8,000-meter-plus peaks, it has the third highest death rate.

Since the 1990s, commercial mountaineering has developed rapidly on a global scale.

It is no exaggeration to say that, provided you have the time and the money, even if you are blind or one-legged, there will be commercial exploration organization willing to try and take you to the summit of Qomolangma, the highest peak in the world.

But, the Karakorums are not the Himalayas, and Chogori is not Qomolangma. This great peak is for expert climbers only. Here, no commercial mountaineering organization will provide you any services, and even top-class mountaineers will choose their climbing partners with a particularly eagle eye. The leader of a Japanese K2 team said sternly when organizing his team in 1982, "We are professional climbers, and all know that if we run into trouble at a height of 8, 000 meters on K2, it is absolutely impossible to get help. If you do not have the confidence and determination to face possible trouble, you should not go!"

This is Chogori! In the eyes of the top-class mountaineers, it is the most beautiful peak; it is its matchless danger that seduces them. This is also the reason why, following last century's enthusiasm for the Himalayas, the focus of professional mountaineering has now shifted to the Karakorums.

The Chinese team bid farewell to K2 in 2000 following an unsuccessful attempt. A strong Chinese Tibetan expedition failed again in 2002 in the teeth of an unexpected blizzard, just when it was within sight of success at a height of 8,400 meters. On July 27th, 2004, seven Chinese Tibetans finally scaled the summit at their third attempt.

Renna, an outstanding Tibetan climber (sadly killed by a rock fall on May 27, 2005 while attempting the last unscaled 8,000-meter peak, Jiashulbrum 1) said that he resolved in a third attempt on K2: succeed or die trying.

This is what the great Chogori means to the world's top-class mountaineers.

Chogori is surrounded by dozens of high peaks. By its eastern side are Mount Buluo'at (8,051 meters), Mount Jiashulbrum 1 (8,080 meters) and Mount Jiashulbrum 2 (8,028 meters). More than 20 other peaks stand 7,000 meters high. There is an abundance of mountaineering resources.

# Number *8*

# Kangrinboqe Peak

## *Home of All the Gods*

Kangrinboqe has a reddish large level platform at mid level, with jagged edge from ice and snow weathering. On the platform is a ring of cut troughs. Its permanently snow-capped summit commands all other peaks.

The Gandise Mountains lie from east to west in the south of Tibet. Among its steep cliffs and glaciers is its main peak, Kangrinboqe, located in Pulan County, Ali Prefecture in Tibet. It is a world-acknowledged holy mountain and regarded as the centre of the world by Hinduism, Tibetan Buddhism, Bon (the primitive religion of Tibet) and ancient Jainism.

The 6,638-meter Kangrinboqe is the source of four of Asia's major rivers. From the snow-capped summit rise the Shiquan (which becomes the River Indus), the Maquan (which becomes the Yarlung Tsangpo River and then the Brahmaputra), the Xiangquan (which becomes the Sutlej River) and the Kongque (which becomes the Ganges). Kangrinboqe's crystal-clear and white snow-capped summit and Mount Namnani, which Tibetans call the "Mountain of the Goddess," face each other from afar. Between the two lie the beautiful holy and pure Mapangyongco Lake and the changeable Devil Lake — La'angco.

Kangrinboqe is formed of several thousands-of-meter-thick layers of ordinary gravels, pebbles, grit and conglomerate. The different properties of these strata, tectonic changes from different directions, and long-time natural weathering have combined to form today's odd-looking "Mountain of the Goddess." Among the myriad of peaks, Kangrinboqe shoots directly skywards, its icy, snow-covered summit merging as one with the white clouds. The natural platform halfway up the mountain, the result of prolong weathering, looks like a hanging ladder flanked by sheer precipices leading to the clouds. It makes the whole mountain even more majestic and imposing and worthy of the name of the "heaven-made divine palace."

There are five temples in Kangrinboqe's vicinity — the Nianri, Zhilapu, Songchu Jiangzha, and Sailong temples. Kangrinboqe has always been an enchanting place for pilgrims and explorers, but up till today, not a soul has been able to scale the holy mountain or dared to trespass into the centre of this world.

Laqu Valley at the foot of the mountain.

China's Ten Most Beautiful Mountains

Number *9*

# Mount Tai
*Totem of Ancient China*

Mount Tai's status as the first among China's five sacred mountains originates in mythology. After the death of Pan Gu, creator of the universe in Chinese mythology, his head was turned into Mount Tai and the mountain became the leader of the five sacred mountains.

As every Chinese knows, it is at Mount Tai that human culture and nature are most perfectly and harmoniously blended. It has been worshipped by people since antiquity, and regarded as the symbol of social stability and national unity. A saying about the Chinese people goes that "If Mount Tai is at peace, the whole country is at peace." It was the only mountain in China where ancient emperors offered sacrifices to Heaven and Earth. Seventy-two emperors and sovereigns went to Mount Tai, meeting with royalty and nobles, bestowing high ranks, and making inscriptions on stone tablets. Men of letters made pilgrimages here, composing impromptu poems and writing inscriptions. There are over 20 complexes of ancient architecture and over 2,200 stone tablets and steles on Mount Tai, making the mountain "first under the sun." It has always been a source of inspiration for artists and scholars.

The Mount Tai panorama begins with the Middle Gate to Heaven. Standing here and looking north, we saw the whole mountain, forested and fortified, its steep staircases hanging high, just like a huge Chinese ink painting where light and dark set each other off to perfection. Without noticing, we reached the pine woods where the 18th century Emperor Qianlong wrote the inscription: "The Finest Place on Daizhong (i.e., Mount Tai)." The stone steps are hidden under the woods, their edges overgrown with moss. Both stones and moss are dark in color and it takes just a glance to know that they carry the dust of years. The surface of the steps is moistened by water from the springs.

Reaching the Arch of Immortals Ascending, and looking up, the staircase of the Eighteen Hairpin Bends looks just like a scaling ladder to the sky, hanging between Xiangfeng (Soaring Phoenix) Ridge and Feilong (Flying Dragon) Rock and swinging in the air. Climbing this stone staircase felt like heaving myself up every step of the way.

As soon as we came to the Street of Heaven, the heavy fog suddenly disappeared; the tourists seemed to have descended from the sky, strolling at their ease. As we approached the Ancestral Hall of Azure Clouds, having passed the Imperial Sacrificial Altar and the Confucian stele with the line of "On top of Mount Tai, the world looks small," a light wind blew up, and the sun came out flooding the street in sunlight. Looking down to the foot of the mountain, everything became "a small world." Everything was visible: fields and households, rivers and mountains, as if freshly purified, a paradise world of peace and simplicity.

After passing the Azure Cloud Temple, the Grand View Peak cliff inscriptions appeared. There are still over 1,500 cliff carvings on the mountain, mainly in the temples and along the two sides of the "Hairpin Bends." It can well be called a "Calligraphic Museum of the Chinese Dynasties." The Grand View Peak has the mountain's largest collection of rock carvings from past dynasties. They include "the sky is as high as the

Rock carving

The "Slow Eighteen Hairpin Bends" go from the foot of the mountain to the Dragon Gate, the "Neither Quick Nor Slow Eighteen Hairpin Bends" go from the Dragon Gate to the Arch of Immortals Ascending, and the "Quick Eighteen Hairpin Bends" to the South Gate to Heaven. There are a total of 1,630 steps.

mountain," "only the sky is above," "ascend the peak to attain perfection." The matchless beauty of the calligraphy aside, the bold and uninhibited manner of the words alone is enough to show the imposing presence of Mount Tai.

The ancient theory of the "five elements" combines the season, colors and position to determine the good or ill fortune. Mount Tai is situated in the east, belongs to spring, and is the incarnation of the Green Emperor. The east is the place where all things grow. The four seasons begin with the spring, when everything comes back to life and grows. The beginning of spring is Tai (peace), so Mount Tai naturally became the place for offering luck and happiness. Therefore, the ancient people also believed that Mount Tai was the place of immortals, the mysterious paradise, the symbol of China's ancient civilization and belief.

# Number *10*
# Emei Mountain
## *The Rise from A Basin to the Heaven*

Outside the red walls of the Baoguo Temple, tall dark trees on two sides shade out the sunlight and keep out the fierce summer heat.

The Baoguo Temple is the entrance to Mount Emei. It was first built by the Taoist Ming Guang. Its original name was the Hui Zong Hall, meaning the hall where Confucianism, Buddhism and Taoism come together. They can all regard the majestic Emei as their common spiritual home, where they fuse as one. Visitors could not but extol its "greatness."

What you see of the mountain ultimately depends upon how you decide to go up it.

In the past, there was no choice. Whatever great mountain you climbed, you had to go up every step for yourself. Even the Tang Emperor Taizong himself, the ruler of a mighty land, took several days to get to the summit on foot. Today, visitors can drive, take a cable car or walk.

Walking from the Wannian Temple to the Qingyin Pavilion, you feel as if you were in a pure and empty world. Gently-flowing brooks on two sides, and two small bridges connect at this meeting place. Emei is so huge that even just this section of it seems to encompass a universe. The bird sing, breezes waft, springs

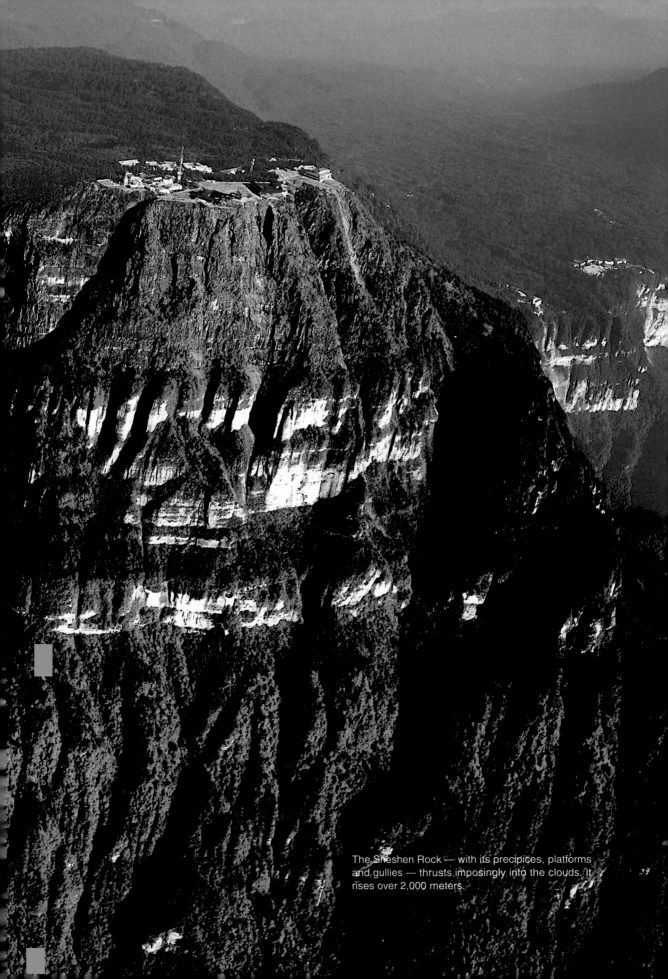

The Sheshen Rock — with its precipices, platforms and gullies — thrusts imposingly into the clouds. It rises over 2,000 meters.

The Wannian Temple is one of the eight major temples on Emei. It was first built in the Jin Dynasty (265-420), and was called the Puxian Temple. The name was changed to Baishui Temple in the Tang Dynasty (618-907), and then to Baishui Puxian Temple in the Song Dynasty (960-1279). Kept in the temple are the pattra leaf sutra, a Buddha tooth relic and an imperial seal, honored by Buddhists as the "three Buddhist treasures on Emei." (left)

The mountain is located in the southwest of the Sichuan Basin, seven kilometers from Emeishan City. It extends 23 kilometers from north to south, covering 115 square kilometers. The western slope is gentle, the eastern one steep. Its main peak, the Wanfo (Ten Thousand Buddhas) Summit, stands 3,099 meters above sea level, 2,600 meters above the plain at its eastern foot. (right)

gush and leaves fall. Their beauty is so simple that words can hardly describe them.

The Qingyin Pavilion means the pavilion of gentle singing and is a quote from a poem by the Jin Dynasty (1115-1234) poet Zuo Si: "Why use string and wind instruments when there is gentle music from the mountains and waters?" Indeed, the terms high peak, flowing water, empty valley and serene mist can all be used to describe this place. In a pure, exquisite world, why play an ancient zither!

In fact, as long as you are at Emei, you are immersed in an atmosphere of harmony. Both the works of nature and of man can reach magnificence. And the two are so inseparable so that you can appreciate their beauty from many angles.

When we reached the Golden Summit, we saw a big piece of flat ground, like a huge rock had landed from elsewhere and embedded itself into the mountaintop. Its 3,000-meter height is just right. At the bottom of the mountain, we were in short-sleeves, but here at the top, we wrapped up in warm outerwear. But Emei pierces through the clouds and mist just like this, greeting winter and summer like this. No wonder that it too aspires to the status of "Number One mountain under the sun." This preeminence lies in its great abundance of natural sights and cultural legacy.

Below the Sheshen Rock was a sea of heavy clouds. In the far distance, glowing streaks emerged, changing hues, as the red sun thrust out to rend apart the dark mass of clouds. The cloud sea quickly turned dark blue. As the sun rose, the feeling of heaviness gradually lifted, and the sea of clouds changed back to proper clouds.

In fact, this process is repeated every day, but for those witnessing the sunrise on the Golden Summit, it must be the most beautiful.

The significance of the Golden Summit to Emei is like the perfect happy ending to a story. At this moment, Emei is just like a benevolent and kind-hearted old man, at peace with himself and with the world. Azaleas, monkeys and tourists, they can all find happiness on the mountain.

In fact, however you get to the top, you will always see the beauty and greatness of Emei! ▯

# China's Five Most
# Beautiful Lakes

**Ranking**

1. Qinghai Lake               (Qinghai)
2. Kanas Lake              (Xinjiang)
3. Namtso Lake             (Tibet)
4. Tianchi Lake            (Jilin)
5. West Lake              (Zhejiang)

On the vast Qinghai-Tibet Plateau, waves on Qinghai Lake tell tales of this beautiful body of water.

# Number *1*
# Qinghai Lake
## *An Inland Sea*

It is birds that have lived around the Qinghai Lake for the longest time, complimenting the lake and shoreline scenery, and being complimented in return. Visitors keep their distance, showing their respect for the real residents of the lake area.

With the coming of November, flocks of sheep can walk safely on the ice. The frozen lake shrinks the distance between the pasturelands on either side and the experienced shepherds bore holes through the ice allowing the sheep to drink the lake water below.

Over a thousand years ago, so the beautiful story goes, the Tang Dynasty (618-907) Princess Wencheng married the Tibetan king Songzan Gambo. Before she set off on her long journey to Tibet, the Tang emperor gave the princess a magic mirror, telling her that whenever she missed home, she should look into the mirror and her home, the city of Chang'an, would appear in it. Having covered quite a distance on her journey, the princess and her entourage arrived at the Sun and Moon Mountain on the borders of ancient Tibet, where she began to feel homesick. Producing her magic mirror, she did indeed see the image of her home, and realizing that she would probably never be able to return, tears began to roll down her cheeks. Just then, she remembered her sacred mission of cementing friendship between the two ancient kingdoms through marriage and cast the mirror away. Where the mirror landed, a beautiful lake appeared — the Qinghai Lake. The princess pressed on across the mountains. As she trudged on westwards, her tears became a river flowing west, following her footsteps. Now it is known as the Daotang River.

In history, people referred to the Qinghai Lake as the "West Sea", while the Tibetans, Mongolians and the ancient Beihe tribe all had their own names for the lake. Western Queen Mother was said to be the female chieftain of the ancient Qiang tribe who lived in the lake area 3,000 years ago. Once she invited King Mu of Zhou, who came in a carriage drawn by eight horses to visit Yaochi — another name for the Qinghai Lake. Western Queen Mother is seen as the goddess of the lake and the myriads of migrating birds that keep returning there year after year are the same birds that kept a lookout for King Mu of Zhou.

Beautiful legends like this one made the Qinghai Lake sacred in the eyes of emperors. According to historical documents, many emperors, starting with Tang Dynasty rulers, came here to offer sacrifices and erect memorial tablets to show their respect for the lake. In the eighth century, the Tang Emperor Xuanzong gave the god of the lake the title "Duke of Guangrun" and formally named the water Qinghai Lake. Lake worship ceremonies became regular and elaborate established events during the Qing Dynasty (1644-1911), ceremonies used

to be conducted at remote locations began to be held at the lakeside. People believed that the 18th day of the 7th lunar month was the birthday of Western Queen Mother, which became the official day for the services, as ceremonies had been held on this day ever since the time of the Tang Emperor Xuanzong. During the Republican period (1911-1949), senior political and military figures such as the Kuomintang prime minister T. V. Soong and the northwest warlord Ma Bufang officiated at memorial services to worship the lake. Now the ceremony has returned, but as a folk cultural activity.

The legends are beautiful to be sure, but the facts, as we all know, are that the Qinghai Lake is China's largest inland lake and its largest salt water lake. It was created, some 40 million years ago, as a result of the collision of the Indian and Eurasian plates and the lifting of the Himalayan Sea to create the mountain chain. Geological studies show that rivers used to empty into the lake and then drained out into the ancient course of the Yellow River in the southeast. Later, continued movement of the earth's crust saw the rising of the landmass east of the lake which blocked the flow of the lake water, creating a drainless lake which only received water but had no outflow.

Being 3,260 meters above sea level, and with a circumference of 360 kilometers, the lake has a water area of 4,340 square kilometers and contains 77.8 billion cubic meters of water. It is encircled by mountains on all sides — the Datong Mountain in the north, the South Qinghai Mountain in the south, the Xiangpi Mountain in the west and the Sun and Moon Mountain in the east. The east-west flowing Daotang River empties into the lake.

People who have never been there often imagine that its water is blue, but come close, you'll discover that the lake water is by no means

During July and August, rape comes into full flower, as the Qinghai Lake shows off its most dazzlingly beautiful scenery. This is the time, too, that migrating birds get ready for their southbound journey.

a single color — at different times of day, during different seasons, and when viewed from different angles, its waters appear in different colors — light green, blue, green, gray, orange, yellow.... So wide a range of different colors in a single lake casts light on why it was referred to as the "Fairy Sea" during the Han Dynasty (206 BC - AD 220) some two thousand years ago and why it was described as "a scene that rightly belongs in Heaven."

Equally interesting is the hill, known as Haixin, or Mid-lake Island, right in the heart of the lake. With an area of one square kilometer, this island stands over 30 kilometers

This scene can only be witnessed between March and May when birds come over here to breed on the lakeshore and islets. Their arrival injects the lake with boundless vitality.

Przewalski's gazelles are amongst the world's most endangered animals, with a population of only about 300. They are under first-class protection in China and can be seen only in the area around the Qinghai Lake.

distant from the south shore, measures 2.3 kilometers from east to west and 0.8 kilometers from north to south. Its top rises a few dozen meters above the surface of the water. The strong wind on the lake, as sharp as a knife, has carved the rocks into pointed pagoda shapes. The Mid-lake Island is also known as Longju Island or Little Dragon Island. Legend has it that if a female horse was driven to the island when the lake was frozen during winter, it would be pregnant with a baby as good as a "little dragon". The fact is that adequate snowfall in winter and spring and ample precipitation in summer and autumn provide plentiful water resources for grass around the lake, making it a vast and fertile grazing pasture. The "Qin horses" raised locally were known for their strong bodies and fast speed as long as 2,000 or more years ago during the Warring States Period (220-280). During the Sui Dynasty (581-618), people cross-bred the horse here with Kazak and Fergana horses to develop a unique breed known as the Qinghai horse, which was most popular for fighting wars. During the Tang Dynasty that followed, the Sun and Moon Mountain became a place for horse and tea trading and the horses thus bought were enlisted in the cavalry.

During the Tianbo reign period (742-756) of the Tang Dynasty, forces under the command of the famous general Gegehan launched a surprise attack by night and took Shibo, breaking into the heart of the Tubo Kingdom and occupying the area around the lake. They had a fortress erected on the Mid-lake Island, but with the passage of time, there is no trace of it visible. The islet, surrounded by water, remote from the "dust of the world," is like a beautiful Buddhist holy ground and as early as the Han Dynasty, religious devotees began to have temples built there. When the lake froze over, stocked up with food supplies, they would cross to the islet to meditate and recite Buddhist sutras, and this tradition is still followed today, as Buddhist

Perhaps to escape the hassle of migrating birds on Egg Island, cormorants build their homes on the Haixipi Island on the opposite side of the Qinghai Lake. This solitary rock is a virtual symbol of the Bird Island. The desolate environment and the vitality of the cormorants are reminders of the vast and wildness of the Qinghai Lake.

monks worship Buddha and incant sutras, in their pursuit of Buddhahood.

There are three other islets in the lake. Actually they are three huge rocks, known to locals as the "cooking pot supporting rocks," It is said that when the Tang Dynasty monk Xuan Zang passed here on his journey to India to bring back Buddhist scriptures, he placed his cooking pot on the rocks. Their distance from the shore has so far protected the islets from human intrusion and allowed them to remain bird paradises.

The most charming islands in the lake are the Egg Island and the Haixipi Island, both lying in the northwest of the lake, not very far from the oasis of Buh River, the largest of its kind, whose water empties into the lake. Facing each other, the two islands are also called "Bird Islands" because of the large number of birds residing on them.

The Egg Island, also known as the Lesser West Hill, rises barely 7.6 meters above the water level. Small as it is, it is home to the greatest number of birds, over a hundred thousand of them, including the bar-headed goose, great black-headed gull and red-neck gull. Every spring, huge flocks of these birds come to this traditional home of theirs to build nests and raise their chicks. The whole islet is densely populated with birds and many bird eggs have given rise

to its name.

The Haixipi Islet, high in the east and low in the west, is four times the size of the Egg Island, roughly 4.6 square kilometers. Its relatively flat terrain means there are large numbers of visitors. On its eastern side edge, a huge rock stands over the water like a great bell, its back thickly covered with cormorant nests. It looks just like a cormorant fortress in the Qinghai Lake.

The majority of the population of the Bird Island are birds rather than human residents. With the coming of spring and of warm air currents from the Indian Ocean, birds from the islands of South Asia fly north across the Himalayas during their annual migration. For many the Qinghai Lake is their destination and the Bird Island is paradise for them. For as far as the eye can see, there is the spectacular of thick flocks of birds wheeling through the air, busy hunting food, building nests, laying and hatching eggs. This unique sight has made the island the most popular tourist spot on the Qinghai Lake.

The main food for these birds is a kind of carp that thrives in the waters of the Qinghai Lake; it is unique to the lake and famous for its tenderness and flavor.

The lake is surrounded by vast expanses of pastureland where herds of sheep and cattle graze. Generation after generation of Tibetan people live around this lake.

China's Five Most Beautiful Lakes

Number *2*

# Kanas Lake
## *Palette of the Gods*

This frigid highland valley lake, nestling at the foot of the Youyi (Friendship) Peak of the Altay Mountains, is actually the widest section of the Kanas River, a tributary of the Erix River. The Erix originates in the Erix glacier, winds its way through the mountains becoming slow and gentle once it flows into this narrow strip of lowland. On its east and west banks are European primeval coniferous and birch forests, creating the scenery typical of forested areas in Scandinavia and Russia.

The wooded valley, stretching for over 2,000 square kilometers from the lake, is China's only area of ancient frigid forest. It is home to over 1,000 plant species, 300 kinds of animal and 100 kinds of bird, many of which are rare protected species. In the lake are eight varieties of rare cold water fish, including the huge and ferocious hucho taimen, capable of swallowing a whole duck in the lake waters. On occasion the fish have even attacked and taken baby calves on the lake banks, and are thus known as Lake Monster, intensifying the lake's mystery and color.

Number *3*

# Namtso Lake

*Where One Whispers into the Ear of the God*

People say the Namtso Lake also has its moods. When you feel happy, it will only add to your pleasure, and when you feel sad, it will bring you consolation. Here at Namtso Lake, you lose all interest in sightseeing; all you can do is relax and think deep thoughts.

On the southern bank of Namtso Lake, the main peak of the Nyainqentanglha Mountains dances between the clouds. The lake and the 7,162-meter-high snow mountain set each other off here, the goddess of the lake and the mountain peak both are partners in protecting pilgrims coming here to pray.

Known as the "Lake of Heaven," the Namtso Lake lies in the north Tibetan plateau north of the main peak of the Nyainqentanglha Mountains. The lake, 4,720 meters above sea level and 55 meters deep, covers an area of 1,961.5 square kilometers, making it the highest of Tibet's three largest lakes and the second largest salt lake in China.

Some two million years ago, drastic movement of the earth's crust caused the Qinghai-Tibet Plateau to rise by a huge degree. As a result of the intense pressures exerted in this process, some strata were folded into high mountains whilst others fell, creating valleys or basins. The Namtso Lake was a result, first, of the movement of the earth's crust, exacerbated by glacier movement. In the lake's early days, it had a much wider surface area and a lower elevation than it has today. The climate then was much warmer and more humid too, and the rippling lake was just like a sea. As the earth's crust continued to rise, so too did the lake. Some 10,000 years ago, the plateau turned cold and dry and the lake's water sources decreased, resulting in the lake shrinking in size. There are three shorelines around the lake, the highest of which is 80 meters higher than today's lake shore.

Summer is the most active time at the Namtso Lake, when wild animals, among them yaks, gazelles and hares, graze happily on the broad grasslands and many migrating birds arrive from the south, to lay their eggs, hatch and raise their broods on islets and lakeshore. Fish often leap out of the water, revealing their silvery scales. Leisurely herders tend their horses, sheep and cattle, filling the valleys with their lovely echoing songs.

Because of the extreme cold here, the lake freezes in October and the ice does not melt until May the following year. When it does melt, the ice emits thunderous cracking noises that can be heard miles away, and is one of the sights of Namtso.

The Namtso Lake teems with fish that have fine scales or no scales at all. The majority of the lake dwellers are from the carp and eel families; they are however unlike their cousins in waters on the plains, having evolved from their original forms, over the course of two million years, adapting to plateau conditions. Many still have the primitive shape of large head and small tail.

Peninsulars jutting out into the lake are home to many sites associated with prominent monks from different sects, with many sacred rocks and trees of spiritual significance. The mountains around the shore have ancient mystical drawings. Visitors to these spots will be rewarded not just with the beauty of nature, but with a sense of mystic serenity that accompanies it. Standing on the bank, eight meters apart, are two stone pillars, about 30 meters high, one of them with a fissure big enough to accommodate a man. They are said by some to be symbols of *yin* and *yang* while others claim they are the guardians of the lake. To followers of Tibetan Buddhism, it is a matter of great significance to circumambulate the lake and pray to the mountain god of Nyainqentanglha during the Year of the Sheep because the Good Luck Peninsular on the lake's east bank represents the sacred body of Sakyamuni, and is where 3,000 Buddhist deities congregate. The goddess of the lake is also the queen of the mountain god and each of the couple was born in the Year of the Sheep. A circumambulation performed in this particular year means one will receive great fortune and protection. It takes about a week, not including time for sightseeing. One test of the circumambulants' sincerity is for them to come to the peninsular, Sakyamuni's "body," to pray and then throw into the lake a *katag* white silk scarf, as an expression of sincerity. If the *katag* sinks into the water quickly, it is an indication of the spotless sincerity of the well-wisher and that the holy Buddha has accepted the disciple's prayers. If it remains floating, or only half sinks, it means the disciple is not sufficiently sincere and pious or that unpleasant things await. Some tourists often take the test here too, but only if they are sure there is no one around that they know, and then it's a nervous wait to see if the *katag* sinks.

Then, there is also the ceremony of sacrifices to the water gods. For Tibetans, the water gods are invisible but ubiquitous. Even in a water pot as small as a horseshoe, there may well be dozens of water gods. The god of all water gods lives in this sacred lake. These deities are highly magic, with power over poverty and fortune; but they are very tight-fisted and quick to anger. At the slightest provocation, they will not only prevent you from gaining wealth but also send diseases and disasters your way too. When making offerings, apart from five types of grains, other treasures must be offered to the water gods, and expensive medicines too. So, pilgrims to the lake always bring along a "sacrifice kit," a bottle containing all the necessary offerings and sutras, which they cast into the lake.

## Number *4*

# Tianchi Lake

## *Calm after the Storm*

In antiquity, Changbai Mountain was a volcano and history records three eruptions since the 16th century. Violent eruptions left behind a huge crater in which, as time went by, a lake was formed. The lava flows became 16 mountain peaks around the lake, seven of them within the Democratic People's Republic of Korea and nine in China. The Tianchi Lake is the largest volcano lake in China and also the source of the Songhua, Tumen and Yalu rivers. Its high altitude, 2,150 meters above sea level, gave rise to its name which translates as "Heavenly Pool."

Springtime green willows and peach blossoms at the Bai Juyi Causeway.

China's Five Most Beautiful Lakes

Number 5

West Lake

There is culture in virtually every drop of water in the West Lake. Indeed the rich accumulation of history nourishes every inch of the surrounding land and the hearts of lakeside residents. Dancing lights and quiet lapping waters together produce a moving serenade.

The West Lake derives its name from the fact that it lies west of the city of Hangzhou. Over hundreds of years, it changed from a bay to a lagoon, and then, before the Tang Dynasty (618-907), to a completely inland lake. During the ensuing Song (960-1279), Yuan (1206-1368), Ming(1368-1644) and Qing (1644-1911) dynasties, the lake underwent repeated building and repairs. By the end of the 20th century, it had grown to an area of five to six square kilometers. In the 21st century, work began on the rebuilding of the Duke Yang Causeway, increasing the lake surface area to 6.5 square kilometers and its depth from 1.65 meters to 2.27 meters.

*Literature*. And it is here too that one hears the tale about a beauty and the love story of Su Xiaoxiao and the deeds of the heroine Qiu Jin, a women's right fighter and killed by the Qing court in 1907, tales of eminent monks and poets, offering the visitor an additional note of history. For a greater understanding of the profundity of Chinese culture, the seals and paintings created by the Xiling Engravers Society are a lesson in traditional Chinese art. Here one gets a sense of the lake's expanse and the depth of local history and culture. Gazing down from this vantage point to the lake below, cast your eyes on the lake's three causeways and three islets and you'll appreciate why this place was described as a heavenly city. You would be well advised to take

Visitors to the West Lake invariably feel like tasting tea and reading here. The West Lake is part and parcel of people's lives.

The first place visitors to Hangzhou should head for is Gu Shan (Solitary Hill), spending a day or two on this, the key to the scenic West Lake, and only then fanning out to the lake scenic sites.

Here the visitor will experience the depth of history as symbolized by the Wenlan Pavilion and the *Complete Library in Four Branches of* in the Zhejiang Provincial Museum and Art Gallery for a panoramic view of Zhejiang's civilization. And after that, sample the delights of the West Lake cuisine at the Louwailou Restaurant. From there, a walk along Lingyin Road, the Bai Juyi Causeway or the North Hill Road will reward the visitor with scenic surprises.

The West Lake scenery has been as tender and beautiful as this since ancient times. "The light of water shines in the sun, magic the haziness of the hill in the rain." The eternal power of poetry captures the beauty of the lake and safeguards our reminiscence.

Although there are many other West Lake "must see" sights, I believe a trip on the water is most essential, because, it is by taking to the water that gets you closest to the core beauty of the West Lake.

The Bai Juyi and Su Dongpo causeways represent the rich collection of poems created by these two poetic geniuses of ancient China. Without going there, how can we experience the true spirit of their poetry? The three islets on the lake are the land of immortals, the recreation of an ideal world, and you must go in person. This way, one can enrich one's sense of the best and most beautiful parts of Chinese civilization.

If you want to see the old West Lake, why not check out what the "westward project" has created? The aim of this massive project, launched in 2002, is to return the lake its former glory. This natural winter scene shows why the West Lake exerts such a pull on people's heart strings.

you leave your hotel room. Height is not what matters, but the spirit.

In history, Hangzhou was known as the "Buddhist land in the east," for its flourishing religious life. Many of the temples that used to stand around the lake are gone and those that do remain have acquired a much more solemn atmosphere. Taoism and Christianity also have their own history here and coexist peacefully by the lake, each attracting its own followers. There are people too who burn incense and pray, not necessarily out of their belief in an afterlife. Every religious building is a hall of art. Many important events in the history of Buddhism, Taoism and Christianity took place here and visiting these religious sites will enrich one's knowledge of history.

The beauty and profundity of Hangzhou cannot be described in just a few words, but they can be seen and felt. A trip on the lake will introduce the city and vice versa. Lake and city are a single entity. Take a trip on the water and you fall in love with the city.

The Confucius Temple here is little visited but its steles are really worth seeing. Having gone through the busy area of Qinghefang, a few more steps brings you there. And you really should try the Hangzhou tea. The Hangzhou tea you can have at the West Lake cannot be matched elsewhere.

As for museums, the Hu Mansion and the studios of several master painters will lead you into the heart of this city, let you feel the heartbeat of the city and feel the pulse of the spirit of the place. 🞑

In the early 20th century, someone praised Hangzhou's color, saying that the city's beauty lay in the jade green color of the West Lake. Hangzhou has on three sides hills each with its own grace. As you stroll among them, you forget their physical being. The appreciation of the hills begins with your very first step, the very moment

Appreciating danxia formations calls for a poetic soul — to sense
a magical rhythm, the movement of the earth's crust.

# China's Seven Most Beautiful Danxia Landscapes

## Ranking

1. Danxia Mountain            (Guangdong)
2. Wuyi Mountain             (Fujian)
3. Dajin Lake                (Fujian)
4. Longhu Mountain          (Jiangxi)
5. Langshan Mountain       (Guangxi and Hunan)
6. Zhangye Danxia Landform   (Gansu)
7. Chishui Danxia Landform    (Guizhou)

Danxia topography, named after Danxia Mountain in Guangdong Province, is created by the collapsing and weathering of red sandstone and conglomerate. Danxia landforms have many common features, including flat or slightly tilted tops, one or more sheer sides, but gentle slopes at the foot.

China's Seven Most Beautiful Danxia Landscapes

Number *1*

# Danxia Mountain
*China's Red Stone Park*

Danxia Mountain, located in Renhua County, Guangdong Province, with its walls and tiers of red rocks and cliffs, like danxia (red rays of the sun), from which its name derives, has been compared to a ruby sculpture park. It is known as "China's Red Stone Park."

That Danxia Mountain is special has been known for many years. Early in the 1930s, the late geologist and member of the Chinese Academy of Sciences, Professor Chen Guoda, after a thorough study of the red stone mountain regions of South China, gave the name danxia to this kind of topography, of which Danxia Mountain had the most classic features. Fellow academics accepted the concept, which became popular in the field of geography. Over the past 70-odd years, China's geologists and geographers have identified 715 danxia landforms in China (according to the latest statistics from Professor Huang Jin), Danxia geomorphology has developed into a sub-discipline of geomorphology and Danxia Mountain has become China's research base for danxia landforms.

Defined in narrow terms, Danxia Mountain goes as far as Zhanglao (Elder) Peak, Hailuo (Conch) Peak and Baozhu (Pearl) Peak in the north. Defined more broadly, it covers a mountainous area of 290 square kilometers (180 of which are of typical danxia topography), composed of red stones, and called Danxia Mountain Geopark. Located in a basin south of the Nanling mountain range, the park encompasses four scenic areas of Danxia Mountain in the north, Shaoshi in the southeast, Bazhai in the west and Jinjiang River in the central area. There are over 400 rock peaks, rock castles, rock walls and rock bridges of various sizes, standing in graceful disorder in the geopark.

Bazhai Peak, at 618 meters above sea level, is Danxia Mountain's highest peak, which is not high in mountain terms, but all the peaks are formed of sheer and perilous cliffs, many of them hundreds of meters high, rising straight from the plain or riverbank, full of power and grandeur.

These steep red cliffs, most of them too precipitous to climb, are the symbols of Danxia Mountain. Even today, only a few cliff paths are available for visitors, and only a few of the summits may be climbed. However, mountain paths and fortifications left by the ancients are often seen on the 400-odd hilltops. The present cliff paths have been built on the foundation of ancient paths and plank roads. They have been widened and fitted with railings, but they still take your breath away.

Danxia Mountain is full of scenic wonders ...curious mountains, cliffs, stones, caves, natural

The Yangyuan (Male Organ) Rock and Yinyuan (Female Organ) Rock are among the many rocks on Danxia Mountain resembling human organs and figures. (above) There is no mystery about how they were formed — in exactly the same way as every peak and cliff on Danxia Mountain (right page), but the latter was not so successfully sculpted by Nature.

bridges and valleys ...all simply incredible. The mountains are noted for their different shapes ... a sequence of castles, cones, walls, pillars, and pagodas. Especially in the morning mist or above a sea of clouds, you feel as if you are part of a mirage or in a fairyland jeweled palace. Some resemble human figures in different postures, others look like birds or beasts; but all are Nature's masterpieces. They include the Yangyuan (Male Organ) Rock, famed as the "Most Curious Rock in the World," and the honeycomb front of the Longlin (Dragon Scale) Stone in the Jinshi Cave, whose colors differ with the seasons. There are bryophytes living in the small holes of the honeycomb and the more water they absorb, the greener they become. The

The fascinating mushroom-like formation is the result of weathering of different rock strata; they are not classic danxia formations, but do add interest.

Yangyuan Rock, Yinyuan (Female Organ) Rock, Wangfu (Longing for Husband to Return) Rock and Longlin Rock are regarded as the "Four Beauties of Danxia Mountain."

As a rule of thumb, the mountains of north China are grand, and those of south China are delicate. But Danxia Mountain is both grand and delicate, combining the characteristics of northern and southern mountains. The mountain is covered with sub-tropical evergreen forest, lush and green all the year round. Originating in the immense forest of Nanling, the graceful Jinjiang River winds its way through the mountain, enhancing the landscape. The river looks like a superb wine flowing out of the forest, with watery reflections of bamboo, trees and rocks, a rural landscape full of the feel of the south, a landscape no whit less beautiful than that of Guilin.

Danxia Mountain is a place of towering cliffs and deep valleys that are home to verdant trees and limpid springs. Walking on the forest trails, one enjoys a feeling of detachment and seclusion, so it is an ideal place for those who want to cultivate their mind and develop their characters. Since the Sui (581-618) and Tang (618-907) dynasties, Danxia Mountain has been a magnet for visitors, drawing countless literati to make exquisite engravings on cliffs and steles, and monks and priests to build temples. So far, more than 40 cave temple sites have been found, including the newly reconstructed Biechuan Temple and the carved temple in Jinshiyan Cliff.

Danxia landform's rock walls and cliffs are formed of red sandstone and conglomerate. How did Danxia Mountain come into being? Research shows that about 100 million years ago, there used to be a huge inland basin here. Water carried silt from the surrounding mountains to the basin. As the result of global high temperatures the basin dried up and in these arid conditions the sediment oxidized and turned rust color. Then some 70 million years ago a 3,700-meter-thick red-colored layer formed on the basin, known as the chalk bed. On the top, there was a 1,300-meter-thick solid layer, i.e., layer of Cretaceous system, from which the peaks of

In south China, danxia formations have always mingled with human habitations; below towering cliffs, there you have villages and farms. Refugees see them as a natural sanctuary as well as a sacred place where Gods and Buddha are believed to live.

Danxia Mountain gradually took shape.

Since 30 million years ago, orogenic movement has lifted the whole basin many times. Water flowing down through fissures cut through and eroded the sedimentary rock, the slope broke and receded, leaving behind the red fragmentary rocks we see now — danxia landforms. According to experts, orogenic movement is still going on in the Danxia Mountain area, with an average rise of 0.87 meter every 10,000 years over the last 500,000 years. Beautiful Danxia Mountain is still growing.

The Jiuqu Stream snakes its way through Wuyi Mountain; the peaks on its banks are typical danxia landforms. Wuyi Mountain boasts 36 majestic peaks and 99 rocks, in various shapes and postures. Due to the humid and warm climate, the peaks are emerald green.

China's Seven Most Beautiful Danxia Landscapes

Number *2*

# Wuyi Mountain
## *Second to None in Southeast China*

The peerless scenery of Wuyi Mountain in the north of Fujian Province combines the strange shapes of Huangshan Mountains, the elegance of Guilin, the grandeur of Mount Tai, the steepness of Huashan, and the beauty of Hangzhou's West Lake. Covering an area of 70 square kilometers (54.4 of which are danxia topography), the Wuyi Mountain Scenic Area has an average elevation of 350 meters, boasts 36 extraordinary peaks and is circled by the beautiful 9.5-kilometer-long Jiuqu (Nine Zigzag) Stream. Wuyi Mountain is composed of hills of red sandstone and conglomerate. The scenery on both sides of the Jiuqu Stream is typical danxia topography, with flat tops, precipitous hillsides and towering peaks. Due to the warm and humid climate, and a good ecological environment, the tops are lush and green. Red cliffs, green waters, each enhancing the lustrous beauty of the other... every view a handsome prospect.

# Number 3
# Dajin Lake
## *Spectacle of "Danxia on Water"*

Take a boat and drift on the Dajin Lake, enjoying beautiful scenes of green trees and red rocks, startled by the strange danxia shapes and intoxicated with the landscape of lakes and mountains.

Situated in Taining County, Fujian Province, in the central part of Wuyi Mountain, the Dajin Lake covers an area of 461.8 square kilometers, 166.9 of which are danxia topography. There are four danxia scenic spots here. Going from northeast to southwest they are: Shangqing Stream, Jinhu Lake, Dragon King Cave and Eight Immortals Cliff. The Jinhu Lake and the Shangqing Stream are China's largest danxia landforms on water. Characterized by deep incised gorges and many incised meanders, the Dajin Lake danxia area has a wealth of different shapes. Fissured in all directions, the topography of the Dajin Lake has further undergone weathering and erosion by wind and water, giving rise to the red cliffs, square mountains, pointed peaks, stone pillars and walls, incised meanders and gorges that constitute the unique danxia landscape. Threaded through by the meandering waters of the lake, the place is a rare phenomenon of "danxia on water."

# Number 4
# Longhu Mountain
## *Cradle of Taoism*

Situated in Yingtan, Jiangxi Province, Longhu (Dragon and Tiger) Mountain has a danxia area of 80 square kilometers, and is one of the most evolved danxia landform areas in China. Geologically it is a Mesozoic fault basin, in which thick strata of purplish-red conglomerate, sandstone and volcanic rock were formed. Subsequent scouring and weathering ultimately shaped the landscape here into what it is today ...a wealth of flat-top summits, hog back mountains, stockades, walls, ridges, cliffs, honeycomb caves, upright caves, rock pillars, rock peaks, peak forests, natural bridges, rock arches and "elephant trunks."

A feature of most of China's danxia landforms, because of their relative elevation, is majestic and precipitous. Longhu Mountain, however, is in its senior years in danxia topographical terms, so the relative elevation is low, 240 meters at the most, and thus appears graceful and enchanting. The danxia formations, in various shapes, are mainly distributed over Longhu Mountain and Xianshuiyan (Celestial Water Rock) scenic areas, covering an area of about 40 square kilometers. The Luxi River flows through the scenic area, linking the danxia sights

Surrounded by water, these typical danxia peaks stand along the banks of the Luxi River, looking mild and graceful. In topographical terms, the Longhu Mountain danxia is in its senior years.

on the banks. Additionally, it is celebrated as the cradle of Chinese Taoism, with many coffins suspended on the cliffs of Xianshuiyan, dating back nearly two and a half thousand years to the Spring and Autumn Period (770 BC-476 BC) and the Warring States Period (475 BC-221 BC).

# Number 5
# Langshan Mountain

All touching scenes are wonders of Nature. The peaks seem like ten thousand horses galloping ahead. Standing on the commanding height, one can overlook the whole scenic area, fully enjoying the beautiful danxia landscape.

In the heart of Yuecheng Mountain, where Hunan and Guangxi meet, there is a long, narrow basin of red conglomerate and sandstone, which took shape in the early Cretaceous period of the Mesozoic era, about 100 million years ago. Here, in the scenic area from Langshan Mountain, where Zijiang River (a tributary of the Yangtze) originates, to Bajiaozhai, you can find the danxia landform, which straddles Xinning County in Hunan, where it covers an area of 77.5 square kilometers and Ziyuan County in Guangxi, where it covers an area of 125 square kilometers. The Zijiang and Fuyi rivers flow northward from the basin into the Dongting Lake, their banks as pretty as a picture.

Langshan Mountain is thick with danxia

peak forests — like ten thousand bamboo shoots soaring into the sky, or ten thousand horses charging; its outstanding feature is its many deep-cut narrow valleys; because the sandstone has a larger proportion of limestone and conglomerate, the karst features are quite clear.

In the Bajiaozhai Scenic Area, there are over a hundred weirdly-shaped towering mountains, jagged rocks, red peaks, caves and valleys. One such, Conch Mountain, is composed of four awl-shaped peaks, each over a hundred meters high and covered by exquisite whorls, just like gigantic conches. Standing on a commanding height to look upon the panorama, all you can see is fold after fold of mountains, rising and falling like waves.

# Number 6

Because of aridity the Zhangye danxia landform differs from that of south China. Dry and desolate, without any vegetation, geologists call this "window lattice and palace-shaped danxia topography." (right)

The Zhangye danxia formations are set off by magical colorful hills. (below)

# Zhangye Danxia Landform
*Palaces Created by Nature*

The Zhangye danxia landform is concentrated predominantly in Linze and Sunan counties in Gansu Province. It is both the largest and the most typical of China's arid area danxia landforms.

Danxia landforms in Kangle Township, Sunan Uygur Autonomous County, are the best evolved examples in China of window lattice and palace forms. They can be seen only in the arid areas of Gansu and Qinghai provinces. The danxia formations are surrounded by colorful hills, which seem to rise and fall like waves; with rock strata of different colors mixed in graceful disarray, it is an imposing and magnificent sight. The Zhangye's palace danxia formations and its colorful hills cover about 300 square kilometers.

Karst Peak Forest in Guilin, Guangxi

# China's Five Most
# Beautiful Peak Forests

## Ranking

1. Lijiang River Landscape        (Guangxi)
2. Wulingyuan Peak Forest        (Hunan)
3. Wanfenglin Peak Forest        (Guizhou)
4. Sanqing Mountain        (Jiangxi)
5. Luoping Peak Forest        (Yunnan)

# Number *1*
# Lijiang River Landscape
## *A Landscape Gallery*

The Lijiang River, part of the Zhujiang (Pearl River) system, originates in the Mao'er Mountain, the highest in southern China. Its course is 437 kilometers long.

The river is internationally known for the 83-kilometer stretch between Xiangbi (Elephant Trunk) Hill in Guilin City to Bilian (Green Lotus) Peak in Yangshuo County, Guangxi Zhuang Autonomous Region.

The Lijiang River area, which is typical of karst landscape and Guangxi sub-tropical karst topography, boasts diverse beautiful landscapes, peak forests, karst caves, deep pools, dangerous shoals, precipitous crags and rushing waterfalls. The picturesque peak forests along the river were formed by limestone rising from the seabed and

About 325 million years ago, today's Guilin and Yangshuo area was just a vast expanse of water. Movement of the earth's crust pushed the limestone, deposited on the ocean floor, above the waters to become dry land. The special landscapes of peak clusters and forests, subterranean streams and karst caves gradually emerged as the result of wind and rain erosion.

The Lijiang River, like a green silk belt, threads through the grotesque peaks, everywhere is permeated with local feeling.

undergoing years of erosion by continual high temperatures and rain. As their hardness and abruptness softened away, they merged with the life force of all creatures, composing an elegant picture of green towering peaks.

The beauty of the Lijiang River lies in its clear and graceful waters and its curious rock formations.

In the sunshine, its waters take all shades of green that keep on changing constantly — one moment like emerald, the next the colour of young leaves. Not only has the river created all creatures around it, it has also transformed water — this colorless, ordinary material — into a beautiful enchanting spirit.

The peaks here are neither tall nor steep. Dotted along the Lijiang River, they form a smoothly meandering line of dark green. The peaks follow on one after another, each close upon the heel of the one before, but each has its own story and associations. They stand together, shoulder to shoulder, keeping watch over the area, bringing endless blessings, and witnessing its great changes.

The banks of the Lijiang River are inhabited by people of a dozen or so ethnic minority groups, including Zhuang, Yao, Dong, Miao, Shui and Maonan. For thousands of years, their unique traditions and culture, together with the picturesque and poetic Lijiang River, have intoxicated many men of letters.

# Number *2*
# Wulingyuan Peak Forest
## *A Superb Painting in the Remote Mountains*

If anyone talks about a scroll painting of world-shaking beauty over 300 square kilometers in size, they must be referring to Wulingyuan.

The name Wulingyuan comes from its geographical location north of the Wuling Mountains on the border between the provinces of Hunan and Guizhou. During the mid and late Devonian Period, quartz sandstones were deposited at Wulingyuan, where the sea and the land interfaced. Great changes took place with the passage of time. Due to the rise of the earth's crust, erosion and weathering, some mesas gradually became peak clusters and forests while others were leveled to the ground before finally being eroded into gullies and valleys. In every respect — scale, completeness, variety of forms, and biodiversity — Wulingyuan is a priceless legacy handed down by Nature to mankind.

Now a World Natural Heritage site, the Wulingyuan Scenic Area encompasses Zhangjiajie, Tianzi Mountain, Suoxiyu Valley, and a few other newly developed spots.

Every visitor to Wulingyuan will visit the Shili (Ten-*li*) Gallery at the foot of Tianzi Mountain.

The Shili Gallery has no actual paintings or

It was not until the 1980s that Wulingyuan became well-known at home and abroad, but because of its grotesque peaks and wandering valleys, it was quickly hailed as "a pearl hidden in the remote mountains."

The towering and dense stand of quartz sandstone peak forests at Wulingyuan impresses visitors with its boundless majesty. Many peaks have acquired splendid names, among them: Valley Bend of the Spirit Hall; Peaks in a Long Scroll Painting of the West Sea; Heavenly Goddess Presenting Flowers; Qu Yuan Chanting Verse while Strolling; and, Arhat Peak. Peaks without a name also have their own features, which allow free rein to one's thoughts and imagination.

galleries, but stretches for 10 *li* (about three miles), covered with narrow mountain paths. The sides of the valley are lined with peak after peak and from the bottom of the stream rocks pile up into the sky, forming some 200 weird statues of every shape — humans, birds, animals and objects. So, as in a gallery, one moves through the valley feasting on its frequently changing sights, as if enjoying superb paintings and poetry.

At Zhangjiajie, the clouds and mountains form a natural scroll painting. The sun's rays slant across the peaks, white clouds drift around the mountainside, and lush primeval forest cloaks the peaks and valleys in shades of green.

Like the majesty and magnificent Shili Gallery, the Jinbianxi Brook has sights to delight the eye at every step, but is more tranquil and elegant in appearance. Wandering in the lush forest beside the brook, glimpsing the jade stream and the glittering color stones in the water, you

can quite easily feel that the brook must lead to the Peach Blossom Valley, the paradise of the great poet Tao Yuanming. Perhaps it is this lovely dream that draws endless visitors to the stream.

The Heaven Terrace on Taizi Mountain, surrounded by countless peaks, gives panoramic views of all of Wulingyuan.

It is the grotesque peaks that are Wulingyuan's impressive feature.

Within its 360 square kilometers, Wulingyuan has over 3,000 sandstone pillars and peaks, most of them over 200 meters in height. When the thousands of erect-towering peaks that make up the sandstone forests suddenly appear, one is lost for words to describe the imposing grandeur of the spectacle.

These peaks seem to share similarities in shape and spirit with all things and creatures on earth.

From the highest (Rabbit Watching the Moon

Peak) to the lowest (Stream Winding around Four Gates Peak), the grotesque formations come in every size, height and shape; there is a dancing fairy, an old man culling medicinal herbs, a dragon rising from the sea, and a sword thrusting into the sky. Nature wielded its brush freely here, leaving behind countless sights to inspire the infinite imagination and pious worship of worldly beings — the South Column to Heaven, Golden Whip Cliff, Five Fingers Peak, Sacred Needle for Calming the Sea Peak.

At Wulingyuan, every peak is a life. When the rain passes and the skies clear, the peaks are faintly discernible, wreathed in clouds and mists from the valleys. Then no one could deny that Wulingyuan is really a living wonderland on earth.

Wulingyuan is known for its "3,000 peaks and 800 waters."

The peaks are surrounded by water — waterfalls cascading down from high cliffs, rivulets snaking through thick grass, boat-bearing forest lakes formed by long accumulation.

The grotesque peaks and graceful waters each lend beauty to the other. Springs bubbling up through the cracks between rocks, shy streams in deep secluded valleys, green-shaded lakes, and waterfalls tumbling down the cliffs, all in perfect and lovely contrast with the red sandstone.

The moment you step into Wulingyuan, beautiful scenes keep coming up, minute by minute, along the way. Who needs way markers to roam such a bewitching landscape? Walking here freely, being intoxicated, marveling in and drinking it all in will be the delight of a lifetime.

The beauty of waters and mountains lies in naturalness and freedom. Any deliberate attempt to achieve perfect beauty is in vain. Only the spontaneous emotion that touches the heart is eternal.

China's Five Most Beautiful Peak Forests

Number *3*

# Wanfenglin Peak Forest

*Arcadia on the Plateau*

Xingyi City in Guizhou Province is among the most representative examples of the evolution of karst topography in China. Wanfenglin (Forest of Ten Thousand Peaks) in Xingyi takes up an area of 2,000 square kilometers, about two thirds of the Xingyi total.

As early as 300 million years ago, the area of Wanfenglin was part of the Yunnan-Guizhou ancient sea. After several orogenic movements, bulged limestone rocks underwent the combined effect of burning sunshine, rain, dioxide and organic acids, in the process forming marvelous sights, such as karst caves, peak forests, natural craters, rift valleys, earth crevices, stalactites and stalagmites. From whatever aspect you judge it — aesthetic value, completeness of the karst topography evolution process, diversity, scale and concentration of cone-shaped peak forest, or the classic nature of each spectacle — Wanfenglin Peak Forest deserves its reputation as one of China's wonders.

Wanfenglin Peak Forest is located at the middle and lower reaches of a "beautiful scar on earth" — the Malinghe Gorge. It has an eastern part and a western part. The forest spreads out like a fan from the edge of the Yunnan-Guizhou

The dense peak forest and a vast expanse of fields enhance each other's beauty — an extraordinary natural scroll painting of elegant and open composition.

Plateau at an altitude of over 2,000 meters. The peaks are categorized according to the shape: liezhen (array), baojian (sword), qunlong (dragon), luohan (arhat), and diemao (piled up hats). The forest extends to the fault zone of the Nanpanjiang Basin where part was submerged, forming the Wanfeng Lake. The water and peaks dotted by craggy karst rocks and strangely shaped trees create views of extraordinary magnificence and enchantment.

In the main, the mountains here are not high, but the "bamboo-shoot" serried peaks present an irresistible spectacle. Looking at it from above, you can see unfurling a natural scroll painting of elegance and openness: the green-grey peaks and yellow and green fields each enhance the other's radiance and beauty; the wandering Nahui River threads through the villages like white silk stringing pearls together. Then you understand why Buyi and Miao folk songs describe this place as their heart's bliss.

The forest's eastern part is characterized by brilliant fields, the western part by graceful waters. A perfect rural landscape, the forest stands like an arcadia on the Yunnan-Guizhou Plateau.

# Number 4
# Sanqing Mountain
## *The Most Beautiful Granites on the West Coast of the Pacific*

Sanqing Mountain is situated on the boundary of Dexing City and Yushan County in the north of Jiangxi Province. Covering an area of 229 square kilometers, it is famed for the three main peaks — Yujing, Yuxu and Yuhua — which look like the Sanqing (three pure) Taoist deities sitting side by side on the summit. Yujing, at an elevation of 1,816 meters above sea level is the highest peak.

The mountain, in the junction zone of the Yangtze and Cathaysian plates, underwent over a billion years of geological evolution, in the process forming granite peak forest topography, unequalled anywhere in the world.

Its beauty lies in its simplicity and naturalness, its specialness in its combination of form and spirit. Painstakingly sculpted by Nature, that superb master artist, Sanqing boasts such unique sights as the Goddess of Spring Peak and Huge Boa Emerging from the Mountain Peak.

With the most completely evolved granite fractures in the world, Sanqing is veritable geological museum and is said by experts to have the most beautiful granites on the west coast of the Pacific.

Three peaks in a row at Sanqing Mountain

Rape blossom, villages and green peaks ... indispensable elements of the enchanting landscape that forms the natural garden of Luoping.

Number **5**

# Luoping Peak Forest
*A Natural Golden Garden*

Hidden among the serried mountains where Yunnan, Guizhou and Guangxi meet, lies a marvelous landscape called Luoping Peak Forest.

Because of its unique location, Luoping County, in the east of Yunnan Province, has been called the East Gateway to Yunnan or the Strategic Gateway to Yunnan and Guizhou.

In spring, in the third month of the year, vast swathes of rape come into bloom in Luoping.

There are patches, undulating waves, snaking lines and coiling spirals of these flowers, together forming a boundless sea of lustrous gold.

Yudai Lake, Lashan Lake and Wanzi Lake, set like three brilliant mirrors in the midst of a sea of flowers, enhance the luxuriant green of Baila Mountain. Dotted about the sea are karst cones in all shapes. White clouds partially cloak the verdant mountains and streams flow quietly through the villages.... ▯

# China's Ten Most
# Beautiful Gorges

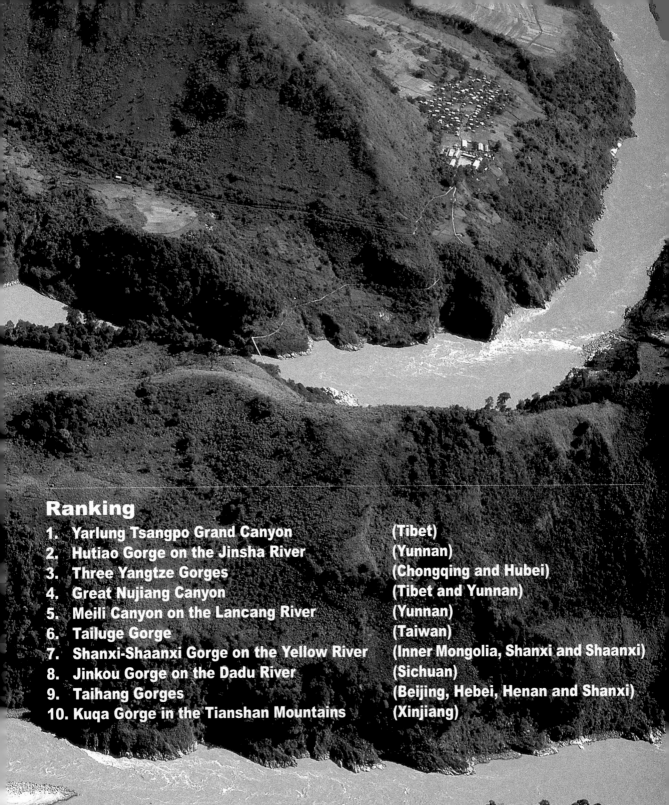

## Ranking

1. Yarlung Tsangpo Grand Canyon                      (Tibet)
2. Hutiao Gorge on the Jinsha River            (Yunnan)
3. Three Yangtze Gorges                            (Chongqing and Hubei)
4. Great Nujiang Canyon                           (Tibet and Yunnan)
5. Meili Canyon on the Lancang River         (Yunnan)
6. Tailuge Gorge                                  (Taiwan)
7. Shanxi-Shaanxi Gorge on the Yellow River   (Inner Mongolia, Shanxi and Shaanxi)
8. Jinkou Gorge on the Dadu River              (Sichuan)
9. Taihang Gorges                               (Beijing, Hebei, Henan and Shanxi)
10. Kuqa Gorge in the Tianshan Mountains    (Xinjiang)

The Yarlung Tsangpo Grand Cahyon is the largest green canyon in the world.

Number *1*

# Yarlung Tsangpo Grand Canyon

The Yarlung Tsangpo River, with its entrance at Pai Township in Menling County in southeastern Tibet, cuts through the Himalayas that stands in its path, making an unparalleled unique U-turn around the mountain of Namjagbarwa, before finally reaching Baxika in Medog County, and creating the famous Yarlung Tsangpo Grand Canyon. The actual length of the canyon is 504.6 kilometers and its deepest point (6,009 meters) is at Zongrong Village where the river, Namjagbarwa and Mount Lile intersect. Near Dege Village, one side of the canyon is as deep as 7,057 meters. The overall average depth of the Yarlung Tsangpo Grand Canyon is 2,268 meters and in the core section the average depth is 2,673 meters. At the entrance to the canyon

The phenomenon of the moisture passage at the Medog section of the Yarlung Tsangpo Grand Canyon.

A unique plank bridge in the Yarlung Tsangpo Grand Canyon. (left)

The Bayu river section in the Yarlung Tsangpo Grand Canyon — riverbed cutting into the bedrock, valley sides rising vertically, hurtling currents, sheer rockwalls, and waterfall cascading 200 meters down the cliff, is like a bolt of white silk. (right page)

the river is 660 meters across, gradually reducing to 35 meters at its narrowest point. The sharpest gradient of the river surface is 7.535 per cent. All the figures go to show beyond any doubt that the Yarlung Tsangpo Grand Canyon is the world champion. Other great canyons, such as the Colorado Canyon in the United States, which is 370 kilometers long and 2,133 meters deep, and the Colca Canyon in Peru, with a length of 90 kilometers and a depth of 3,200 meters, are not in the same league.

Besides, in the region of the Yarlung Tsangpo Bend there is strong mantle plume action producing the rare phenomenon of "thermal eddying." With an annual rise of 30 mm, this is one of the world's fastest rising regions.

As the Yarlung Tsangpo Grand Canyon cuts right through the Himalayas, it becomes the largest moisture passage for the Indian Ocean monsoon to enter the Qinghai-Tibet Plateau. The enormous moisture intensity almost equals all the moisture carried in summer from south of the Yangtze River to the north. As the result of this moisture passage along the canyon, the tropical mountain environment extends northwards for an extra six degrees of latitude, thus forming a large green land in southeastern Tibet, and the third largest forested area in China second only to the

The perfect harmony and dazzling splendor of the Yarlung Tsangpo Grand Canyon, Namjagbarwa, and the Zenonglong Glacier on the western slope of the mountain.

Northeast and Yunnan. Around 60-70 per cent of Qinghai-Tibet Plateau living species can be found in the canyon. It presents the world's fullest vertical range of natural zones — from the polar frigid zone to the tropical monsoon rainforest zone in low river valleys; monsoon marine (temperate) glaciers falling from the high mountains; four waterfalls in the river course, and in terms of unit length the richest water resource in the world. It is indeed the world's greenest canyon — no other famous canyons can boast these things.

The average annual rate of flow is 2,000 cubic meters per second at the entrance near Pai Township; by time it exits at Baxika it is 5,200 cubic meters per second. That of the Colorado River can be measured in hundreds of cubic meters per second, and it is almost the same with the Colca Canyon; neither can rival the Yarlung Tsangpo Grand Canyon. In terms of a section of waterway, the average discharge of the Yarlung Tsangpo River is 4,425 cubic meters per second, way above the Colorado River's 67 cubic meters per second. With an average velocity of 16 meters per second, the Yarlung Tsangpo River runs rapidly with rising and falling currents, more treacherous than any other canyon.

The beauty of the Yarlung Tsangpo Grand Canyon is beyond compare. The unique U-turn it makes and its being the largest moisture passage on the Qinghai-Tibet Plateau put the canyon among the ranks of the world's rarest natural wonders. Its unique natural environment and species diversity make up the colorful and unmatched scenery of the Yarlung Tsangpo Grand Canyon — primal, natural, simple, magical....

In many places suspension cable is the only means of transport. With the surging current below, using the "flying ferry" requires great courage.

Sheer cliffs flank the gorge. The swiftly rushing river seeks a way out, its rolling waves roaring like thunder, spray flying in all directions — a soul-stirring, breath-taking scene.

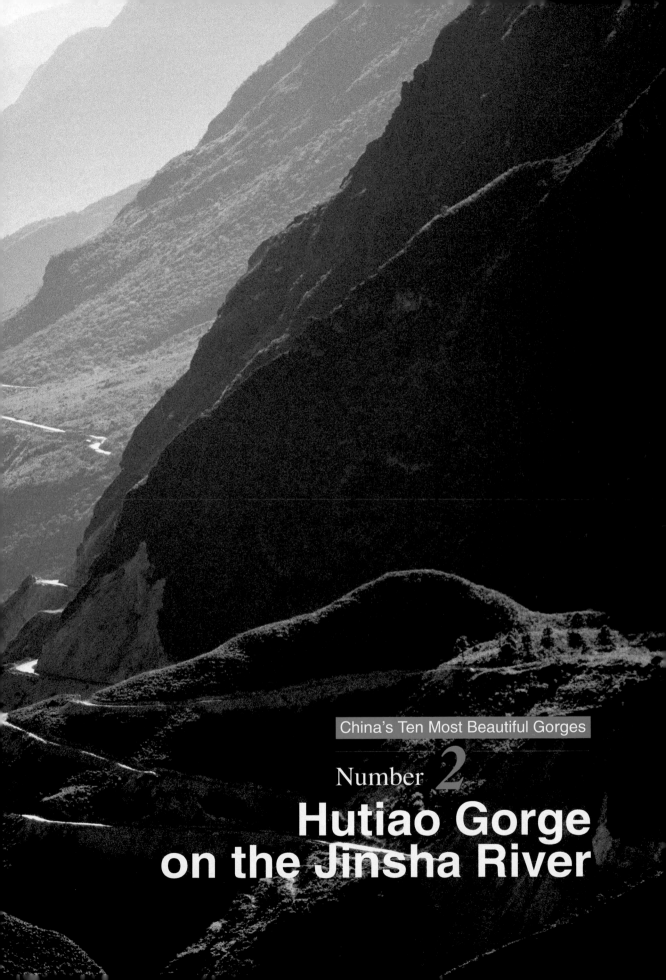

China's Ten Most Beautiful Gorges

Number *2*

# Hutiao Gorge
# on the Jinsha River

Hutiao (Tiger-Leaping) Gorge is internationally famous, far better known in the world than the province in which it is located. Many people abroad have not heard of Yunnan Province, but they have heard of Hutiao Gorge.

This great gorge inspires awe and nobility of spirit. I have walked here many times but what impressed me most was my experience two summers ago, when I walked through the gorge in intermittent heavy rain for over 20 kilometers.

I drove out from Shangri-La and as we were about to enter the gorge, suddenly the terrain opened out. I could see the Yulong (Jade Dragon) and the Haba snow mountains, that originally had looked like a single whole, now standing apart like a pair of huge curtains drawn open, their sheer faces opposing each other across an expanse of the cloudy sky. Such a soul-stirring scene! I seemed to hear the sounds of hundreds of thousands of years before, when the earth drew back on both two sides, the thunder of mud, sand, colossal rocks and mighty torrents coming rolling down. The entrance to the gorge was all turmoil and action, whilst the Jinsha River hidden far below kept silent. All this was for the Jinsha River.

The average elevation of the Jinsha River inside Hutiao Gorge is 1,630 meters above sea level, and its bank is 3,733 meters at the highest point, a difference of over 2,100 meters. The gorge consists of upper, middle and lower sections. Our

The famous Tiger-Leaping Rock, bisecting the rolling current as the roaring river makes its way around it. Emblem of the upper gorge, it is the most beautiful point in Hutiao Gorge.

cross-country vehicle advanced along the road beside the gorge — a dangerous road with white and yellow fallen rocks scattered everywhere. The great change process that started in remote antiquity was still continuing. Suddenly, the road ahead was blocked by a flood from the Haba Snow Mountain that had deposited several huge rocks on the road. Most of the road was under water. I decided immediately to get out and walk through Hutiao Gorge. I crossed the torrent and started walking. Landslips continued here and there, giving off the fresh smell of stones. Black clouds blotted out the sky, making it dim in the gorge, and then another rainstorm caught me, drenching me from top to toe. After walking a few kilometers in the rain, it stopped, and the gorge was restored to its original tranquility. Then suddenly I heard noises above and spotted lots of rocks and stones, big and small, jumping after each other like footballs and rolling into the Jinsha River several hundred meters ahead of me.

Aerial view of Hutiao Gorge showing how the Jinsha River divides the Yulong and Haba snow mountains.

The gorge was full of hidden danger. Not knowing when more rocks would roll down, I was quite edgy and walked quickly, away from danger, as if being pursued by those rocks. About two hours later (I can't be more precise since I lost all sense of time in the gorge and was just aware that it was getting darker), I reached the Hutiao Gorge Scenic Area. This 28-kilometer-long stretch is the major tourist area, with the famous Tiger-Leaping Rock below. Although I was exhausted, the sound of hundreds of tigers roaring below me revived me. It was raining again, and Tiger-Leaping Rock was submerged. I stood by the mighty torrent, its vapors surging upward and I dared not get too close. I could see that the Jinsha River was as smooth as a mirror upstream but when it reached Tiger-Leaping Rock, the mighty river suddenly fell, exploded, fragmented, and gushed out. It seemed that what had been pent up for a long time was suddenly erupting, several currents were surging, rushing and roaring like crazy tongues or banners fluttering in the wind. I shivered and drew back, for fear that those tigers would suddenly turn on me. Back on the road, I felt the peace of heart that had experienced great sadness or happiness. "I have been to Hutiao Gorge, and I am no longer who I was before: I become more open-minded, and my life is more natural." Cultivating the mind and character, nourishing purity of spirit, and feeling at one with nature... these things cannot be achieved in a study.

It was getting dark. A Naxi driver took me to Lijiang that same night. He drove in silence while I meditated in the dark interior. This experience made me understand the appeal of Chinese culture. The world of nature is a church of the Chinese spirit, from which great poets and artists derive their understanding of life and draw their creative inspiration, and which in turn becomes their masterpiece works. In this sense, Hutiao Gorge is a great Chinese church, like Notre Dame in Paris, a place where the heart and soul can rest.

Number *3*

# Three Yangtze Gorges

The Wuxia Gorge, the most precipitous section of the Three Yangtze Gorges, is a dreamland in the dying rays of the setting sun.

The Qutang Gorge, the shortest of the three, is surrounded by steep high mountains, sheer and imposing. On both banks wistaria drapes the cliffs and the trees are tinged with color.

The Three Yangtze Gorges stretch from Baidicheng in Fengjie County, Chongqiang Municipality eastward for 192 kilometers to Nanjinguan in Yichang City, Hubei Province. However, it is not a single entity and most sections are separated by broad valleys. The aggregate length of the gorge sections — the Qutang, Wuxia and Xiling gorges — is 90 kilometers.

The westernmost of these, the Qutang Gorge, extends for about 8 kilometers between Baidicheng and Daxi. Though the shortest, it is the most spectacular of the three. The Chijia and Baiyan mountains face each other from opposite sides of the Yangtze. At its narrowest point the riverbed is just a few dozen meters wide, but the valley is over 1,000 meters deep. These land features make the Kuimen Gate, the upstream entrance to the Three Gorges, like the "throat" of Sichuan Province. The middle gorge — the Wuxia Gorge — is 45 kilometers in length from the Daning River in the west to Guangdukou in the east. This is the longest and most complete of the three, and is often called the "Great Gorge." It is renowned for its remote and peaceful landscape beauty and for its changing clouds and rain. The 12 peaks of the Wushan Mountains that flank the Yangtze stand like a continuous screen

— a landscape to stir the spirit. Strictly speaking, the easternmost Xiling Gorge consists of two sections: the westerly one stretches 15 kilometers from the Bingshubaojian (Military Books and Precious Sword) Gorge at Xiangxi (Fragrant Stream), via the Niuganmafei (Ox Liver and Horse Lungs) Gorge, and ends in the Kongling Gorge at the Miaohe River; the easterly one extends 20 kilometers from the Dengying (Lantern Shadow) Gorge at Nantuo to the Huangmao (Yellow Cat) Gorge at Nanjinguan. Between the two lies the Miaonan Wide Valley, the longest valley in the Three Gorges area. The world-famous Three Gorges Dam stands at Sandouping, at the point in this valley where Yangtze is at its widest.

The Three Gorges came about as the result of China's physical geography. Thousands of streams and rivers on the Sichuan Basin seek to empty into the ocean in the east, but between the second and third steps of China's geological staircase they are impeded by the Qiyao and the Xuefeng mountains. However, this threshold of undulating, folding mountains cannot resist the tender toughness of the river — ultimately the Yangtze fights its way through, out to the ocean and the world beyond.

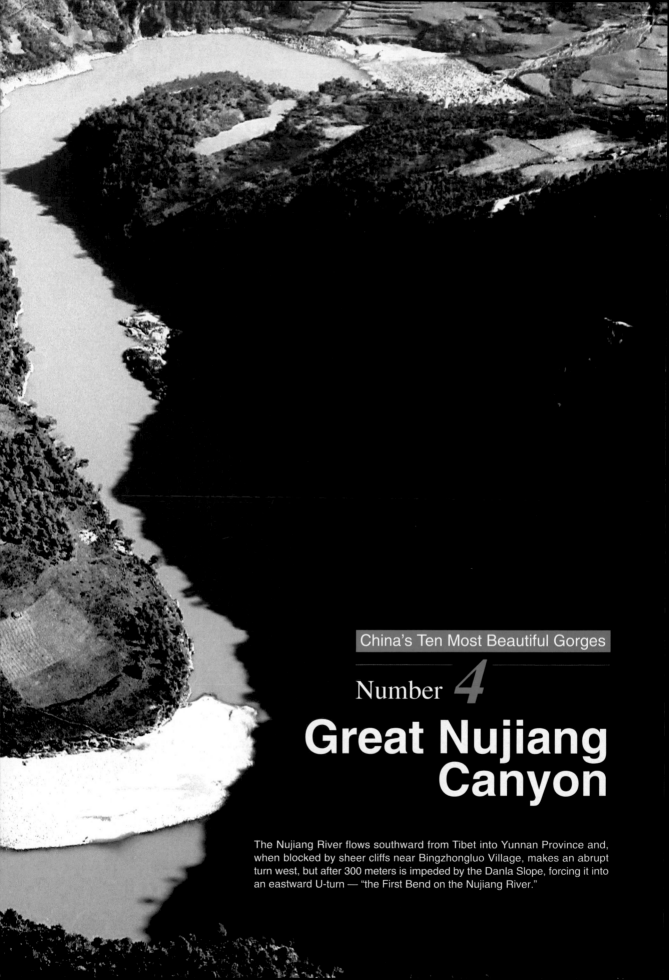

Number *4*

# Great Nujiang Canyon

The Nujiang River flows southward from Tibet into Yunnan Province and, when blocked by sheer cliffs near Bingzhongluo Village, makes an abrupt turn west, but after 300 meters is impeded by the Danla Slope, forcing it into an eastward U-turn — "the First Bend on the Nujiang River."

The Great Nujiang Canyon from the air. This dreamland is one of the most mysterious canyons in the world.

Here the river is wide and flows gentle — not a trace of the angry Nujiang River that its name (Nu means anger) implies, just a sense of harmony with nature. (right)

The Great Nujiang Canyon is a "longitudinal" valley, lying parallel with the run of mountain ranges that give rise to the natural wonder of the Three Parallel Rivers. This is because the northeast edge of the Indian Plate collided with the Eurasian Plate, creating a series of large north-south splits in what is today's northwestern Yunnan and eastern Tibet. The Great Nujiang Canyon starts from Cawarong at Zayul County in Tibet and stretches south for some 300 kilometers to reach Liuku, capital of Nujiang Lisu Autonomous Prefecture in Yunnan Province. Flanked by the Biluo and Gaoligong snow mountains, this is the most perilous section of the Nujiang River; it is over 2,000 meters deep on average, the deepest point being between the 5,128-meter-high Luchulaka Peak of the Gaoligong Mountain and the 4,784-meter-high Zhuzipo Peak of the Biluo Snow Mountain, where the valley bottom is 1,650 meters above sea level, giving a height difference of 3,478 meters. The riverbed in the Great Nujiang

Canyon is usually 100-150 meters wide in the canyon but is just a few dozen meters across at its narrowest. In this deep-cut valley, the Nujiang River breaks through the stone gates, ravines and cliffs that would pen it in, and the many dangerous shoals in its path provoke a continuous earth-shaking roar.

The area of the Great Nujiang Canyon is famous for cultural diversity. The largest community of the Lisu ethnic group lives here and it is the only place where Nu and Derung ethnic groups live; 20 other minorities are represented here, among them Primi, Bai, Yi, Naxi, Tibetan, Jingpo and Dai. The Ancient Tea Horse Road along the canyon is some 1,000 years old. Many ethnic groups and religions coexist, but Christianity and Catholicism are all very popular with those ethnic minorities — a cultural and geographical phenomenon worth pondering.

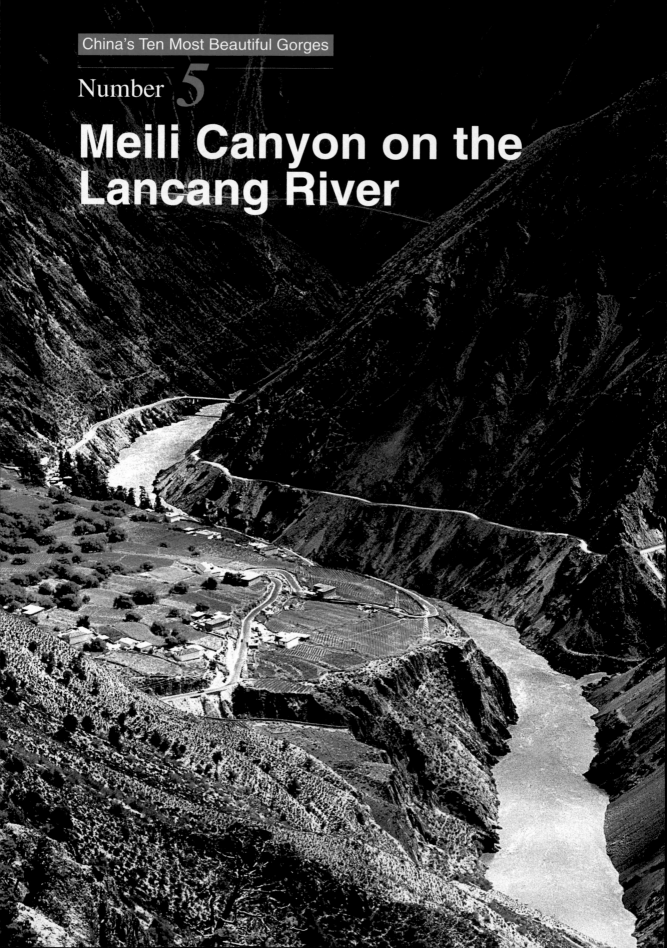

Number *5*

# Meili Canyon on the Lancang River

The Lancang Canyon is located in Deqen County, Yunnan Province, stretching from Foshan Township to Yanmen Township, over 100 kilometers to the south, and has the largest elevation difference in Yunnan. The river surface in the canyon is 2,006 meters above sea level; on the left bank rises the Kawagebo Summit (6,740 meters) of the Meili Snow Mountain and on the right the Zhalaqueni Summit (5,460 meters) of the Baima Snow Mountain, giving a maximum elevation difference of 4,734 meters, within a slope distance of only 14 kilometers. When the Lancang River flows from Tibet into the Meili Canyon, it suddenly narrows, causing a violent rushing torrent. It is a key passage between Yunnan and Tibet. The Meili Canyon area, as one of China's largest and most important nature reserves, the main objects of its protection being such rare species as the Yunnan golden monkey, and natural scenery such as typical Hengduan Mountains mountain-forest vertical zone.

The internationally renowned Lancang River has been dubbed "the Danube of the East." The Meili Canyon on the Lancang River within Deqen County has an exceptionally wonderful geological structure, with precipitous mountains and vertical valleys.

There is a kind of gorge called Zhang valley. It is a V-shaped valley flanked by steep, near-vertical sides, that are practically of the same width apart from top to bottom, almost all of the bottom being occupied by the riverbed. In areas where the earth's crust rises abruptly, rivers flow down between the joints of hard rock strata, and thus a Zhang valley comes into being. The Tailuge Gorge is a typical example.

Number *6*

# Tailuge Gorge

A "kettle cave" in the Tailuge Gorge riverbed. A "kettle cave" is a kind of deep pit scoured out of broken and soft rocks by the gravels brought down by mountain rivers. They can either be at the bottom of a riverbed or on the two sides of the river course.

Look at a cross section of Taiwan Island, you will find that its topography is asymmetrical. The Central Mountain Range lies mostly in the eastern part, rather gentle on their western face with a wide plain in front, while their eastern face is mostly sheer cliffs rising sharply from the western shore of the Pacific Ocean. This came about due to the westward tilting of the Pacific Plate, which in turn caused Taiwan to incline westwards. The Liwu River descends oceanwards, down from its 3,440-meter-high source in the Qilai Mountains, landing right on the world-famous Qingshui Precipice on the east coast of Taiwan where, like a master craftsman, it carves out the Tailuge (Taroko) Gorge. The gorge winds for about 20 kilometers along the course of the Liwu River from Tailuge in the east to Tianxiang in the west, with a gradient of 0.59 per cent; it measures 1,660 meters at its deepest point and between 10-20 meters at its narrowest. Since the cliffs are formed of crisp, hard and solid marble with beautiful markings, they look quite lofty and majestic. The Atayal people, the indigenous inhabitants of the Tailuge Gorge who once had 97 tribes in the Liwu River basin, shaped a unique culture of their own, and Tailuge means "great mountain range" in their language.

# Number 7
# Shanxi-Shaanxi Gorge on the Yellow River

Displayed in all its beauty, the Qiankun Bend on the Yellow River lies on the boundary between Shanxi and Shaanxi provinces.

Once it leaves the Qinghai-Tibet Plateau, the Yellow River flows through mountains, making many twists and turns, falls and continues its course until reaches Taohuayu (Peach Blossom Valley) in Zhengzhou where it suddenly changes from opening up channels and valleys into creating new land; Taohuayu thus becomes the top of the world's largest delta — the North China Plain. Most of the Yellow River gorges occur along Taohuayu.

The upper reaches of the Yellow River to Hekou Township in Togtoh County, Inner Mongolia, and the lower part of its middle lower reaches between Yumenkou and Taohuayu have many famous gorges, including the Longyang, Jishi, Liujia, Hongshan, Qingtong, and Sanmen gorges; but these are separated by many broad valleys and basins. The section between Hekou in Inner Mongolia and Yumenkou in Shanxi Province — the 725-kilometer-long Shanxi-Shaanxi Gorge — is the longest continuous gorge on the mainstream of the Yellow River. The Yellow River runs in a west-east direction in the Hetao area, but it makes a sharp turn here and dashes southward through the Ordos Plateau. Flanked by the Lüliang Mountains to the left and northern Shaanxi on the right, the Yellow River stays deep in the Loess Plateau. The valley is over 100 meters deep on average and the valley bottom declines from 1,000 meters above sea

level to below 400 meters. The riverbed at its narrowest points, such as the Hukou Waterfall, is just 30-50 meters across.

Since silt is carried along down from the Loess Plateau, sand in the Shanxi-Shaanxi Gorge section accounts for 56 per cent of all sand carried by the Yellow River, even though its drainage area represents only 15 per cent of the entire Yellow River drainage area. Perhaps we should say that the real "Yellow" River is created here, where archetypal Yellow River gorge scenes — swift currents, roaring yellow waters, deep valleys — coalesce. The Longmen Gorge above Yumenkou is the most magnificent. With this the Shanxi-Shaanxi Gorge reaches its final climax.

The desolate beauty of the Shanxi-Shaanxi Gorge where the Yellow River flows through the Loess Plateau, captured in this aerial photograph.

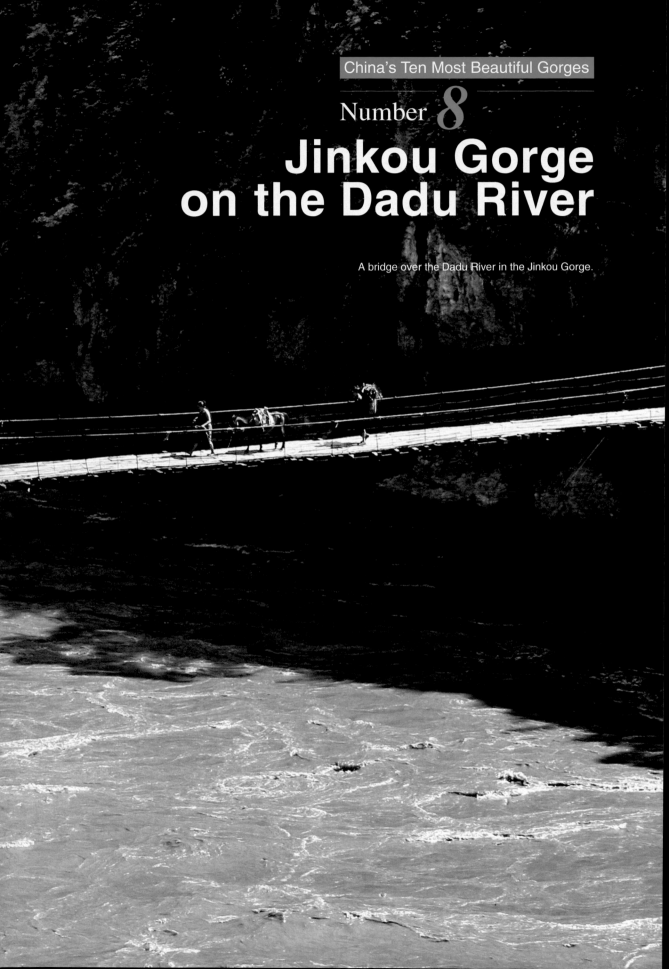

Number *8*

# Jinkou Gorge on the Dadu River

A bridge over the Dadu River in the Jinkou Gorge.

The Dadu River originates in the Bayan Har Mountains where Sichuan and Qinghai provinces meet. After the Lesser Jinchuan River converges with the Large Jinchuan in its upper reaches at Danba, it is called the Dadu River. The river rushes through high mountains and lofty ridges in the eastern part of the Hengduan Mountains. There are gorges with splendid scenery all the way, but it is in the Jinkou Gorge that the Dadu River gorge landscape reaches its climax. The Jinkou Gorge extends eastward for 26 kilometers from the Wusi River in Hanyuan County to the Jinkou River in Leshan City. The valley floor is usually between 70 and 200 meters wide, shrinking at one point to below 50 meters; and the valley shoulders are about eight kilometers across at the widest point. At the exit of the canyon, the river valley is 580 meters above sea level at the lowest point, and Dawa Mountain on the northern bank of the Dadu River is 3,222 meters above sea level, making the canyon over 2,600 meters deep. Continuous, sheer and magnificent, the gorge is a rare and precious sight. The Jinkou Gorge is located on a dramatically rising section of the earth's crust in the eastern part of the Hengduan Mountains, moreover it is where the elevational difference between the first and second steps of China's "geological staircase" is greatest, and is predominantly composed of horizontally stratified hard dolomite. These factors make it one of the most classical examples of a Zhang valley and ravine on China's large rivers, characterized by near vertical slopes, a deep and narrow floor almost completely taken up by the riverbed. The tributary channels feeding in on both sides are fathomless, narrow and precipitous beyond description. The entrance to the Jinkou Gorge has an unusual three-way access: running parallel to the Dadu River are the Jinkou-Wusihe Road and Chengdu-Kunming Railway, and winding through the perilous mountains is the Leshan-Xichang Road built during the Second World War.

The Jinkou Gorge on the Dadu River is a classical example of erosion landform and a rare natural wonder.

# Number 9
# Taihang Gorges

The gorge group of the southern Taihang Mountains, located between the Huguan Pass and Pingshun in Shanxi Province and Linzhou and Huixian in Henan Province, with the White Defile as the mainstream, is typical of the Taihang Gorge system. The height of those ridges is between 1,000 and 2,000 meters. The above photo shows the cliffs of Zhangliang Peak in Jiaozuo, Henan Province.

The Taihang Gorges are outstanding, not just for one section, but because the Juma, Hutuo, Zhanghe and Qinhe rivers and eight defiles create the Taihang Gorge system that stretches 600 kilometers north to south, and 250 kilometers east to west. It is a gorge group rare in China or anywhere in the world for that matter, with both individual aesthetic features and excellent regional qualities.

The vertical composition of the Taihang Mountains is diverse. In the central and southern areas the mountains are comprised roughly of three strata: the base of the Taihang Mountains is formed of 1.8 billion year-old gneiss — a type of ancient metamorphic rock; then there is purple-red quartzite laid down one billion years ago; then limestone laid down 500 to 600 million years ago. The gorges were formed predominantly through the quartzite and limestone of the upper and central parts of the Taihang Mountains, but in terms of

Baligou Gorge in Huixian County,
Henan Province.

topography, the Taihang Gorge system demonstrates an amazing consistency. The strong uprise of the Shanxi Plateau against the North China Plain created mountain fault-blocks, and then downward erosion by water formed typical combinations such as Zhang valleys, jar-like valleys, hanging ditches, long cliffs, and stepped terraces. These, plus the various rock textures, colors and striations, combine to create a scroll painting of the Taihang Gorge group in all its austerity, strength and simplicity.

Mount Wangmang in Lingchuan County in Shanxi Province is the most strategic and inaccessible spot on the fracture zone between the Loess Plateau in the west and the North China Plain in the east — a place of immeasurable sheer precipices, crowded mountain peaks, dangerous rocks and crisscrossing ravines.

Number *10*

# Kuqa Gorge in the Tianshan Mountains

The Kuqa Gorge in the Tianshan Mountains, magical and fantastic, has many "natural sculptures" — masterpieces created by the mountains' melting ice and snow. Some look like "an old man with a stick," and some like "a narrow rift in heaven."

The Kuqa (or Kucha) Gorge is located in the southern part of the Tianshan Mountains, about 64 kilometers north of Kuqa County in Xinjiang. The Kuqa River is a tributary of the Tarim River, and local Uygur people call its valley "Kizilia" which means "red cliffs." A typical earth-rift ravine, the gorge extends more than five kilometers in total, with a main valley and seven branch valleys. It is 1,600 meters above sea level on average and its highest peak reaches 2,048 meters; it is between 150-200 meters deep and at its narrowest point is only 1.2 meters wide. The whole gorge is made up of red sandstone and conglomerate of the Paleogene Period. With the upthrust of the Tianshan Mountains, these red rock strata were subjected to all kinds of folding and bending, added to which water and wind erosion, created the gorge's grotesque, jagged peaks and rocks. Although located in an arid continental area, there are clear gurgling springs in the gorge. At sunrise, sunset as the wind gets up, as mists rise or sounds echo, as light and shade shift and change — its mystery and strangeness is beyond words.

Kuqa is a corruption of the name "Qiuci." The cultural heritage of the ancient Qiuci Kingdom in Kuqa is a delight of the Silk Road. Recently the remains of the Thousand-Buddha Cave created during the heyday of the Tang Dynasty (618-907) were discovered in the Kuqa Gorge. Its grotto murals compare well with those of the Dunhuang Grottoes of the same period. There is a similar but larger gorge — Kuduluke Gorge in Wensu in the southern part of Mount Tomur, the highest peak of the Tianshan Mountains. In the vast tracts of the Tianshan Mountains, indeed all China's northwest, there are more splendid gorge landscapes waiting. ▯

Moonnight in the heart of the Taklamakan Desert, quiet and mysterious.

# China's Five Most
# Beautiful Deserts

**Ranking**

1. **Badain Jaran Desert Interior**      **(Inner Mongolia)**
2. **Taklamakan Desert Interior**      **(Xinjiang)**
3. **Gurbantünggüt Desert Interior**      **(Xinjiang)**
4. **Booming Sand Dune and Crescent Spring**      **(Gansu)**
5. **Shapotou**      **(Ningxia)**

China's Five Most Beautiful Deserts

Number 1

# Badain Jaran Desert Interior

*Curves Drawn by God*

Deep in the Badain Jaran Desert, fold after fold of dunes rise and fall; the wave-like lines seem like curves doodled by God.

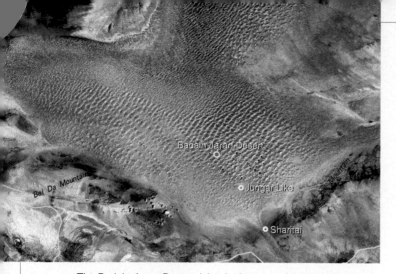

Badain Jaran Desert

Bei Da Mountain

Jungar Like

Sharitai

Walking in the Badain Jaran, one feels like walking through thousands years of history, and like making a pilgrimage to the high Alasha Desert Pyramid. (right)

Among the high dunes of the Badain Jaran are over 140 inland lakes, locally known as *haizi*. Most of them are saline. There are always swampy meadows and salt meadows around the lakes, which are important for grazing. (below)

The Badain Jaran Desert, lying in the west of the Alasha Plateau of the Alasha Prefecture, Inner Mongolia, covers 44,000 square kilometers, ranking third in China. Some 83 per cent of the desert is composed of shifting dunes. The area around the Badain Jaran Monastery, deep in the interior, is the most beautiful part.

Facing its infinite emptiness and unending dunes, you can only feel expansive and still. The world here is simplified into three elements — dunes, camels and vastness.

Walking in the Badain Jaran Desert is like walking through thousands of years of history; it feels like a pilgrimage too, as you face the pyramid dunes of Alasha.

The steep dunes rise up high from the flat ground, one after the other, covering the whole desert. Paths zigzag up the dunes and down to the next; and as for road signs — there are only the dried white droppings of camels to guide you, or simply gut instinct. When the camel's pads step onto the sand drifts, the sand slides down, and the camels too, often slip back a step for every two they climb. You have to lie on your stomach over the camel, holding firmly onto its front hump for fear of falling off. Unlike in the flat gobi, the camels cannot run at will; it takes much time and all their breath to creep over every single dune.

Walking in the desert calls for patience. In fact, there is nothing to worry about. Ahead of

you lies nothing but sand, nothing but loneliness, nothing but one day following another. But walking in desert, there is much space and time for reflection, for letting the mind wander; this vast backdrop is better than lofty mountains and flowing rivers. If you suddenly spot camels in the far distance, you feel a surge of warm emotion. But in just a second, they vanish without a trace.

Throughout a lifetime, one can have countless nights — plain, impulsive, nostalgic, romantic, merry and lively. But the night we camped out on Wuzhumu, deep in the Badain Jaran Desert, I had the feeling I was on the west slope of Qomolangma Peak. Wuzhumu is the highest point in the Badain Jaran Desert, at an elevation of 1,700 meters. The dune rises 528 meters high from the ground, and is the highest sand hill in China. It is also the world's largest area of booming

Only in the Badain Jaran can you see such a magical sight: light and shadow chop and change on the ridges and cols of the high dunes. Look at the shadow of this dune, is it not like a person's profile?

sand. As it slips and slides, the sand emits thunderous booming noises.

Resting my head on sand of the Badain Jaran Desert and thinking back of the past of the western area, it was hard to fall asleep.

At dawn the next day, we remounted our camels and continued our journey on to Bayan Nur.

The dunes here were even bigger. Green saksauls grew everywhere on the yellow sand beside the road, their colors enhancing each other. A yurt visible in the distance took us ages to reach, even though it didn't look that far.

The lake stretched out below our feet, deep and clear. Surrounded by sand, it was like a mother's charming smile, or a teardrop on the sky. There are over 140 such lakes in the desert, with an area of 666 hectares all told — a unique desert sight. Some are freshwater lakes, others are extremely saline. It is a really incredible thing when a lake next to a salty one turns out to be fresh.

It was sunset when we arrived at the shore of Bayan Nur. The sheep dogs barked in excitement while the host family busied themselves preparing food and lodging for the guests. They had no time to exchange more than a word or so of greeting.

During my ten days of jolting through the Badain Jaran, looking out for yurts and colored pennants on the dunes, I experienced a myriad of emotions, sadness and thrills. Badain Jaran is the most beautiful, the most wonderful place in the world. How lucky I was to go there.

The lake amongst the dunes is deep and clear. Surrounded by sand, it's like a mother's charming smile, or a teardrop on the sky. (below)

High dunes are a feature of the Badain Jaran — at least 200 to 300 meters high, and up to 500 meters. There is no other desert in the world with dunes as high as this. (right page)

China's Five Most Beautiful Deserts

Number *2*

# Taklamakan Desert Interior
*A World of Sand on Earth*

In the Taklamakan, the earth opens its arms, revealing itself without reservation.

The Taklamakan Desert, covering some 330,000 square kilometers, is the second largest shifting sand desert in the world. As a "cemetery of civilizations," in the early years of the 20th century, the Taklamakan attracted explorers from all around the world and treasures excavated here and in the Tarim Basin are in the museum collections of more than ten countries.

It is the world's largest underground treasury of cultural relics. The desert destroyed many towns and villages, swallowing lives, legends and details, but left ruins, remote echoes, fragmentary memories and unlimited imaginings. Loulan, Niya, Xiaohe, Milan and Dandanwulike ... these famous ancient cities recorded the prosperity of the Silk Road; after years, they are still like sparks in the wilderness which can light up flames in people's minds. The winged angel mural, the brocade bearing the words "five planets appearing in the east bode well for the Middle Kingdom," the Roman pillar, the Indian Buddha statue, the mummified "Loulan Beauty" ... all these excavated discoveries show that this was the only place on earth where the four great ancient civilizations mixed together.

From just about every standpoint — geography, ecology, psychology and symbolism — the Taklamakan Desert is a fearsome, nightmarish place. It has been called the "Sea of Death." Sparsity and desolation are its only themes, but the most dangerous thing is the lack of water. For a weary and exhausted traveler, even more awful is the seeming boundlessness of this never-ending desert. Once a sand storm forms, roaring and howling, it can even uproot large trees. This is the "fury of God...." Frightful white bones in the desert are all that is left of persons, horses and camels. High hovering vultures looking for carrion, a crouching sand fox, nose still bloody from prey eaten a few hours earlier, a lizard, hiding in the loose sand to escape predators, a scurrying scorpion carrying a brood of tiny scorpions on its back, gruesome wolf spiders, six eyes glittering cruelly, the other two eyes closed.... But none of these could stop people trying to explore this desert. For hundreds of years, an endless stream of expeditions, trade caravans, treasure seekers, robbers and pilgrims entered the desert. They came with different purposes. But the real attraction might be something else — not dead civilizations, gold or treasure, but the scared magic of the desert itself.

The Swedish explorer Sven Hedin once likened the shifting dunes of

Deep in the Taklamakan Desert, are the Hotan, Keriya, Niya, and Andir rivers. Some, like the Hotan River, go through the desert; others run dry and gradually disappear in a fan-shaped area. These rivers form natural "green corridors" in the heart of the desert. (right page)

the Taklamakan to "graves without crosses" and the expedition departures to "funeral processions."

Late in the 9th century, Satuq Bughra Khan of the Qarakhanid Dynasty, who was just 16 years old at the time, was hunting one day in the Taklamakan when he saw a caravan of Muslims, prostrating themselves toward Mecca in daily prayer, oblivious to their goods and baggage scattered around. He was surprised and intrigued. Considering such devout belief and strict discipline would help him realize his ambitions, he became a fervent convert to Islam. Several centuries later, Islam was the only religion in the Taklamakan area. What a coincidence that Islam, born in the Arabian desert, should find a home in the Taklamakan.

The native Keriya and Ywungkax people who have lived deep in the desert for centuries say that the Taklamakan, in fact, is not uninhabitable. Until not long ago, crossing the desert along the old watercourse of the Keriya River, the Uygur shepherds of Yutian County always herded their sheep and camels by the banks of the Tarim River in Shaya, and returned to Yutian once the sheep and camels were fattened up. For them, the wadi in the desert is a road, a road to oasis and life.

The Taklamakan Desert is called the "Sea of Death." Sven Hedin translated it into "if you go in, you won't come out." However, in Uygur, the name actually means "old home."

The Taklamakan, lying in the center of the Tarim Basin, covers 337,600 square kilometers, and is the biggest desert in China. It is also the world's second largest shifting sand desert. Between the Keriya River and the Hotan River in the heart of the desert, the vast sea of sand stretches to the horizon. It is a magnificent sight. (below)

The Taklamakan has an unequalled variety of dunes — pyramid, dome, fish-scale, tower, honeycomb and feather dunes. Almost every dune type that China has can be found in this desert and their changing shapes are a desert attraction. (right page)

China's Five Most Beautiful Deserts

Number 3

# Gurbantünggüt Desert Interior

*Blood Vessels of the Desert*

Shaped by the wind direction, the linear dunes of the Gurbantünggüt Desert stretch ten kilometers from north to south, looking like tree branches or the desert's blood vessels.

The Gurbantunggut lies in Xinjiang's Junggar Basin. Some 48,000 square kilometers in area, it is China's second largest desert. (first right)

Fixed or semi-fixed sand ridges cover 97 per cent of the desert. Some 100 plants grow in the desert, many of which make good sand-fixing plants and pasture grass. About a quarter of the annual precipitation falls in winter. (second right)

There are several thousand hectares of well-protected virgin saksaul forest in the depths of the Gurbantunggut. (below)

I grew up in a small village at the edge of the Gurbantünggüt Desert. When I was young, I used to like sitting on a haystack, looking north toward the desert for a bit and then south toward the Tianshan Mountains for a while. Sitting between these two, I had a sense of being trapped. From where I lived, the Manas River wriggles its way northwest along the edge of the desert, before finally disappearing into the desert. It is the dividing line between desert and oasis. I never went to the end of the river. By the time I grew up, it had almost vanished, its course intercepted by several dams along its upper and middle reaches. All that now remains of the famous Manas River is just a dry riverbed left as a spillway.

The Gurbantünggüt Desert is the northwest wind's masterpiece, the image of the invisible wind on the ground. From west to east, a northwest wind, as wide and as long as the desert, lies in the Junggar Basin. I have taken National Highway 217 from Kuytun to Urho and Hoboksar many times. Along the route, the Karamay Gobi is certainly the start of the Gurbantünggüt Desert, as it is here that the strong northwest wind starts blowing up sand and making dunes. The start of a large desert is not as grand as you would think: there is endless desert, but no high dunes, just an occasional small dune standing on the desert, like a solitary animal facing east. When the wind blows, it

Shaped by the northwest wind, the linear, regular sand ridges in the west of the desert stretch from northwest to southeast.

seems to run, but it is still there when the wind stops. But perhaps what we now see is not the one that was there originally. The sand, filling everything between earth and sky, runs, runs and runs, forming the awesome Gurbantunggut Desert not far away.

In Qitai County where the west wind abates, the sand drops, forming larger dunes than elsewhere. Connected with the hills of the Jiangjun Gobi, vegetation there thrives. A mix of saksauls, purple willows, agriophyllum pungens, camel thorns, and diversiform-leaved poplars grows upon the dunes.

When it reaches the Jiangjun Gobi, the northwest wind is blocked by the Baytik Mountains between China and Mongolia, and turns south towards Hami (Kumul). The desert expands southeastward, following the wind. Once past Urho, known as the "devil's city", the wind turns to another famous Xinjiang "devil's city" — Longcheng — and enters Lop Nur.

The Karamay Gobi and the Jiangjun Gobi represent the head and tail of a huge desert, and the start and end of the strong northwest wind. The Shawan area in the middle of the Gurbantunggut Desert where I used to live is the most mature part. The dunes here are full, regular and stable. And because of the all-year-round, ceaseless northwest wind, they all face east. This fact is a very important piece of desert lore; if you get lost in the desert, you can take your bearing from the dunes. If you know the dunes all face east, you can climb a high dune, and figure out the direction. At the entrance to our village, the Manas River makes a bend, leaving a small lake, bordered by the dunes. Great swathes of purple willow grow on the banks, covering vast areas. When the purple willows come into bloom, their red fire spreads from the water's edge right up to the sky. Nowadays, thanks to a ban on tree-felling and grazing, the vegetation has started to recover and Mongolian gazelles, Asiatic wild asses, wolves, wild boar and other animals come here in great number to drink. Several years ago, an oil prospecting team built a road from east to west in the heart of the desert. Regular cross-country vehicles can use it.

The dunes of the Gurbantunggut Desert are fairly uniform. Full-grown sand ridges account for 80 per cent of all fixed and semi-fixed dunes.

## Number *4*

# Booming Sand Dune and Crescent Spring

## *A Thousand Years of Watching*

The Booming Sand Dune and Crescent Spring, five kilometers southwest of Dunhuang, create an amazing desert view. (below)

The dune's name (Mingshashan) comes from the booming noise made by the sands when people climb up. The spring's name (Yueyaquan) comes from its crescent form, cradled in the dunes. For a lake near a dune to survive for a thousand years is a unique desert phenomenon. As it is near Dunhuang, it has a temple on its bank, adding to its fame. (right)

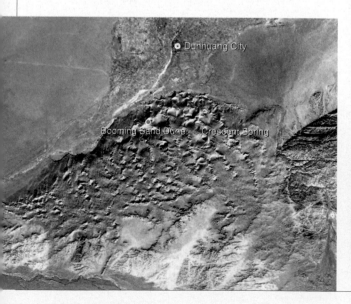

Dunhuang City

Booming Sand Dune    Crescent Spring

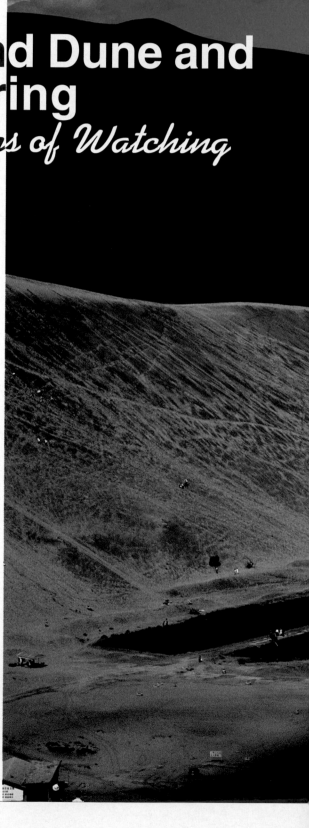

Number **5**

# Shapotou
## *Slowing the Steps of the Drifting Sands*

On one side of the Yellow River is the Loess Plateau and the other side is the Tengger Desert. The vast desert, long river, high mountain and oasis together make a magnificent sight. The sand-fixing miracle made by the desert-control experts for safety along the railway has spread the name of Shapotou throughout the world.

Shapotou lies in Zhongwei City of Ningxia Hui Autonomous Region, southeast of the Tengger Desert and north of the Yellow River. (below)

A majestic, infinite sea of yellow sand, trimmed with a wide belt of green. At Shapotou stands a dune one hundred meters high; southward-facing, the dune curves inward at its center. When tourists go sand-sledging, the sand thunders, giving rise to the name Shapo Mingzhong — "Sounding Bell on the Sand Slope."

The Baotou-Lanzhou Railway, built 50 years ago, has become part of the scenery. Shapotou epitomizes the harmonious coexistence of man and desert adapting to the laws of nature. ⏻

Shapotou means Sand Slope Head, this name coming from the
2,000-meter-wide and 100-meter-high sand riverbank.

# China's Three Most
# **Beautiful Yadan Landforms**

**Ranking**

"Yadan" is a precipitous hillock in the Uygur language, a kind of wind-eroded landform. Of all the Yadan landforms, the magnificent rocks of Urho are the favorites of photographers. The setting sun gives Urho's jumble of crags and boulders a fiery red hue, as if a castle were burning.

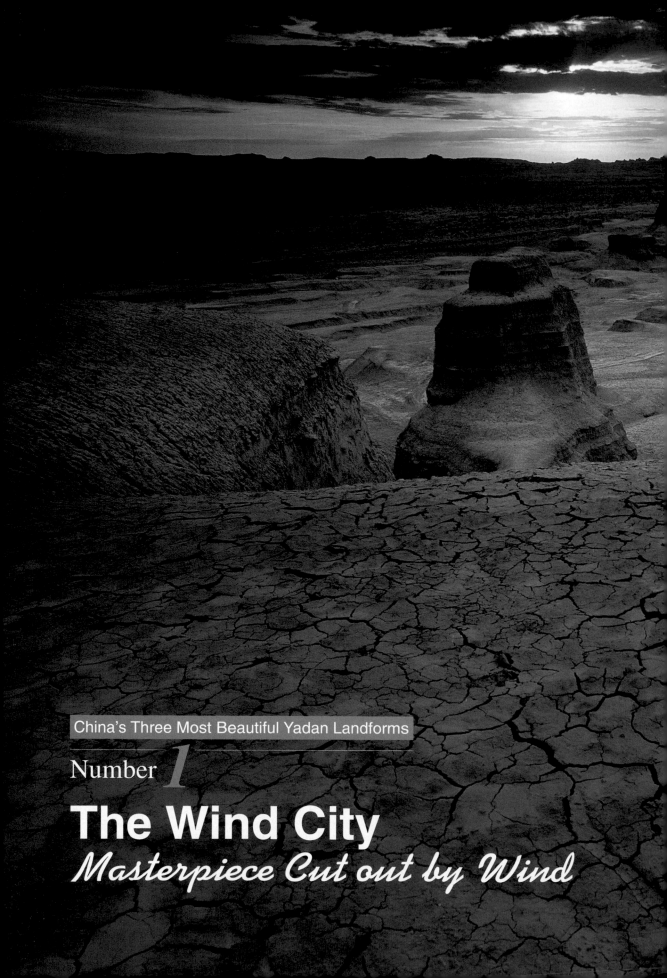

China's Three Most Beautiful Yadan Landforms

Number *1*

# The Wind City
## *Masterpiece Cut out by Wind*

The rocks of the Wind City of Urho are densely distributed in huge quantities.

Some 110 kilometers from the oil city of Karamay lies a striking natural sand formation called Yadan with an area of 10 square kilometers known as the Wind City of Urho. It suddenly looms out of the desert as you drive along National Highway 217. Placed in graceful disorder by a mysterious force, the "city" is embellished with stimulating colors — red,

Urho is a bleak sight in winter. (above)

A typical cave of the Urho region, carved out by the wind and rain. (right)

A block of solid mudstone. (left)

Battered by centuries of wind, the soil is spongy in Urho, exposing a multitude of colorful rocks. Sometimes, sparkling agate can be found here. (below)

grayish-green and grayish-blue.

It is called the "Haunt of Devils" in both the Mongolian and Kazak languages. When a howling wind suddenly arises, it whips up sand, rolls stones around, and darkens the sky and the earth, causing people in ancient times to believe that demons haunted the Wind City.

The desolate formation has a multitude of

A wind-eroded rock pillar in the shape of a dolphin.

The landform in the Wind City of Urho came into being after prolonged erosion of rock stratums, which vary in degree of hardness. The howling of the frequent winds has given the area the name of "Haunt of Devils."

shapes, large and small, high and low, beautiful and ugly. Some look like medieval European castles; some are like lofty pagodas; some are like clouds of dense smoke; others are like crawling tortoises or snakes. There are thousands of gorges and crisscross gullies winding through the Wind City. In the bright sunshine, the Wind City is a dazzling and impressive sight. On rainy days, it is covered with mist, suggestive of fear and danger. In winter, it looks unusually peaceful in its blanket of snow, like a sleeping child.

In northwest China's Xinjiang Uygur Autonomous Region many abandoned cities can be found, including Jiaohe, Gaochang and Loulan. However, unlike them, the Wind City of Urho is without any trace of a human presence.

The Wind City is lovely and terrible, miraculous and weird, imbued with a sense of loneliness and wildness, making a striking contrast to bustling modern cities. Generally speaking, beauty is harmonious. But the Wind City is in graceful disorder. And whereas beauty is usually refined and elegant, the Wind City is rough and natural.

# Number *2*

# Bailongdui
*Where Dragons Gather*

No one knows why these giant white dragons have gathered here. Maybe they are guarding the secrets of Lop Nur. (above)

The Yadan landform of Bailongdui (White Dragon Dunes) is located in the north of Qarkilik County, Xinjiang, to the northeast of Lop Nur. Covering an area of 1,000 square kilometers, it is most difficult to reach among all the Yandan landforms. Without a guide, no one would be able to find his way out of this labyrinth. (right)

China's Three Most Beautiful Yadan Landforms

Number *3*

# Sanlongsha
## *A Fleet in Desert*

The great variety of Yadan landforms at Sanlongsha is a feast for the eyes. It is a masterpiece of the romance of desolation in Nature, and adding to its attraction are the nearby ruins of the long-lost Loulan Kingdom. ▯

Situated in the east of the Aqqik Valley, Sanlongsha (Three Sandy Ridges) is part of the Yadan landforms of Lop Nur, and they cover about 100 square kilometers. Under the noonday sun, Sanlongsha looks like a group of millstones or a huge sparkling glossy ganoderma.

The sand dunes of the Yadan landform of Sanlongsha are evenly arranged, like a fleet of ships sailing in formation.

# China's Eight Most
# Beautiful Coastlines

## Ranking

| | |
|---|---|
| 1. Yalong Bay | (Sanya, Hainan) |
| 2. Yeliu | (Keelung, Taiwan) |
| 3. Chengshantou | (Rongcheng, Shandong) |
| 4. Dongzhaigang Mangrove Forest | (Qiongshan, Hainan) |
| 5. Changli Golden Beach | (Hebei) |
| 6. Victoria Bay | (Hong Kong) |
| 7. Chongwu Beach | (Hui'an, Fujian) |
| 8. Dapeng Peninsula Beach | (Shenzhen, Guangdong) |

Saw-tooth rocks seen from Xiyong Hill on the Dapeng Peninsula, Shenzhen, at daybreak.

The pristine beach attracts tourists all year round.

# Number *1*

# Yalong Bay
## *Paradise on Earth*

The tranquil Yalong Bay lies by a mountain to the north whose gentle slopes are covered with lush vegetation. Verdant and yellow leafy plants all grow humbly, keeping their heads down in submission to the frequent and ferocious visits of typhoons. At the foot of the mountain is a wide expanse of flat land, also green and lush, thanks to the ideal climate. Hidden amidst the greenery are the upswept eaves and painted beams of luxury hotels. Alongside stretches crescent-shaped Yalong Bay.

The south of the bay is dotted with three islets named, from east to west, Yezhu, Dongpai and Xipai. Small as they are, they create a line of protection for the quiet bay against the surging waves. Covering 66 square kilometers, the bay has a nine square-kilometers area of coral. The sea water is so clean that people can see clearly 10 meters down and spot tropical fish of all sizes and colors swimming through the coral reefs.

White sand beach at Yalong Bay.

"Yalong" is not the original name. It was first called "Yalang" by the local Li ethnic people. Long, long ago, there was a small village on the bay, where people lived a peaceful life until that peace was broken with the arrival of sea monsters that plundered the village, killing people and abducting women and cattle. One of the villagers vowed to drive away the monsters, and went to practice martial arts deep in the mountains for nine years and nine days. Then he returned home with a group of strong beasts he had trained. Hearing the news, the monsters were so scared they dared not come back.

One night, when a fierce wind blew and the seas billowed, the villagers fled for refuge to the mountains, leaving the hero and his beasts guarding their home,

not returning until all was calm. They found the hero and his beasts all transformed into rocks. His wolf, brandishing its claws and baring its teeth, looked very fierce, so the locals named the bay "Yalang" or "wolf cub."

Today, the bay is known for its wide expanse, gentle waves, refreshing air, and in particular, for its fine white sand. For hundreds of years, its crescent beach, stretching eight kilometers from east to west, has nurtured the eyes and lungs of people from near and far.

The transparency, pH value and dissolved oxygen in the water are all up to top standards. Nothing could lurk in the pure water. When standing in it, you can see your toenails clearly, like shells on the sand.

# Number *2*

# Yeliu

## *Works Created by Waves*

The magical erosion effects of tides and winds, and the movements of land and sea have created this fascinating seashore, where a rich variety of 180 mushroom-shaped rocks presents photographers with a marvelous scene.

Yeliu is a cape in north Taiwan, projecting some 1,700 meters into the sea. Standing on the Camel Rock in the southwest, you'll find the cape like a tortoise about to swim into the sea, hence the name "Yeliu Tortoise."

Yeliu means Wild Willow and the place has always had something wild about it. The peerless shapes of its rocks are a result of the caressing and lapping of waves and wind throughout the ages.

According to geologists, six million or 20 million years ago, due to the effects of orogenic movement, two faults emerged on the sides of today's Yeliu, and the original seabed was squeezed upwards above the ground. Scoured by wind, rain and wave action, the fault belt collapsed into the landmass, becoming a bay, the central prominent section becoming what is Yeliu cape today. Along the banks, cuesta escarpment, wave-cut cliffs and sea caves also emerged. The hard inner core of fossilized life forms that had lain undisturbed for centuries below the sea now started to be exposed under the weathering of the northeast monsoon winds and the washing of tides. Once soft surface rock was eroded, they were exposed to the air. Their shapes inspired the names they were given, among them beehive, bean-curd, mushroom, window and ginger formations.

The first section, at the eroded terrace entrance to the promontory, has the greatest diversity of grotesque rocks, their different geological strata eroding differently to create different shapes. Those nearest to the coastline look like ginger, the rocks along the inner side of a sea-cut trench are like windows, and those further inside look just like mushrooms. From the moment a rock first rises from the ground, it undergoes three periods — no neck, thick neck, thin neck until finally, when the thin neck can no longer bear the weighty head, it snaps off, announcing the ending of the rock's life. The iconic Yeliu landmark, the Queen's Head Rock, is said to be in its old age and geologists estimate it will collapse within 20 years.

A bird's-eye view of Yeliu.

The Queen's Head Rock, a Yeliu landmark.

Mushroom rocks are the most numerous type at Yeliu, but the most unique has to be the Candlestick Rock, the only one in Taiwan and one of the few around the world. Standing by the shore between the terrace and the hillside, the rock suffers scouring waves all year round. When the northeast monsoon blows in autumn and winter, terrifying waves pound on the rock. For centuries, the ceaseless currents have tempered the hard rock, smoothing its surface and shaping it into a huge candlestick.

The hill to the left is the best spot for a panoramic view of Yeliu. The grotesque rocks line up as far as the cuesta in the distance. The green mountains, golden marine terrace and blue sea combine to create fresh and colorful views.

While enjoying the strange rocks, don't forget to look down at the land beneath your feet. You can find fossils of ancient marine organisms, especially arthropods, since this was once the seabed. The most common are sea hedgehog fossils; dotted here and there are starfish and oyster fossils too.

On the way between the first and second areas, you come to the sea cave called Mazu Cave or Wangye Hall. It's said that two statues were once found here. Legend has it that 200 years ago, on the 16th day of the fourth lunar month, a statue of the goddess of the sea Mazu was found by the Yeliu villagers at the cave and later was enshrined in a temple five kilometers away. Another statue belongs to Chen Yuanguang, worshipped as "Sage King" by local people for his merits in reclaiming Zhangzhou and other places in southern Fujian. His statue is now enshrined in a temple by Yeliu Port.

To pray for peace and bumper catches, the local fishermen invite Mazu to their home on the date of the finding of her statue. People say that on the morning the goddess comes to Yeliu, it's always sunny and the tide is on the ebb, but that when she leaves, rain will fall and the tide will come in to submerge her cave.

Grove of 180 mushroom rocks, each two meters high and one meter in diameter.

Local fishermen believe the rain to be the tears of the goddess who is reluctant to leave.

Go past the Bird Rock and further toward the cuesta, you'll find yourself at the tip of the promontory, feeling extremely free and relaxed. A high point of your trip to Yeliu has been reached.

Near Yeliu Geological Park is a small fishing village that has existed since long before this place became well known. At dawn, the fishermen drive their boats out of the harbor and at dusk, they return. Some trade their catch at the harbor, but most will be sent to the tables in nearby restaurants. The small fishing boats put out to sea and return every day, busy but aloof from the renowned scenic spot a stone's throw away. The serenity here may be another aspect of Yeliu's appeal.

On the 16th day of the fourth lunar month, the Yeliu villagers invite Mazu to their home and pray for peace and bumper catches.

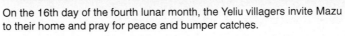

Wave action has scoured the bedrock into many "bean-curds."

China's Eight Most Beautiful Coastlines

Number *3*

# Chengshantou

*Longing to Embrace the Sea*

A bird's-eye view of Chengshantou.

Chengshantou, known as "the end of the earth," sits at the easternmost point of the Shandong Peninsula. It is also called "China's Cape of Good Hope."

Extruding into the sea, the cliffs have been cut steep by mighty waves and storms down the ages. Seething waves breaking upon the reefs can rise up to seven meters high. In the reserve area are also sea caves, sea pillars and other marine-cut landforms, as well as the red continental sedimentary bedrock at nearby Liukuang, all highly valued by Chinese and overseas geologists. Chengshantou's zigzag coastline, its many bays and headlands, and abundant plankton food, attracts flocks of swans and other rare birds to go over winter here. It has become one of the world's four major swan habitats.

A small harbor at Dongzhaigang.

China's Eight Most Beautiful Coastlines

Number 4

# Dongzhaigang Mangrove Forest
*Green-waved Coastline*

In 1986, the mangrove forest at Dongzhaigang at Qiongshan on Hainan Island was listed as a nature reserve under state protection. In 1992, it became China's first place on the world list of major wetlands.

The mangrove is an evergreen tree that grows along tropical, sub-tropical tidal shores or river estuaries. At high tide, they are totally submerged or only their tops are visible, and when the tide recedes, they show themselves as dense thickets. Both trees and shrubs have

Mangrove trees and their tangled masses of arching roots.

Fishing by the mangrove forest.

reddish brown bark and green leaves.

There are more than 40 mangrove species in the world, of which 24 grow in China (Guangdong, Hainan, Taiwan and Fujian) and 19 at Dongzhaigang. The overgrown mangroves at Dongzhaigang are like green waves along the coast. The place is also home to 159 kinds of bird and is an important resting place on the migration routes of many birds.

Number *5*

# Changli Golden Beach
## *Where the Desert Meets the Sea*

Blue sea beyond the golden dunes.

The Changli Golden Beach lies in northeast Hebei Province. It was formed 2,000-3,000 years ago by sand brought by the Liugu River that empties into the Bohai Sea in neighboring Liaoning Province.

Originating in the Yanshan Mountains that extend from northeast Beijing eastward to the Bohai Gulf, the river deposits huge quantities of silt into the sea, which drifts southwest with the current, driven by the strong northeasterly winds and piles up along the west coast of the gulf. The sand is then blown up by the northeast wind and after a short distance falls down on the beach, creating dunes.

In the slow process of accumulation down the ages, the dunes have got bigger and higher. The gentle sea-facing slope has a gradient of 6-8 degrees, whilst the steep escarpment on the other is 30-32 degrees. There are all together 40 chains of dunes, forming a rare landscape 30 kilometers long and 4 kilometers wide, and 44 meters high at the highest part. The fine, glittering sand has earned the beach the accolade "golden beach."

Golden beach below the waves.

# Number 6

# Victoria Bay

## Skyscrapers Mirrored on the Sea

Ten thousand years ago this place was an extension of the mainland mountains. Later, the mountains sank into the sea, forming the bay which separates Hong Kong Island from the mainland. It was given its present name by the British conquerors after their Queen Victoria 150 years ago.

The Victoria Bay is 1.3 kilometers wide, 10 kilometers long east-west, and has a water area of 59 square kilometers. Thanks to its advantageous location and conditions and massive development since the mid-19th century, it has now become a famous international center for finance, transportation and shopping.

# Number 7

# Chongwu Beach
## *A Vista of Hui'an Women*

The beach is on the southern Chongwu Peninsula, 24 kilometers southeast of Hui'an County. Standing at the highest part of the nearby ancient Chongwu City, you can get a view of the crescent bay and bathing beach, embraced by mountains on three sides. Hui'an women, wearing their yellow bamboo hats, bright-colored scarves, silver waist belts, short jackets and fat trousers, are another beautiful scene at Chongwu.

The place is known for its combination of pleasant beach views, ancient city and special local customs. The old white granite city, now under state protection, is an intact Ming (1368-1644) structure. The unique and ingenious construction skills have made the city "an example of historic systematic engineering."

Hard-working Hui'an women.

A panoramic view of Chongwu Beach.

Number *8*

# Dapeng Peninsula Beach
*A Virgin Land by the Bustling Metropolis*

The Dapeng Peninsula lies in east Shenzhen, and has a coastline of 133.2 kilometers. The granite hills on the peninsula are precipitous, with grotesque rocks and peaks. Along the tortuous coast are a dozen beaches, such as Xiasha, Xichong, Dongchong and Judiaosha. The sands are fine and the water is deep, ideal for surfing and sailing. This is the only virgin place yet to be developed in this bustling economic special zone. ❑

Xiyong Beach on the peninsula. At high tide the waters rise from between the two sand dunes into the lagoon.

# China's Six Most
# Beautiful Waterfalls

## Ranking

1. Tsangpo Badong Waterfalls     (Tibet)
2. Detian Waterfall     (Guangxi)
3. Hukou Waterfall     (Shanxi/Shaanxi border)
4. Jiulong Waterfall     (Yunnan)
5. Nuorilang Waterfall     (Sichuan)
6. Huangguoshu Waterfall     (Guizhou)

The Jiulong Waterfall in Luoping, Yunnan Province

The Yarlung Tsangpo is one of the most important rivers in China, with water reserves that rank second in China. In the heart of the Yarlung Tsangpo Grand Canyon, along the 20-kilometer uninhabited section between Shishing La to where the river is joined by the Parlung Tsangpo, there are many U-turns and steep cliffs. Four waterfalls represented by the Tsangpo

Number *1*

# Tsangpo Badong Waterfalls
## *Recluse in the Grand Canyon*

The Bailang (White Wave) Waterfall has the biggest headfall in the Tsangpo Badong Waterfalls and of any along the mainstream of the Yarlung Tsangpo River so far.

Badong have been discovered here. For so many majestic waterfalls occur along such a short but zigzag stretch of river is not only unique in China but a rare phenomenon anywhere. The Tsangpo Badong Waterfalls are the most spectacular, primitive and mysterious waterfalls in China.

In the deep and precipitous Yarlung Tsangpo Grand Canyon, waterfalls several-hundred-meter-high can be seen right along the river valley.

In October 1998, I led the first team of the Yarlung Tsangpo Grand Canyon science group, trekking for some 20 days from Pai Township in Menling County, along the Yarlung Tsangpo River towards its lower reaches, climbing over the Shishing La Pass and finally reaching the foot of the Tsangpo Badong Waterfalls on the mainstream of the Yarlung Tsangpo. My heart quaked at the sight of these wild falls slamming into the river from a 35-meter steep cliff at a rate of 1,900 cubic meters per second.

The Yarlung Tsangpo has a total length of 2,840 kilometers and is the 23rd longest river in the world. In terms of flow, it ranks seventh — 16,290 cubic meters per second, as much as 76,600 cubic meters per second at its largest flood flow, ranking fourth in the world. It starts in the Gyima Yamzoin Glacier on the north slope of the Himalayas, meanders along the foot of the Himalayas from west to east before meeting the foot of Namjagbarwa (7,782 meters), the main peak of the eastern Himalayas. Its way is blocked by Gyalabele (7,294 meters) snow mountain — then it pushes its way through the gap between the two mountains. In so doing it forms the precipitous Dorje Pagmo Valley east of Gyalabele. This mysterious valley, situated in the west of the Yarlung Tsangpo Grand Canyon, is home to four great waterfalls: Tsangpo Badong, Tsatan Muni, Chokor Tolang and Rongdrak waterfalls. The most spectacular is the Tsangpo Badong Waterfall at the entrance of the Dorje Pagmo Valley.

On November 16, 1998, when we crossed the Shishing La Pass and peered down over the Yarlung Tsangpo River from a height of 3,000 meters, our eyes beheld a wonderful sight: here the Yarlung Tsangpo River turns north and its 200-meter breadth is suddenly squeezed to some 100 meters. The roaring river surges and rolls with white billows into the Dorje Pagmo Valley, and crashes against a section of 30-odd-meter-high bedrock. Packing a punch of several thousand tons of water per second, it flies down from the bedrock like a maddened wild horse, smashing down at the foot of the cliff and splashing water everywhere. Clouds of white mist rose from the river up to where we stood. Seen from above, the whole river looked like a long white belt and seemed that the steep cliffs on both river banks were collapsing. As the river continues down, it encounters another steep cliff, so it has to swerve left and push its way through an even narrower passage before vanishing behind the cliff. This is the Tsangpo Badong Waterfalls. In fact it is a cluster of three waterfalls. The first waterfall at the upper reaches is the Tsangpo Badong Waterfall with a width of 117.7 meters and a headfall of 33 meters. The second is Bailang (White Wave) Waterfall which measures 62 meters across. Its headfall of 35 meters is the biggest of any waterfall found so far on the mainstream of the Yarlung Tsangpo. The width and headfall of Tsangpo Badong

In the dry season the Tsangpo Badong Waterfall is 117.7 meters wide with a headfall of 33 meters which might reach 40 meters in the flood season. So far, scientists cannot make measurements of the Tsangpo Badong Waterfall during the flood season.

Number 3 Waterfall are relatively small.

But, it's not easy to get close to and unveil the mysterious Tsangpo Badong Waterfall. To do so we had to trek for two days in the unending primeval forest. Finally, after hacking through the thick branches on a cliff edge, the Tsangpo Badong Waterfalls appeared before us. Between the almost perpendicular banks stood a 33-meter-high cliff, with a huge rock towering on the east side and splitting the river into two flows, which, colliding and clashing with each other, made a thundering sound as they flooded down. At times, the sunlight hit the river, immediately creating a rainbow across it. Although it was dry season at the time, the river flow was still enormous. We could tell by the watermark that during the summer flood season, the river could submerge the entire bedrock and the headfall can be as much as 40 meters. Just imagine that power!

Once past the falls the Yarlong Tsangpo continues to surge down. At the backwater at the foot of the western bank, are several huge craters formed by the grinding of huge sandstones driven by the power of the torrential current. Finally, the river water crashes into the wall of the bedrock, launching itself from the 65-meter-wide, 35-meter-deep second stair on the west side, and creating the Bailang Waterfall. This, the most splendid waterfall on the mainstream of the Yarlung Tsangpo River, is also the most mysterious waterfall in the world — no one had ever caught a panoramic view of it, apart from the photographer who was shooting from a helicopter.

The Bailang Waterfall hides beneath a steep slope, the bedrock, which was once the Yarlung Tsangpo riverbed, abandoned when the river cut its way around the side. Standing on this smooth rock, we saw water vapor rising up and heard a thundering roar but saw no waterfall. In order to photograph the waterfall, our photographers had to be lowered by rope with the help of the mountaineer members of the team. Protected with ropes, I approached the edge of the rock and peered down at the Bailang Waterfall. Sticking out my head, I was amazed by the flying waterfall below. From down below on the west side of the bedrock, the river launches itself forward, then hurtles down, disappearing into the abyss of the canyon. White water vapor rises from the bottom of the canyon like a mushroom cloud after an atomic explosion, and then disperses above the canyon.

At this point, the Chushur-Tsethang section of the Yarlung Tsangpo River suddenly appeared in front of my eyes. There the Yarlung Tsangpo river valley broadens out to between six and eight kilometers wide. There are many riverlets running in the valley and it is impossible to tell which is the mainstream. Leather boats are floating down with the current. During the flood season, the river is like a vast lake. The Tibetan people dig channels from the riverside, taking its water into their fields and forests. The Yarlung Tsangpo is so tranquil there. But here what we saw was a wild torrent!

Standing on the smooth rock riverbed, I listened to the roar of the river, smelled its scent permeating the air, my body quivering with the canyon and river. There and then I clearly understood what kind of waterfall is the most beautiful — a waterfall with all the power of a thunderbolt. Why? Because it is the true embodiment of Nature's might and majesty, awe-inspiring and stirring, and makes human beings more rational.

The Yarlung Tsangpo Grand Canyon is precipitous, misty and mysterious. The average flow of the river section of Yarlung Tsangpo Grand Canyon is ten times that of the Colorado River's 67 cubic meters per second.It has turbulent currents and many waterfalls.

China's Six Most Beautiful Waterfalls

Number 2

# Detian Waterfall
## Transcending National Boundaries

The changes of history bring a tinge of mystery to Detian Waterfall on the China — Vietnam border.

The Detian (Virtuous Heaven) Waterfall is situated on an international border — between Shuolong Town of Daxin County in Guangxi, China, and Yuxi of Chongqing County in Cao Bang, Vietnam. The Guichun River serves as the natural national boundary from Detian Village to Shuolong. The Guichun, which originates in Jingxi County, Guangxi, is about 150 kilometers long, and runs into Vietnam for 35 kilometers before crossing back into China. Indeed the name Guichun, which comes from the local inhabitants, means "returning to the country and meeting the source." The Guichun becomes a waterfall when it comes to a cliff at Putang Islet

near Detian and the waterfall is named after the village. The Detian Waterfall has an overall headfall of 70 meters over three cascades, the largest being over 200 meters wide and with an average flow of 50 cubic meters per second, five times that of the Huangguoshu Waterfall in Guangxi.

Geologically, the site is stratified dolomite, a relatively soft rock that is prone to collapse during the flood season, resulting in the waterfall changing form frequently.

It can provoke different reactions at different seasons. During the rainy season when the Guichun River is at peak flow in June and July,

The small waterfall beside the Detian Waterfall lies entirely in Vietnamese territory. The Vietnamese call all waterfalls Ban Gioc and, taking their cue from their cross-river neighbors, the Chinese call this small waterfall Ban Gioc Waterfall. In summer when there is plenty of rain, the two waterfalls look like a strong broad-shouldered male lover and a slim female lover. In winter when the waterfalls have smaller flows, they are like twin sisters.

the waterfall is mighty, powerful and inspiring, angrily roaring and billowing, not allowing anyone near. Try getting close on a bamboo raft, and the earthquaking roar and overwhelming vapor swallow up the air, making it hard to breathe.

If you can't stand the humidity and heat of summer in a sub-tropical monsoon climate and appreciate gentleness and grace, you should visit Detian Waterfall in October or even later, when the paddy fields turn gold. Detian Waterfall at this time looks stunning — like a graceful lady wearing a silk cape. In winter, the sub-tropical zone is rather cold and gloomy and the flow is reduced.

Spring comes early to southern China; the

mountains are covered by green and the kapok is in full bloom. If you want to enjoy Detian Waterfall in spring, you need to get on the road in February. If you stay at the nearby village you can enjoy the murmuring sound of the waterfall at night and, though the flow may still look meager in spring, it will swell out after several rains.

Within a 250-kilometer radius of the Detian Scenic Area — a natural landscape gallery — you can enjoy karst landscapes, rural scenery, canyons and waterfalls, deep river valleys, steep cliffs and roads, lakes and exotic customs.

A combination of wars and range upon range of high mountains have kept this Sino-Vietnamese border area separate from the outside

world. The most dangerous section lies 60 kilometers away from Detian, where the road winds its way through steep mountains towering into the sky. Fortunately, since the completion of the Class 2 highway, it takes only three hours to drive the 196 kilometers from Nanning to Detian and the steep cliffs and mountains and other views en route are a real delight.

After Shuolong, the Guichun River comes into view. The river water is green and crystal clear. On market days, people from one bank take their piglets, chickens and rice on bamboo rafts to the busy market fair on the opposite bank less than 100 meters away. If no one mentioned it, you would never believe that these two sides of the river, with the same mountains, water, trees, crops and villages are two different countries. At the bustling market, people with the same skin color and facial features chat to each other in dialect, as if from the same village. Just around the corner, the Detian Waterfall roars day and night. Scenes like these are particularly heart-warming.

It is commonplace that people from the two countries in the border area inter-marry. To them the Guichun is just an ordinary river instead of an international boundary. People from both banks raise their families, using the river for irrigation, for fishing, and for a nice cool dip after hard physical labor.

To the inhabitants of the border area, the past wars were not as horrible as outsiders imagine; even during the fighting, they refused the local government's evacuation orders and insisted on staying put.

Life nearby the Detian Waterfall is peaceful and harmonious, like the tranquil Guichun River itself. But though the fighting is a thing of the past, the border area remains mysterious as ever.

The mist, floating in the air some 100 meters in front of the waterfall, never disperses.

Number *3*

# Hukou Waterfall
*Myriads of Scenes in a Kettle*

The Hukou (Kettle's Mouth) Waterfall on the Yellow River is located in the Shanxi-Shannxi section of the Yellow River valley, 165 kilometers from Linfen City and 45 kilometers west of Jixian county seat. It is one of the world's few yellow waterfalls and has a fall of about 30 meters; at its widest it is over 1,000 meters across, and has an average flow of 1,010 cubic meters per second. The rolling Yellow River suddenly narrows at this point and plummets down, with a thundering roar, yellow waves, and rising mist.

The Yellow River is the symbol of the Chinese race, honored as the mother river, and the Hukou Waterfall is the most spectacular natural view on the Yellow River — a precious treasure gifted by Nature.

In winter, the Hukou Waterfall is partially frozen, creating a special kind of beauty. The ice on the banks resembles powerful lions about to bathe in the waters of the Yellow River which is howling, majestic, stirring....

# Number 4

# Jiulong Waterfall
## Flying Streamer on the Red Earth

The Jiulong (Nine Dragons) Waterfall, in Luoping County, eastern Yunnan, originates from the Jiulong River. It has ten tiers, and an average annual flow of 18.13 cubic meters per second. Every tier is different; some are powerful, some steep, some gentle, and the scene changes with the change of season and flow. Each tier is connected with the next by shoals or pools, giving rise to the saying "Jiulong has ten ponds, it is unique in the south." The most spectacular cascade is the fan-shaped Shenlong (Sacred Dragon) Waterfall, 112 meters wide and with a headfall of 56 meters, at the foot of which is an unfathombly deep round pool. Behind the curtain of water lies a cave some 10 meters deep. Luoping lies in the border area of Yunnan, Guizhou and Guangxi, where it is said "if a rooster crows, it can wake up three provinces." The waterfall surrounded by mountains and patchwork fields is a real countryside picture. Some two kilometers upstream of the fall are two governing reservoirs that can control the flow of the waterfall around the year; these have a certain impact on the natural features of the waterfall.

The Jiulong Waterfall during the flood season. Red earth accounts for over half of Yunnan's area, and the province is known as the "Red Earth Plateau." In the flood season, the water flow increases dramatically, carrying with it lots of red earth and dyeing the waterfall red.

In fact, the Jiulong Waterfall has more than ten tiers. If you walk further from the uppermost tier, you'll see three small-drop cascades. In this picture, taken from a hill a few hundred meters in height, some small waterfalls cannot be seen, making it look as if there are only five tiers.

China's Six Most Beautiful Waterfalls

Number **5**

# Nuorilang Waterfall
*A Length of Brocade in the Jungle*

The Nuorilang Waterfall is one of China's major travertine waterfalls. Its rolling waters swoop down, stirring the whole valley. Also called a "forest waterfall," its waters flow out of the dense forest, the trees and waterfall both separate and yet combine into one, like a green loom ceaselessly weaving a cloth of white silk.

At Jiuzhaigou Valley in northern Sichuan, it is a peerless experience to walk along the water, fed by distant clear and freezing snow water, that submerges old trees and dry roots, flows through desolate grassland and into the tranquil Jinghai Lake, sneaking out of the jungle and finally racing down over a fault cliff to create the fabulous Nuorilang Waterfall. Flowers, grasses and conifers thrive at the foot of the cliff, the vegetation muffling the noise of the flying waterfall like a soft sponge, thus making the scene look both wild and restrained at the same time — like a group of wild strongmen tamed by a beautiful maiden. In the far distance, rise steep snow-capped mountains, elegant green hills, limitless lush forests, peaceful lakes, blue sky and

floating white clouds.

Of all the charming waterfalls in Jiuzhaigou, the Nuorilang Waterfall is the most stunning. It is about 2,365 meters high above sea level, 325 meters across at its widest point, with a headfall of 30-40 meters and an average flow of 5.8 cubic meters per second. The faulting here has formed steep slopes and waterfalls, and, because of abrupt changes in the water velocity, carbon dioxide in the water is released, forming travertine deposits on the steep slopes and creating a major, multi-level travertine waterfall. It has altogether 18 lakes separated by delicate travertine dikes. The water flows over and runs down in tiered cascades and as the water from all the lakes rushes out of the forest, it crashes down as the spectacular Nuorilang Waterfall. It is a rare "forest waterfall" as the cliff down which

The Nuorilang Waterfall is most colorful in autumn. Perhaps Nature, impressed by the clear waters, has dyed the trees many colors, fusing them into this stirring water scenery.

the waterfall runs is covered with thriving trees. As the seasons change, the lakes take on a new appearance. In spring and summer, dense willows and bright flowers crowd the banks and the waters are full of life; in autumn, seasonal red leaves and colorful fruits create a charming lakeland scene; in winter, the waters freeze, glittering with beauty and purity.

When night falls, the waterfall shows its other charms. In the darkness, the mountains become quiet and solemn; the lakes both big and small gleam dark blue; in the mist, the only thing stirring is a silvery white belt, moving gently to the murmuring of water. Although surrounded by limitless darkness, the waterfall is still a sacred streamer, full of life-force, like the pulse of the plateau.

The best time to enjoy the Huangguoshu Waterfall is summer and autumn when its flow increases dramatically. Then the waterfall is very powerful, sometimes splashing water vapor hundreds of meters into the air cloaking the area around the waterfall in permanent drizzle or mist. In the sunshine, rainbows often appear, creating a veritable fairyland.

China's Six Most Beautiful Waterfalls

Number *6*

# Huangguoshu Waterfall
*Matchless Vigor and Power*

Originating from the Dabang River, a tributary of the Beipan River in the Pearl River system, the Huangguoshu (Yellow-fruit Tree) Waterfall is 81 meters wide, has a headfall of 77.8 meters, and an average flow of 9.12 cubic meters per second. From the top of the fault cliff, the river water flies through the air, plunging with earth-shaking power into the Xiniu (Rhinoceros) Pond. A 134-meter-long water curtain cave lies secreted behind the main fall. The cave has six "windows," five "sitting rooms" and three springs and from within you look through the "windows" at the rushing waterfall on the other side. It is a real wonder. But in recent years, this wonder can be seen less and less.

The area of the Huangguoshu Waterfall is of karst topography and water leakage is common, making it very difficult to maintain a big flow. For half of every year the waterfall relies on natural rainfall, but for the other half supply is dependent on a reservoir upstream. During the dry season, the waterfall reservoir discharges water in the daytime but not at night. Even so, this is not a complete solution and now a larger upstream reservoir is being constructed. ⬚

# China's Six Most
# Beautiful Glaciers

**Ranking**
1. Rongpo Glacier                    (Tibet)
2. Tomur Glacier                    (Xinjiang)
3. Hailuogou Glacier              (Sichuan)
4. Midui Glacier                    (Tibet)
5. Telamkanli Glacier             (Xinjiang)
6. Touming Mengke Glacier      (Gansu)

Serac forest at the Rongpo Glacier.

China's Six Most Beautiful Glaciers

Number *1*

# Rongpo Glacier
*Bidding Farewell to the Highest Peak*

Central Rongpo Glacier below Qomolangma.

The Himalayas act as a natural screen, blocking the northward movement of southwesterly monsoon air currents and making the north side of the range and the Tibetan Plateau dry, with little precipitation. The Rongpo Glacier has the physical properties of a sub-continental type glacier. It neither grows much nor retreats much, being more stable than the marine glaciers on Himalayas' southern slopes, and is ideal for mountaineering tourism.

The Rongpo Glacier is located in a wide, open area at the foot of Qomolangma (Mount Everest), extending between 5,300 and 6,300 meters above sea level. Consisting of two big glaciers, the Western Rongpo and Central Rongpo, it has a total length of 22.4 kilometers and covers a total area of 85.4 square kilometers. The largest glacier in the Qomolangma Nature Reserve, it is also the world's most completely developed and best preserved form of valley

Qomolangma seen from the serac forest.

deep at certain points. Looking southward from the glacier, Qomolangma appears as a gigantic pyramid standing above all the other mountains, while the two branches of the Rongpo Glacier look like a huge tree, holding the peak on its top.

The Rongpo Glacier has many bowl-shaped cirques and hanging glaciers. It boasts a great number of glacial lakes, ice cliffs, ice caves and crevasses, presenting marvelous and unique sights. Mountaineers have called it the world's largest "alpine park." The action of three natural elements on the northern side of the Qomolangma, namely low latitude, arid climate and high elevation, have helped create the world wonder of the high altitude continental Rongpo Glacier and its serac ice forest. According to glaciologists, the serac ice forests of the Qomolangma and Gasherbrum areas are the most magnificent in the world.

Standing surrounded by these crystal towers in every size, shape and pose — great sculptures made by nature, it is like being in a fairyland palace of jade.

glacier.

The Rongpo Glacier is one of the most magnificent sights in Tibet. Its ice lobe has an average width of 1.4 kilometers and an average depth of 120 meters, reaching over 300 meters

China's Six Most Beautiful Glaciers

Number 2

# Tomur Glacier
## *The Snow Peak's Gift to the Arid Desert*

### A Difficult Journey

We arrived at Kongbair, the leading edge of the Tomur Glacier in the Tianshan Mountains, on the afternoon of September 23, 2004. Kongbair at 3,200 meters above sea level was the starting point for our arduous trek to climb the final section of the retreating glacier.

Our route was complicated by the piles of till and many crevasses on the surface of the glacier, both products of glacial movement and melting. We followed the guide very closely, taking careful steps on the glacier, experiencing a dread that can hardly be put into words. On the high plateau, you have to be unhurried, taking steady steps so as to conserve your physical energy. Walking over the till gave

The snow-capped Mount Tomur is situated in the north of Wensu County, Aksu Prefecture in Xinjiang Uygur Autonomous Region. Its name means "iron mountain" in Uygur. At an elevation of 7,439 meters, Tomur is the highest peak of the Tianshan Mountains and also one of the largest centers of glaciation in China. Tomur's glacier area accounts for a quarter of all the total glacier area in the Tianshan Mountains.

every one of us blisters on the feet and, with backpacks weighing over 20 kilograms, every step forward was made at a great cost. The September daytime temperature on the glacier was only about 5°C. After less than five minutes' rest, I was freezing all over and had to press on.

## Fantastic Scenery

At 7 a.m. I stepped out of my tent. What excitement to see the glaciers intertwining on the horizon, beneath a perfect blue sky — like silver dragons dancing in a deserted valley.

The temperature was about -20°C. Even inside the tent a thin film of ice had formed and outside the biting wind lashed cruelly at our

Mount Tomur has 510 glaciers. It is not only a region where modern glaciers develop but also one of the regions where traces of ancient glaciers are well preserved.

faces. Around 8:15 a.m. the snow-covered summits were suddenly bathed in the red glow of morning sunshine.

Today's itinerary was to take us further along the northern slope towards the heart of the glacier. I had assumed that this section would be easier going, but it was by no means the case.

We encountered a dozen or so U-shaped stony gullies on the way, all a dozen meters deep. Walking over the rocks, weighted down with our backpacks, was immensely difficult — it was a terrific struggle to go on.

The glacier stretched upwards towards 3,800 meters altitude. Seven hours after our morning

Ice

Ice bridge

departure, suddenly, from a wonderful perspective, the glacial landscape unfolded before our eyes.

In these snow-capped peak surroundings, glaciers wiggled and curved their ways on the snow mountains like flying jade dragons. Under the rays of the sun, ice peaks glistened and glaciers surged. Such a world of power and wonder!

This group of glaciers looked as majestic as the Great Wall of China, as disciplined and orderly as a military phalanx. I was totally moved at the sight of them.

Since a Chinese expedition team conquered Mount Tomur for the first time on July 25, 1977, the peak's magnificent and mysterious scenery has begun to be known to the world, attracting many visitors and photographers.

### Facing the Peak,
### I Am Moved to Tears

Our journey was yet over. The next day, we continued towards a section of the glacier where we could enjoy a view of the summit of Mount Tomur.

Waiting for us on the way ahead were fathomless open and concealed crevasses, and glacial tills blocking the way; the hidden river gurgled on beneath our feet and from time to time the sound of collapsing glaciers reverberated in our ears. Every spine-chilling step forward made my hair stand on end!

Two and a half hours later, we finally arrived at the center of the glacier's leading edge.

It was a soul-stirring moment when the magnificent Mount Tomur finally came into view. The white cloud over the summit drifted off, lifting the last veil. Rising erect into the sky, it mirrored the far distant Hantengri, 6,995 meters above sea level. It gives birth to the Aksu River, the largest tributary of the Tarim River, and is

the life source of the Aksu oasis.

With boundless sky above and limitless ground below, this stunning mountain stands proud and defiant in its pure white world of ice and snow, radiant, lustrous, brilliant.

I knelt and kowtowed to this vast world. There and then I left behind my frivolous youth and lack of reverence for nature.

Ice mushroom

Even as we started out, making our way through a stretch of virgin forest, the Hailuogou Glacier still seemed to me like an unattainable dream. Tall green trees, towering skyward, lined the mountain path. Anywhere and everywhere, there was sweet spring water... gushing out from underground, forming crystal-clear streams, or pouring down rocks as a delicate water curtain.

On a crag was built a small log cabin that served as the viewpoint station, and an excellent vantage point it was, facing the snow-capped peak opposite and with the 10,000-year-old glacier below. I was lost for words to describe my emotions at setting foot on the glacier for the very first time — they were nothing like what I'd anticipated. The ice waterfall looked slightly blue in the sunlight. Glacial arches, in many shapes and attitudes, and ice mushrooms too, created a veritable wonderland of ice; the surface of the glacier itself felt more like a thick swathe of rock debris, covering the ground densely and deeply, making you sometimes feel that what lay beneath your feet was no different from the other mountain terrain you'd previously crossed.

Hailuogou boasts a great many glaciers, three of which are much larger than the rest. The biggest, some 14 kilometers long, is Glacier No. 1 or, as it is commonly called, the Great Ice Waterfall. Having gone up the glacier for three kilometers and then round the forest of black pine, we could see the ice in the distance: it was 1,100 meters wide with a drop of 1,080 meters, like the Milky Way pouring down from the sky. Without seeing it for yourself, you could never find words adequate to describe its uniqueness and magnificence.

It is said that in spring and summer when glacial movement is most active, you can hear ice breaking away from the glaciers several hundred times a day. The biggest avalanche involved some one million cubic meters of ice. When a glacial avalanche happens, blue lights glimmer, the ground shakes, and hundreds of thousands of ice blocks running down, colliding, filling the valley with a fog of snow.

Hailuogou is located in Luoding County, Gaze Prefecture in Sichuan Province. It has the largest ice waterfall ever discovered in China, and its drop is amongst the biggest of any glacier in the world, a match for the renowned 1,100-meter-drop ice waterfall in the Glacier National Park of Canada. The picture shows Glacier No. 1 seen from Camp Four.

China's Six Most Beautiful Glaciers

Number **3**

# Hailuogou Glacier
*Refusing to Melt*

# Number 4

# Midui Glacier
## *Ice and Snow in Paradise*

Midui Village in July. (right)

Huge bow structure formed in the Midui Glacier melt area.

The Midui Glacier is located in Yupu Township, about 100 kilometers east of the county seat of Bomi in Nyingchi Prefecture, Tibet.

A monsoon marine glacier, the Midui Glacier is formed from the convergence of two world-class ice waterfalls, sandwiching a stretch of lush

green virgin forest. It looks as if Nature's hand itself had taken up a brush to paint a splashed-ink landscape.

Glistening, soul-stirring ice cliffs are everywhere at the head of the glacier; at its leading edge extends into sub-tropical evergreen broadleaf forests.

The glacier descends through four distinctly different seasons of scenery. Here snow mountains, glaciers, forests, lakes, villages and temples co-exist in harmony, creating a sequence of unique vistas: the worlds of atmosphere, of ice and snow, of rocks, of water, and of living creatures.

Below the Telamkanli Peak (7,441 meters) in the Karakorum Range, the Telamkanli Glacier extends for over 28 kilometers, covering an area of 124.53 square kilometers. Its leading edge is 4,520 meters above sea level and the snowline is at 5,390 meters. Its net ice reserve is 26.774 cubic kilometers, equivalent to a water reserve of 2.2758 billion cubic meters, a veritable solid "water tower."

The most remarkable and attractive sight on the Telamkanli Glacier is its serac forest, with pinnacles dozens of meters high. This extends for some 11 kilometers, starting at 5,200 meters

An ice cave.

As the Telamkanli Glacier is located in the interior, the surface on the upper section of the glacial lobe is pristine. Serac and ice sculpted forms can be seen everywhere.

above sea level and descending towards the glacier's terminus. The connecting pinnacles on the glacier join up to form magnificent ice peak after ice peak, often accompanied by crystal clear ice lakes below. Further down are countless inter-

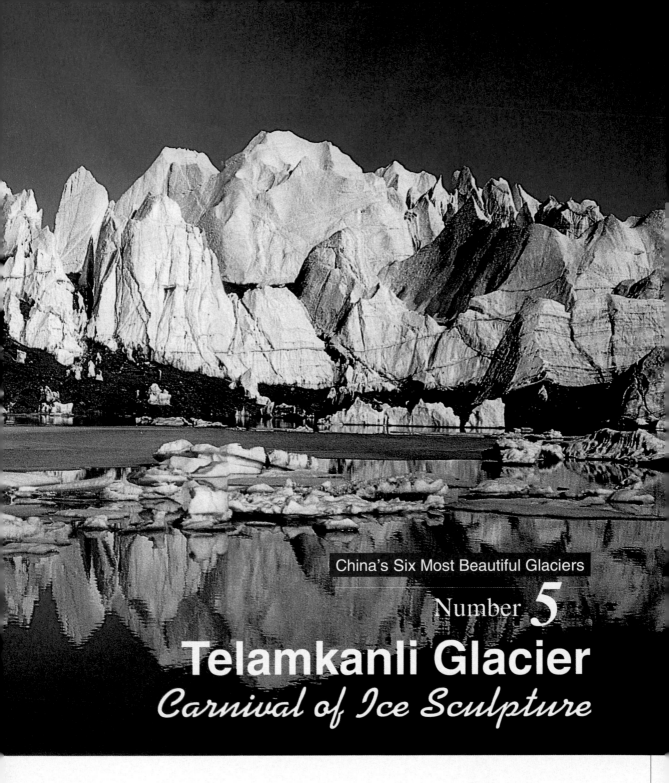

China's Six Most Beautiful Glaciers

Number 5

# Telamkanli Glacier
## Carnival of Ice Sculpture

connecting "ice alleys" that turn the serac forest a glacial labyrinth. Most of the stand-alone pinnacles are pyramid-shaped, their points thrusting into the sky like sharp swords, crystalline and pure, like hand-carved jade. In the serac forest, one can also see glacial karst landscape — ice caves, big high ice tables, ice bridges, ice mushrooms and ice shoots, creating a unique glacier garden.

China's Six Most Beautiful Glaciers

Number **6**

# Touming Mengke Glacier
*A Sweet Spring in the Desert*

The Touming Mengke Glacier covered with snow.

As Touming Mengke developed in an arid environment, it has the physical properties of a typical continental glacier. The glacier's only loss of heat comes from evaporation and because it hardly melts, the glacier has changed little. Its stability is demonstrated by its average annual retreat of only 0.94 meter, estimated by movement of the glacier markers between 1985 and 2002.

The Touming Mengke Glacier, the largest valley glacier in the Qilian Range, is 10.1 kilometers long and covers an area of 21.9 square kilometers. It can be found in Laohu Valley on the northern slope of Daxue Mountain in Subei County, Gansu Province. Its main peak is 5,481 meters above sea level. In Mongolian, Touming Mengke means high and vast.

Heading south from Yumeng, we crossed a "devil's land" of Yadan wind-eroded landscape before reaching the Changma Basin. Daxue Mountain came into view immediately. Under the clear blue sky, the feather-shaped glaciers seemed like dancing silver snakes, dazzling and fascinating, on a desert which seemed to have been devastated by fire.

At the terminus of the glacial lobe, Touming Mengke, for the first time, revealed itself fully before us.

Stretches of serac forest stood in the quiet valley, like groups of sculptures made by the magic fingers of the legendary Queen of Ice and Snow. Between 20 and 30 meters high, they stood on a steep hill, forming a huge ice wall that almost blocked our view.

Touming Mengke is a large gentle slope. In terms of scale it can not compete with the Insukati and Tomur glaciers, but the well-known

"July 1" Glacier, Xinjiang No. 1 Glacier and Yulong Snow Mountain No. 1 Glacier are all only a tenth of the area of Touming Mengke.

On this quiet glacier I experienced a long trek that will live forever in my memory. In 2001, when we climbed the 5,150-meter-high "July 1" Glacier in the Qilian Range, we reached the top with only one camp. But this time, as with the ascent of Muztagata Peak, the climbing team had to make camp three times before reaching the top.

There is a saying that on perilous peaks dwells beauty in her infinite variety. The landscape on the ascent was soul-stirring: the frozen waterfall hanging like an upside-down Milky Way; the crisscross ice gullies, isolated ice mushrooms; mysterious ice caves....

Touming Mengke is an alluring, ever-changing scene. But it requires indomitable spirit and superhuman strength to climb the ice and snow and whilst doing so I had no time to take in the beauty along the way. The hardest but the most beautiful moment I recall was when the lead group ahead of me dwindled to the size of indistinct dots whilst the following members of the team lay out of sight behind me. Wind blew, snow flew. The space between heaven and earth seemed huge. Everything was quiet, pure and indescribably free, as if in a world of illusion.

Touming Mengke is a double branched U-

shaped glacier and we climbed only the eastern branch. After reaching Camp 3, situated 5,180 meters above sea level, I did not follow my three teammates to the top for fear that, being totally

Walking on the glacier.

exhausted, I would hold them back. When I asked them later what they had seen from the top, they answered, eyes gleaming with curiosity, "Another huge glacier."

Once the Qilian Expedition Team carried out a surface blackening experiment on Touming Mengke; its purposes were to accelerate glacier melt and to utilize the glacier more effectively. But now there are deep concerns about the foreseeable melting of glaciers. Change is perhaps the way of the world. As for me, once I had envisaged the development of such tourist activities as skiing and gliding at Touming Mengke. But now, the more I know about it, the more I hope it will retain its ancient vastness and tranquility forever. ☐

# China's Ten Most
# Beautiful Forests

## Ranking

1. **Tianshan Mountain Xueling Spruce Forest** (Xinjiang)
2. **Changbai Mountain Mixed Korean Pine and Broadleaf Forest** (Jilin)
3. **Jianfeng Ridge Tropical Rainforest** (Hainan)
4. **Baima Snow Mountain Azalea Forest** (Yunnan)
5. **Bomi Gangxiang Nyingchi Spruce Forest** (Tibet)
6. **Xishuangbanna Tropical Rainforest** (Yunnan)
7. **Luntai Huyang Poplar Forest** (Xinjiang)
8. **Libo Karst Forest** (Guizhou)
9. **Xing'an Larch Forest** (Heilongjiang and Inner Mongolia)
10. **Shunan Bamboo Forest** (Sichuan)

The most beautiful views on earth always hide themselves away in remote mountains and deep valleys. But the range after range of peaks and summits of the Tianshan Mountains are no barrier to man's pursuit of beautiful sights. The background of the remote snow peaks and the nearby grassland seems to accentuate the beauty of the Xueling spruce, old and hardy but green and luxuriant, freely filling the air with their fragrance and moisture.

The Xueling spruce has existed for 40 million years and is like a living fossil on the Tianshan Mountains. From late October on, cold snow-bearing winds from Siberia start arriving. Blanketed in whiteness, all is quiet; the spruce trees with their elegant crowns stand like an awesome military phalanx.

China's Ten Most Beautiful Forests

Number *1*

# Tianshan Mountain Xueling Spruce Forest

The first time when I heard the name "Xueling spruce" I was captivated. In Chinese, its elements translate at "Snow Peak Cloud Fir" which has a very romantic ring to it.

The Xueling spruce grows mainly in the snow peaks on the northern and southern slopes of the Tianshan Mountains, the western part of the Kunlun Range and mountain areas of the Junggar Basin, its range extending 1,800 kilometers east to west. Along with the western Tianshan, it also goes into Kyrgyzstan. It is the most important mountain evergreen conifer forest in the arid region of Central Asia. The Xueling spruce grows in the mountains between 1,500 and 2,800 meters above sea level. The trees are tall, between 20 and 30 meters when mature —up to 60 or 70 meters in the most favorable environments. Recently, among growth ring samples, researchers of the Institute of Desert Meteorology found a Xueling spruce with annular rings dating back 651 years. This is the oldest tree ever found in Xinjiang and is well worthy of its name "King of Xinjiang Spruces."

Several years ago, when searching for three Hong Kong climbers missing in the Bogda Peak disaster, we went deep into the Tianshan Mountains. Scanning widely, we found the Xueling spruce standing closely in lines and rows, following the rise and fall of the hills, one after another, like countless green piano keys playing the music of tinkling streams. The tall spruces were kept company by roses, honeysuckle and other bushes.

I felt it very plainly that every tree was exerting its utmost to grow upward. Here there is sunlight and sky, while a poor fallen tree gradually decomposes down below, becoming the soil for a young spruce. The sapling, absorbing both its nutrients and ambition, gets taller every day. That is its child, completing the parent's unfinished business.

There came a sudden downpour. We rushed for shelter under the Xueling spruce. Stroking the rough trunk and looking up, we discovered that its branches reached out in an orderly and regular way from the ramrod straight trunk. The branches and foliage stretch upward rather than outward, forming long and narrow crowns.

The soil beneath us was not as deep as I had expected. It was just some leaf mould and thin earth. The trees had rooted themselves deep into the cold, hardy rock. The roots changed direction following the grain of mountain rocks, filling every tiny gap in the rock, groping for water down in the unknown darkness. The girth of a century-old Xueling spruce takes four or five people with outstretched arms to encircle. I know that the root of a tree steadily anchored on a rock cliff should be several times larger than the visible crown. The received wisdom that the height of a tree determines how far down its roots go does not apply here. In places we know and places we don't know, its roots move silently, binding the mountains like cords. Is there any power that can shake a tree if that tree has merged with the mountain as an organic whole? The Xueling spruce of today is the result of the complex work it put in yesterday.

In this pure symphony of snow peaks, glaciers and mountain lakes, the powerful chorus from rows of orderly Xueling spruces, in this jade blue song... the world falls silent.

The Xueling spruce grows widely on the northern slopes of the Tianshan Mountains between 1,500 and 2,800 meters above sea level. This evergreen conifer points to the sky, highly and straight; some reach as much as 60 to 70 meters, giving rise to the name "sky gazing tree." In the northwest of China and desert areas of Central Asia, the evergreen Xueling spruce grows sturdily despite the harshness of the desert.

Number 2

# Changbai Mountain Mixed Korean Pine and Broadleaf Forest

The combination of Korean pine trees, broadleaf trees and other trees shows us a unique beauty of the Changbai Mountain. Along the Jingjiang Valley on the western side of the Changbai Mountain, there is a wide variety of plant species. Besides the native Korean pine, there are also the Amur linden, Mongolian oak, Japanese elm, maple, birch and more. Thanks to a favorable growing environment, the forests are dense, full of primeval views. The seasonal changes to the thriving mixed forest adds enchantment to the mountains.

In China, there are only two well preserved primeval forests of Korean pine; one is on the Lesser Xing'an Mountains, the other here on Changbai. The Korean pine's favored medium is black humus earth, and habitats such as gentle slopes, steep peaks, or flat gullies and valleys are all suitable. Its bark is reddish brown with some grayish black texture. The timber has a close-grained, light and soft texture, with a slightly red tinge. The Korean pine gets its Chinese name *hongsong* (red pine) because of its reddish timber. Its best feature is its stable and straight grain so that it won't change shape, regardless of humidity or dryness.

Korean pine is native to northeast China. It is a member of the white pine group, which is characterized by leaves (needles) in fascicles of

Korean pine saplings like shade, growing below the broadleaf forest out of the sunlight. The mature pine likes sunshine, so its trunk rises straight up. The mixed Korean pine and broadleaf forest changes color from season to season, the foliage being particularly beautiful in the fall.

five. It is an old subgenus of pine. In the primeval forest of Changbai, the Korean pine stands tall, together with other species such as littleseed spruce, Korean spruce, Amur linden, birch, and Manchurian ash. Below these trees, there are over 20 underbrush species such as *corylus mandshurica*. At ground level the herbaceous species are even more diverse. Every year, in late June a yellow smoke spreads over the whole primeval pine forest like a vast yellow umbrella. This yellow smoke is the pollen of thousands of tall Korean pines, bearing countless male and female flowers, the male flowers lower down and the female higher up. In early summer, when the flowers open, yellow pollen from the male flowers flies skyward, each tiny pollen grain equipped with two small air cells that make it

lighter than air. Thus it can fly up to the female flower, and to the sky above the forest, drifting with the airflow. This is the yellow smoke we see.

To enjoy and savor the group beauty, the individual beauty and the primeval beauty of Korean pine here you must go to Lushui River. There, in a forest by the river, stands "the King of Korean Pines" — over 480 years old. The tree is 35.5 meters tall and has a 1.24-meter-diameter trunk. According to historical materials, the Changbai volcano erupted in 1597, 1668 and 1702. This tenacious "King of Korean Pines" is not far away from the Tianchi Lake but has survived all these disasters.

The Lushui River seed stand of Korean pine, programmed by the government in 1964, has an area of 11,764 hectares and is the largest in

The Korean pine's unique and vigorous root system acts like a mini-reservoir. In the Korean pine forest, even after two hours of heavy rain, there are no water paths; the rainwater is held in by the extensive root network of the pines, the major reason for their vigor and longevity.

China. It is a natural excellent gene bank.

Primeval forests are very rare in the world we inhabit today. In China's few primeval forests, the Changbai Korean pine primeval forest is very valuable. In a geographical area, the oldest forests undisturbed by human activity are called primeval forest.

A primeval forest is a world. Forests prefer to live in a mixed community. Whether a forest thrives or not is inseparable from its complex inner structure. The "primeval" views of the Changbai Korean pine primeval forest, composed of huge trees of all periods, old and young, dead woods, fallen trees and a deep layer of humus and debris, not only provide all kinds of animals habitats, but are also of incomparable ecological value, in terms of satisfying people's ever-increasing demand to "get back to nature."

The natural evolvement of the eco-system is also the natural evolution process of biology. It is in this process that the Korean pine, with its unique charms, shows its individual, primeval and group beauty.

This primeval forest is significant in terms both of space and time. The excellence and perfection of the Korean pine primeval forest lie not in its great views or excellent timber. Rather they lie in the systematic and clean arrangement of their groups, in their natural rules unchanged for millions of years, in the countless lessons they teach us, and in the courage, spirit and strength that they bring us.

China's Ten Most Beautiful Forests

Number *3*

# Jianfeng Ridge Tropical Rainforest

The Jianfeng Ridge Tropical Rainforest has tall old trees with a complex multiple storey structure. The canopy is uneven, with "forest windows" formed by fallen trees. These provide important conditions for the growth of new trees, and allow beams of light to penetrate the dense primitive rainforest, showing us such wonderful and unique scenes as buttress roots, old trees in flower, and "stranglers."

Located in the southwest of Hainan Island, the continuous and magnificent tropical rainforest of the Jianfeng Ridge Forest Reserve covers more than 400 square kilometers. When you enter the tropical rainforest, you see unique tropical rainforest scenery everywhere. More particularly, the forest has bred 449 kinds of colorful butterflies, far more even than Taiwan — the "Butterfly Kingdom."

In contrast to forests in the north, which mostly consist of one kind of tree, the Jianfeng Ridge Tropical Rainforest has over 250 species per hectare, a higher degree of biodiversity than tropical rainforest groups in India and Myanmar, and the same as those of Southeast Asia and South America.

If you stand at a commanding point and look carefully at the tropical rainforest, you will find that the continuous canopy is uneven. This is because when some tall old trees die, from natural causes or felled by a typhoon, they form a "forest window." Some varieties in the "forest window" gradually recover, bringing about continual change in the vertical structure of the tropical rainforest group, and an uneven-looking canopy.

Being in the tropical zone, the climate changes little and plants can grow throughout the year; different plants blossom and bear fruit asynchronously, making the area spring-like all year round. As winter is not cold, the tree barks are thin and light brown. The more light brown trees there are, the older the tropical rainforest — one of the important differences between these and northern forests.

Another important feature of the forest is aerial gardens, the formation of which is also related to biodiversity. In the tropical rainforest,

(*pseudodrynaria coronans*) are the most special, usually forming balls on the trunks one or two meters in diameter, and under them grow plants such as *vittaria flexuosa* — beautiful and majestic.

Here, many high arbors have buttress roots, some of them as much as four or five meters high. Prop roots, as the name implies, support the plant. Famous plants with prop roots in the Jianfeng Ridge Tropical Rainforest include gaogenying, *dillenia indica* and some banyans.

The phenomenon of "strangler tree" is an

different plants try hard to make best use of natural resources such as sunshine and water, giving rise to various combinations: tall arbor trees, and below these, shrubs and herbaceous plants, along with diverse vines, epiphytes and parasitic plants. Vines usually climb up to the canopy in different ways, while parasitic plants and epiphytes usually grow within tree branches, thus forming aerial gardens. The bird's nest fern (*asplenium nidus*) and rock ginger fern

ecological wonder unique to tropical rainforests. A classic example is *ficus altissima*. After eating the seeds of this plant, birds leave their droppings on the branches and twigs of large trees. In time, the seeds in the droppings take root, sprout, and, nurtured by bird droppings and leaf litter on the bark, they gradually grow into seedlings. When these seedlings grow up, the tree will have aerial roots. On the one hand, aerial roots can grow vertically toward the earth, land and take root, absorbing nutrients from soil and growing into prop roots. The most famous example in the Jianfeng Ridge Tropical Rainforest is the *lushu* tree. However, aerial roots can grow downward, clinging to the trunk of the host tree and, on reaching the earth, grow thicker and thicker, forming a root network that entwines the trunk, finally surrounding the host tree completely, hindering normal growth and ultimately strangling it to death. After the tree dies and decomposes, nutrients from it can supply other trees.

As well as its unique scenery, the Jianfeng Ridge Tropical Rainforest has an outstanding function in protecting the eco-environment. Findings from the state-level Jianfeng Ridge Forest Ecosystem Research Station show that the tropical rainforest is an important carbon dioxide reservoir, as one hectare of tropical rainforest can store over 340 tons of carbon, so protecting tropical rainforests can effectively reduce carbon in the atmosphere. Moreover, the tropical rainforest can effectively regulate water runoff volume and store water brought by rain, typhoons and storms, providing water for agricultural production in the dry seasons and an inexhaustible supply for local residents. Of course the tropical rainforest also plays a very beneficial role in water and soil conservation, climate regulation and environmental improvement. As natural forests are warm in winter and cool in summer with only minor differences in temperature and rich in anions that can help treat illness, the Jianfeng Ridge Forest Reserve has become a perfect destination for eco-tourism, a spot where people can get back to nature.

"Strangler trees" are an ecological wonder unique to tropical rainforests. Go into a tropical forest and you see masses of aerial roots composing magnificent scenes.

# Number *4*

# Baima Snow Mountain Azalea Forest

On the gravel mountain slopes in western Yunnan, there are few evergreen plants, but azaleas grow in abundance. On high mountains and lofty ridges between 2,600 and 4,200 meters, mountain azaleas blossom every year. Their purpose in life seems to be the production of beautiful flowers. They grow in clusters and blossom together, creating an intoxicating "sea of flowers" as spring gives way to summer. (above)

The Baima Snow Mountain, the watershed of the Lancang and Jinsha rivers, rises in the central section of the Hengduan Mountains, and is administered by Deqen County in the Tibetan Autonomous Prefecture of Deqen, Yunnan Province. Mountain azalea forest is not only an important type of the dwarf community, but the most delicate and charming. One of the most widely occurring plant species in western Yunnan, it is low, naturally shaped, and highly decorative. In early summer when the ice and snow has melted, mountain azaleas come into flower across the hillsides, spreading a magnificent cloak over the bleak and bare slopes.

The warm, damp airflow from the Indian Ocean produces favorable water and temperature conditions so the spruces here are like towers... tall, straight, dense and sturdy. Some are as much as two meters in diameter and 80 meters in height. The density of trees per hectare ranks first in the world. (above)

Located at the lower reaches of the Yarlung Tsangpo River, Gangxiang Village in Bomi County has the largest, best, and last primeval forest in China. Whilst it cannot match the elegance of the Tianshan Xueling spruce forest, its primeval nature, density and magnificence are unsurpassable. (right page)

## China's Ten Most Beautiful Forests

### Number 5

# Bomi Gangxiang Nyingchi Spruce Forest

Under the tree canopy, it is pleasantly cool and moist in the forest. Shrubs and herbaceous plants are evenly distributed. Moss thrives, creating a green blanket almost covering the whole forest floor. Rampant vines, 30 or 40 centimeters in diameter, can wind their way up to the crown canopy. Old man's beard, lightly swaying, completes the typical picture of a damp dark coniferous forest. Temperate zone plateau dark coniferous forest as spectacular as this is a world rarity.

In the primeval forest of Xishuangbanna, a huge variety of tropical plants grow so exuberantly that they block the sun. Xishuangbanna's spectacular tropical landscape and pronounced ethic minority flavors make it a highly popular tourist destination.

China's Ten Most Beautiful Forests

# Number *6*
# Xishuangbanna Tropical Rainforest

The Xishuangbanna tropical rainforest is situated in the valley of the Lancang River in southern Yunnan. Blessed by advantageous climatic conditions, it nurtures a myriad of species and is dubbed "wildlife kingdom." The brown woolly fig (*ficus drupacea*) grows everywhere in the forest, its trunk so huge it takes over a dozen people with outstretched arms to encircle it.

Number *7*

# Luntai Huyang Poplar Forest

Luntai County, lying at the southern foot of the Tianshan Mountains and the northern edge of the Tarim Basin, boasts the world's largest, densest and best-surviving "living fossil of the Tertiary Age" — a natural *huyang* (diversiform-leaved) poplar forest of over 27,000 hectares. The *huyang* poplar forest is a common desert forest meadow vegetation in the Tarim Basin, growing from upper to lower reaches of the Tarim river valley. Despite a rather simple structure, the forest has distinct ecological markings of the bio-zone in which it grows. The forest, in the rosy dawn or in the sunset glow, radiates vigor, hope, and mystery, too.

*Huyang* poplars grow only in the desert and have always been engaged in struggle with it. Faced with cruel broiling heat and drought, only these diversiform-leaved poplars still stand in the desert, brimming with energy and life force.

The *huyang* poplar forest near the desert highway at Luntai is my favorite place to visit. The Tarim Basin contains the world's largest area of natural *huyang* poplar forest and this roadside forest of over 2,700 hectares is only a tiny part of the whole. The forest grows along the meandering course of the silt-laden Tarim River, and stretches to the remote horizon. There is a beautiful small lake in the forest that attracts swans and other precious waterfowl. Hares and corsac foxes often haunt the depths of the dense woods.

In Uygur its name means "the most beautiful tree." It is also acclaimed as the "desert hero" for its indomitable life force and amazing ability to put up with drought, sandstorms, and saline and alkali soils.

In autumn, huyang poplars in the wild dress in their most splendid attire of the year. The sturdy trunks and gigantic crowns indicate that they have stored up ample energy. The poplars will withstand the harsh approaching winter with their tenacity and vigor, which is how they have always survived.

The life of desert plants, including the poplars, Chinese tamarisks, sacsaouls and oleasters, is a revelation about life and death, guarding the desolate desert and surviving desperate situations.

When the scorching summer passes and cool breezes come, the forest begins to bestir itself, get excited, and turn golden almost overnight.

The *huyang* poplar forest has always been beyond human imagination. Botanists concentrate on their indomitable survival qualities — enduring droughts, sandstorms, and saline and alkali soils. Folk have made heroes of them for their ability to grow erect for a thousand years, live for a thousand years after falling, and lie and remain undecayed after death for another thousand years.

But without its moment of glory, three thousand years would be meaningless, just an endless torment, a waste of time and energy. Without one magnificent moment its terrible thirst, hideous appearance, cracked bark, decay, despairing moans and silent struggle, its bitter saltiness and strange "teardrops" secreted via its trunk, would be nothing but hopeless bleakness.

So, the tree goes all out to achieve the pinnacle of brilliance. The blazing magnificent, resplendent beauty of the *huyang* poplar forest in autumn can compare with an epic by Homer, a Wagnerian opera or a Beethoven symphony. Its passionate living of life as gloriously and fully as possible before dying is the best tribute to time.

# Number *8*
# Libo Karst Forest

There are diverse landscapes in the Maolan karst forest — among them "forest on rock," "forest on water" and funnel forest. But the forest ecosystem is very fragile. Once damaged, it is hard to recover. Here, life is invaluable.

Since the discovery of the Maolan karst forest in Libo County, this rare and precious land has attracted many biologists, geologists and ecologists. They were so charmed by the karst peak-clusters, funnels and depressions, covered with primeval vegetation, they almost forgot to return. According to experts, the Maolan karst virgin forest is the only one of its kind along the same latitude, displays the true features of sub-tropical zone karst natural environment, and the best preserved in the world.

As one enters the Maolan karst forest, funnels, depressions, cliffs and peak-clusters, blanketed with forest plants, come into view. Here, life is tough,

with poor soils, arid surface and the water table far below. In order to absorb water and nutrients, every plant has an extensive root system. Root hairs, climbing over the rock faces, stretch out in all directions, coiling around each other, creating spectacular natural tree-root sculptures. Indeed, some roots are thicker and several times longer than the tree trunks themselves. Wriggling like snakes and dragons, they make their way down sheer precipices to the ground, or climb up towering cliffs, the area of the root system several times larger than that of the crown. Then there are bryophytes twining around them and red leaves falling on them. Sometimes, the roots are covered with water droplets that ooze from the rocks, just like glistening amber beads. The forest has another wonder —

The Greater Xing'an Mountains of northeast China, ridges and peaks rising one after another, densely blanketed with vegetation, imposing and beautiful. They are home to towering Xing'an larches with their luxuriant foliage and spreading branches. In some places, they are so thick that no light can get through. The tranquil river, reflecting the wooded hills, makes a wonderful landscape painting.

"trees embracing huge rocks." These occur when a great number of contorted tree roots climb over rocks, worm their way into the soil, and, over time, gradually pull out the rocks.

Tree roots in the Maolan karst forest have a peculiar charm, their suppleness and structure reminding visitors of traditional Chinese calligraphy and painting. Legend has it that in remote antiquity Cang Xie unveiled the mysteries of the universe, and so created the framework for Chinese characters. Since, at the time, the ecological environment he lived in was luxuriant and primitive, might it perhaps be that the fantastic tree roots in the well-preserved Maolan karst virgin forest conceal the mysteries of the universe.

# Number *9*
# Xing'an Larch Forest

The Xing'an larch is the main tree in the Greater Xing'an Mountains Forest, part of the circum-arctic coniferous forest that extends within China north to south along the Greater Xing'an Mountains. It is also home to many arctic species, such as the snow hare, elk, cowberry and crowberry. The mountain range is divided into two sections by the Taoer River in Xing'an County. The northern section is about 770 kilometers long, rising gently to the south; it is a coniferous forest zone of predominantly Xing'an larch. The scenery varies as the seasons come and go. It is at its most beautiful in spring and summer. In spring, the emerging buds and purple azalea set each other off. In summer, the area is one vast stretch of dark green, enveloped in mist and clouds. In the past, the Greater Xing'an Mountains gave rise to many different ethnic peoples. Today, there are Oroqen and the Ewenki people still living deep in the woods. This primeval forest in the north Greater Xing'an Mountains, green and majestic, is a treasured land along China's northern frontier.

China's Ten Most Beautiful Forests

Number *10*

# Shunan Bamboo Forest

At Shunan, there are 58 types of bamboo, making up a vast bamboo sea, which washes over 27 mountain ridges and 500 peaks. As well as such common forms as the *mao* bamboo, some rare bamboos occur too, such as the black bamboo. Growing and propagating fast in these favorable conditions, the bamboos create a boundless expanse of luxuriant green sea ... an enchanting and beautiful forest landscape.

The Shunan Bamboo Sea is a huge bamboo forest stretching across Changning County, in Sichuan Province. The central scenic area is mainly *mao* bamboo forest, covering some 4,567 hectares. It is a boundless expanse of green waves, winning it the name of Bamboo Sea. It boasts the largest scenic spot of wild bamboos in the country, and has a wealth of different landscapes, combining natural grace and rich bamboo culture. ◘

# China's Ten Most
# Beautiful Islands

## Ranking

1.  **Xisha Archipelago — Yongxing and Dongdao**     **(Hainan)**
2.  **Weizhou Island**     **(Guangxi)**
3.  **Nansha Archipelago — Yongshu and Taiping**     **(Hainan)**
4.  **Penghu Islands — Penghu Island**     **(Taiwan)**
5.  **Nanji Island**     **(Zhejiang)**
6.  **Miaodao Islands**     **(Shandong)**
7.  **Putuoshan Island**     **(Zhejiang)**
8.  **Dayushan Island**     **(Fujian)**
9.  **Linjin and Nanding Islands**     **(Fujian)**
10. **Hailing Island**     **(Guangdong)**

Islands beautifully set in the South China Sea.

# Number *1*
# Xisha Archipelago
## *Corals Add Beauty to China*

The Xisha Archipelago lies in the northwest part of the South China Sea. The most attractive feature of this group is that there are two arrays of islands; in the east lie the seven islands of the Xuande group, including the main island of Yongxing and the Dongdao Island (Bird Island); in the west are the eight islands of the Yongle group, including Jinyin, Ganquan and Jinqing islands. There are also reefs, sandy beaches and shoals. This island group is known to local fishermen as the "seven easts and eight wests." From the air, they look like two strings of white-ringed sapphires, set into the vast blueness of the South China Sea.

There's a saying to the effect that if you haven't seen the South China Sea, you can have no idea of vastness of the ocean, and if you haven't seen the Xisha Archipelago, you can't appreciate the mystery of the sea. As the Xisha Archipelago is far from the mainland and rarely visited, the surrounding seawater is so clear that you can see 40 meters down.

The South China Sea is located in the tropical zone, its southernmost sector close to the Equator, making the annual average sea temperature a warm 26°C. The temperature, salinity and transparency of the water are ideal for the growth of corals. Therefore, almost all the islands in the South China Sea are encircled

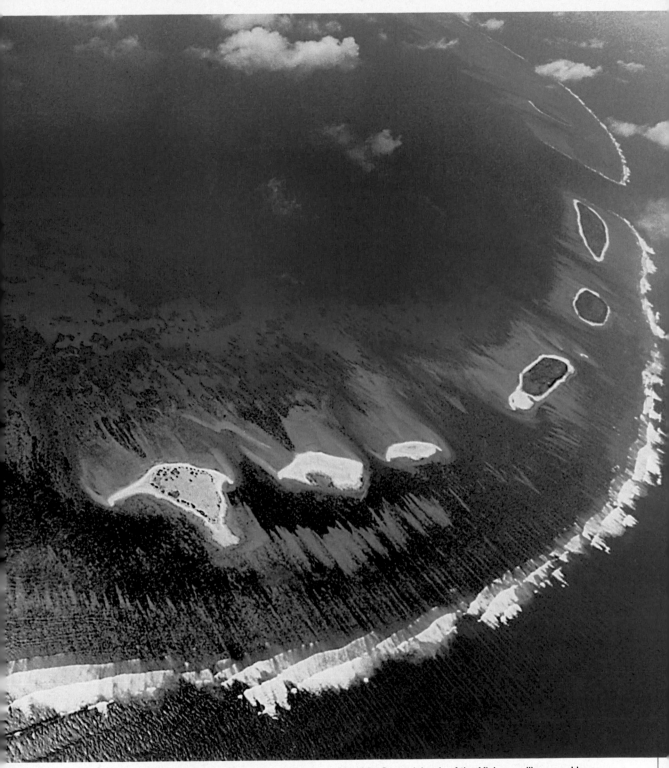

Only Nature could create a masterpiece like this. Seven islands of the Xisha are like a necklace, naturally laid out upon the blue sea, or like seven beautiful pearls in an open shell.

with coral reefs. It is China's main area of reef-building corals and the coral resources are particularly rich in the Nasha and Xisha archipelagos. Indeed the Xisha group alone boasts 127 types of coral belonging to 38 species.

Reef-building corals are formed by reef-building stony polyps and calcium-rich algae, with chinks and cracks filled with shells and masses of polyps. Stony polyps enjoy the reputation of "ocean architects." They are bottom-dwelling tiny tube worms living in tropical and sub-tropical seas. A single polyp is as small as a needle head, but a great colony of them secretes a great deal of calcium carbonate, over time gradually forming huge corals of different shapes and colors. Zooxanthella live inside the stony polyps and if the environment changes, they abandon the polyps, causing the corals to "bleach" and die.

The Xisha boasts over 100 species of stony corals, often named after their shapes — staghorn, brain, rose and mushroom corals. They also vary in color — from red, orange and purple to green and yellow.

Apart from the stony corals, the Xisha islands are noted for their dozens of species of patterned and colored soft corals that cling like sponges to coral rocks. They feel softer than thick carpets under foot. Then, living in the cracks of coral crevices or wherever algae gather, are colorful sea urchins and mollusks of every shape and size, including conches and egg-shaped cowries. Often seen drifting in the Xisha waters are blue "coin jellyfish" because it looks like a coin, blue jellyfish with tentacles, no bigger than two centimeters, resembling the shape of the caps worn by Portuguese sailors in the past, so they are known as "Portuguese soldiers."

In the coral garden beneath the sea, the most attractive and startling thing is the hundreds of different types of fish. Angel fish, huge schools

The heart-shaped Yongxing Islet, set in the blue sea, is dubbed the "Chinese heart" by Chinese photographers. On a foundation of Early Cambrian metamorphic rocks, Yongxing has evolved over 30 million years into a coral island. Its landmass measures 2.8 square kilometers and its coastline 8.12 kilometers.

The Bird Island, the second largest of the Xisha islands, is a paradise for sea birds, thanks to its dense vegetation. The red-footed booby, fondly called "the navigator" by local fishermen, is the most populous bird. With their white feathers and red feet, the birds dart over the island. When they stop to rest, they look just like a patch of snow. (right page, top)

The clear blue waters of the Xisha Archipelago provide an extremely favorable eco-environment. Corals have established a flourishing coral reef ecosystem, as they spread out or cluster together, living in harmony with the sea and with each other. Views like this are very common in the Xisha Archipelago, where coral reefs fringe the islands like dazzlingly beautiful rings. (right page, bottom)

of them, swim about, darting here and there, then "dancing" in the most captivating way. Butterfly fish, the most numerous of all, always swim in pairs. "Clown fish" live together with sea anemones, cleverly using the latter as a protective umbrella to evade predators. Of course they also share their food with the sea anemones. Damselfish and grouper, among others, are very territorial and will not hesitate to attack intruders. The rich bio-resources and the vast area of the Xisha Archipelago complement each other so well, it's no wonder people say "Xisha — one half seawater, the other half fish." In fact, without any interference from man, the natural world would live on and on according to its own laws. On the coral reefs, every living thing seeks to grow and develop according to the principle of "the survival of the fittest." If there were just the corals, without other life forms, it would directly harm the thriving coral reef. These "seabed gardens" — the coral reefs — are an important link in the chain of ocean ecology, a food larder and breeding ground for marine life. These marine creatures are mutually complementary, together maintaining the balance, viability and development of the ecosystem. Between them they create the vitality and beauty of the Xisha Archipelago.

Of the 32 individual islands of the Xisha, the Bird Island deserves special mention. Countless numbers of birds are drawn to the Xisha by the rich resources of marine life such as fish and shrimp: for them the Bird Island is paradise. Boobies, tern and gray-spotted birds love to mix with human beings.

The island is only 1.4 square kilometers in area but is rich in vegetation cover; it stands out as the best-protected natural ecological island of all the Xisha group. It is also a sanctuary for the red-footed booby, whose population amounts to more than 100,000, constituting the largest single group of island residents. In the morning glow or the setting sun, if you sit on the pure-white sand beach, watching these birds darting around like snowflakes, listening to the waves beating against the sand, you will experience the sensation of being as vast and broad as the sea itself.

The red-footed booby is an exceptional flyer. Its light, honeycomb bones give it a reduced body weight for flying. It follows a highly regular routine, going out to sea for food in the morning, returning to the nest in the evening. Its fixed flight times and flight directions are a great boon to fishermen who rely on this bird to get their bearings when out at sea. Thus, the bird has a nice name: "the navigator."

The Xisha islands are on the sea route on the South China Sea and were part of the "Ocean Silk Road." As early as the Sui Dynasty (581-618), Chinese envoys sailed to what is now Malaysia by way of the Xisha islands. In the Tang Dynasty

People say that the Xisha islands are "one half seawater, the other half fish." Indeed the islands are a rich tropical water fishing ground, home to over 400 species of coral and ocean fish. It is a major fishing ground for tuna, mackerel, flying fish, shark and grouper.

Seabirds swooping low, beaches like a white belt... beautiful coral island, a dreamland. Such beautiful views are obtainable only from the air. (top left)

Xisha seabed corals, like bunches of grapes or floral bouquets. The living corals sway with the waves, and the dead corals resemble many-colored forests. (below left)

(618-907), the monk Yijing also went to India via the Xisha. The exploratory voyages by the Song-dynasty (960-1279) navy to the Xisha islands were recorded in the Song Emperor Renzong's "Imperial Preface" to the official histories. In fact, sovereignty of these islands was maintained by China throughout the Song Dynasty and the Yuan (1206-1368), Ming (1368-1644) and Qing (1644-1911) dynasties that came later. Ceramics and coinage from all these dynasties have been discovered here. The Solitude Soul Temple on Yongxing Island, the Earth God Temple and Queen Mother Temple on Jinqing Island and the Bird Island respectively are strong historical proofs of the fact that Chinese fishermen lived and worked on these islands.

China's Ten Most Beautiful Islands

Number *2*

# Weizhou Island
*A Work of Volcanic Sculpture*

Lying south of Beihai City in Guangxi Zhuang Autonomous Region, Weizhou Island is six kilometers from north to south and five kilometers from east to west. Formed of Quaternary Period volcanic rocks and lavas, Weizhou is China's largest and youngest volcanic island. The southern part of the island presents many examples of volcanic topography. These include walls and terraces formed by rocks molten and compressed in volcanic eruptions, grotesque and colorful sights of marine-eroded caverns, hills, pillars and terraces, together creating an ocean fairyland. The northern part of the island is lower, with sand dikes, beaches and rocks. Flatter, more open morphology predominates. On the seabed are corals with fabulously attractive colors. It is features like this that give rise to the name "The Penglai Fairy Island of the South China Sea."

Of all the island groups in the South China Sea, the islands of the Nansha Archipelago are spread out the widest, its coral islands are the most numerous and the average size the smallest. There are over 200 of them, occupying a sea area of 820,000 square kilometers and having a combined land area of about two square kilometers. The largest of them, Taiping Island, covers only 0.43 square kilometer. Seen from the air, it is like a green jade floating on the blue sea. White coral sand encircles the island like a white jade belt. (right)

Islets, sand beaches and reefs are nicely spread out among the Nansha. Like oases, with birds overhead and fish in the nearby waters, they are a virtual never-fading scroll painting of tropical island scenery. Most of the islands are formed by coral reefs of every shape and color. On August 2, 1988, China, at UNESCO's request, established an ocean observatory on the Yongshu Reef , 560 nautical miles from Hainan Island. (below)

# Number *3*

# Nansha Archipelago
*Border Cemented with Corals*

Most of the Yongshu Reef used to be below water, but now a stretch of man-made land provides the space for a 1,000-square-meter two-story building. No matter what happens, the reef is like an unsinkable vessel guarding China's territorial waters.

Number *4*

# Penghu Islands
*Culture and Nature Enhancing Each Other*

Basalt land, the result of cooled volcanic lava, is the authentic face of the Penghu Islands. Sheer cliffs, vertical pillars, wind and sea-eroded formations... the strange and grotesque rocks unique to the Penghu Islands.

Taiwan's largest island county, the Penghu Islands have a total landmass of 127 square kilometers, spread over 64 individual islands.

This is a story behind the name of Penghu: the largest island of the Penghu, together with Chungtun, Paisha and Hsiyu islands, blocks off the very rough (*peng* in Chinese) waters beyond the calm and clear "lake" (*hu* in Chinese) formed by the sheltering embrace of the islands.

Free of any pollution, the Penghu seabed

offers wonderful views, winning it the reputation of "the Hawaii of Taiwan."

Walking on the Penghu's sandy beaches, you will be surprised at their wide variety of scenic charms. Apart from the different color sands, the beaches are noted for being flat and wide, fine and soft. In fact, the special qualities of Penghu sands have resulted in their being bottled as souvenirs.

The Penghu sun is too scorching to be

enjoyed. The northeasterly monsoon comes every year with the punctuality of migrating birds. The six-month-long monsoon leads to the islands being called "wind islands." This, coupled with the salinization of the land, makes it difficult for the islands to support trees. Many islands are without vegetation protection and are quite exposed to the sun. This makes the sky a particularly intense blue, and the sun casts its rays straight down on the islands with dazzling force.

Though there are few trees, huge cacti abound on the hills and slopes, creating a natural scene unique to the Penghu.

The Penghu Islands are not all about sunshine, beaches, sea waves and cacti. For the local people sea basalt is truly Nature's workmanship at its most magic.

Between 17 million and 8 million years ago, the earth's crust in the southern part of the Taiwan Strait went through a period of drastic movement. The Penghu happened to lie on a fissure in the crust. Lava surged up with roaring force and spilled out in all directions, layer after layer, creating elevations dozens of meters high. When the lava cooled down, it solidified into lava rocks (basalt) of strange and beautiful shapes rarely seen elsewhere in the world.

The Penghu Islands are China's only archipelago formed by lava rocks. The Lesser Paisha, Kishan and Dinggou islands have been proclaimed in Taiwan as protected basalt zones. Here, one will be surprised at the fissured, phantasmagoric stone pillars. Hearing the seawater beating thunderously against the basalt is like listening to the heartbeat of life.

Makung Island boasts the only town in the Penghu Islands to have streets. Blown by the monsoon for six or seven months a year, it is a town of low buildings, of only three to six storeies in the main.

Makung Island, seat of the county government, boasts Penghu's oldest street. The centuries-old "four-eye well" is said to have been dug by the troops of General Zheng Chenggong in the 17th centrury. Water can be obtained from all four sides of the well and, on an island where freshwater is scarce, the well is a blessing to local people.

Most of Penghu's early settlers came from Fujian on the mainland, where Penghu people have their cultural roots. Examples of this are the old sea-facing temples whose white walls, green tiles and upturned eaves embody the devotion and trust of people who make their living from the sea. (above)

Much of Penghu life is bound up with fisheries — both catching fish and pisciculture, too, as seen in this marine cage breeding area, which makes use of the marine environment to provide a natural environment for the farmed fish. (below left)

The Penghu Islands are notorious for their strong winds. The climate being dry and windy, hats do not give enough protection against wind and sand and so women working in the fields and by the shore, veil their faces, only their eyes exposed. (below right)

Go down along a stone paved road worn shiny by people's feet, as it leads into a smaller lane, you see huge red lanterns overhead, each bearing the words "First Street of Penghu" in brush calligraphy. This is the oldest street in Penghu and the place where its prosperity started. The "four-eye well" has openings on its four sides, through which one can look down on clear waters, and which appear on the water surface like the images of four full moons. The well is said to have been built by the troops of Zheng Chenggong (1624-1662), the hero general who drove the Dutch from Taiwan and restored the island to Chinese sovereignty in the 17th century. The island is poor in freshwater and the well still provides vital supplies to the inhabitants.

Head further down the winding lane, you come to the Mother Queen Palace, the oldest of its kind in Taiwan, where the Sea Goddess Mazu is worshipped. Over 400 years old, despite the fact that the paint on the pillars and beams has peeled off, and the weathered inscriptions on the stone tablets are too indistinct to read, the temple is still visited by worshippers and offers protection to the Penghu islanders.

Sitting right in the middle of the Taiwan Strait between the mainland and Taiwan Island, since time immemorial the Penghu Islands have been places of contention during times of war and a staging post for people fleeing wars and calamity. Over 700 years have gone by since the founding emperor of the Yuan Dynasty (1206-1368) established an inspection office in 1281 at Penghu, and many ancient military ruins still tell the stories of past wars.

Wang'an Gucuo is the most distinctive old street in Penghu. In southern Fujian on the mainland, houses were typically built with coral rocks. In the same tradition, Penghu fishermen brought coral rocks ashore, letting them weather and age before cutting them into building materials. The ancient houses, old windows, and aged stones used to build houses in this particular street tell the history of how Penghu people lived.

A particular type of wall in the fields deserves mention. Basalt or coral rocks are used to build such walls as windbreaks to protect farmland and vegetable gardens again the sea winds.

Years of history and culture have forged a uniquely strong culture and lifestyle. For centuries, Penghu people have retained the lifestyle typical of south Fujian Province. Despite the passing of time, many ancient rituals and folk traditions still remain popular today — for example, praying for turtles (symbol of health, wealth and happiness) during the Lantern Festival, the Sea Goddess Mazu's touring her land, and the deities welcoming ceremony. Family ancestral temples, found all over the villages, carry on family history and traditions.

"If you grow up in Penghu, you don't realize its good points; only when you've been to many places, can you appreciate how unbreakable are your ties to Penghu." This saying of the Penghu people, who seek to adapt to natural conditions in the most simple and sincere manner, made an ineradicable impression on me.

These "interlinked hearts" show a way of catching fish peculiar to Penghu. The stone structure, built with basalt or coral rocks, serves as a trap for fish and shrimp, which enter the inner area as the tide rises and are trapped inside when it recedes. This fishing method, which also attracts sightseers, speaks of the wisdom of local people.

## Number 5
# Nanji Island
## *A Miraculous Marine Life Park*

It was August when I went to the Nanji Island, a time of year when the island is at its most beautiful. It was around the time of the full moon and friends who had been there before told me that this was the best time to visit; that the seawater then was clear and blue, that it was the best time for lying on the beach listening to the waves and gazing at the round moon, or looking at the distinct water levels on the reefs at low tide and examining the richly colored shells. When autumn and winter come, the water turns a little yellowish and turbid. For most of the year, this part of the sea is influenced by the warm high-saline Kuroshiro Current and the cooler and less saline waters of the South China Sea; in winter it also comes under the influence of low-temperature and low-salt water from the northern part of the East China Sea. Naturally, the warm current from Taiwan and the coastal waters along Zhejiang Province to the west also affect the nature of the water. As a result, as soon as autumn and winter arrive, the number of tourists drops off and business people depart, leaving behind only some 2,000 locals who earn a living from fishing. Occasionally, scholars studying ecology may come for research. This is the time when the Nanji Island "goes into hibernation," quietly waiting for prosperity to come around again next summer.

The island whose shape resembles a galloping muntjac deer is the Nanji (South Muntjac) Island off Wenzhou, Zhejiang Province. Lying in the East China Sea, 30 nautical miles from the mouth of the Aojiang River, Pingyang County, the Nanji consists of 23 islands with a combined land area of 12 square kilometers. Because of its rich marine life resources, it has been listed as a national marine nature reserve.

The Nanji Island is a tourist resort with golden sandy beaches, blue seawaters, strange-looking rocks and intricate caves. Even more impressive is the natural lawn, as soft as carpet.

When I got off the ferry at the Nanji Island dock, I immediately rushed to Dasha'ao Beach, a stretch of fine and soft shell sand 800 meters long and 600 meters wide. It is the only sand of this type in China, indeed it is a rare phenomenon anywhere in the world.

The southern cape of Dasha'ao is the core area of the beach reserve area. Facing the beach is the famous Longchuan Reef. A kind of black-leaf sargassum, the only kind in the world, is found here at the core reserve on this reef island.

In 1990, the Nanji Island was among China's first batch of five national marine nature reserves. In December 1998, the area became China's only marine life reserve designated as a part of UNESCO's world network of bio-sphere reserves.

Tropical mollusca such as pearl oyster and tortoise-shell that are common around Hainan Island are not found along the coast of Fujian, but they do live among the Nanji Island off the coast of the more northerly Zhejiang. The strange thing is that these tropical mollusks cannot be found in the waters either north or south of the Nanji Island. Similarly, tropical algae not found in more southerly waters are present in the Nanji Island, but do not exist to the northern areas of the Nanji. There are many such examples, the reason lying in the fact that warm currents from Taiwan mix with offshore currents along the Zhejiang coast, making this region rich in tropical, sub-tropical and temperate marine life.

The Nanji Island boasts 403 kinds of mollusks, 174 kinds of algae and 397 fish varieties. Because of its unique location in the sea, the island is valuable for marine life research as well as an important data resource of northward migration of southern marine life and southward migration of northern marine life.

In the 1990s, a major survey was made of the Nanji Island, which found 421 kinds of mollusks and 174 kinds of algae. Of the latter, 19 kinds were discovered for the first time in Chinese waters and 22 kinds have been classified as rare species. Recently another four species of algae have been found. There may well be even more types of marine life to be discovered here.

While the Nanji Island is famous in particular for its mollusks and algae, it deserves equal acclaim for its beauty. What lures most holiday-makers here are the rippling seascapes, the natural bathing, a large stretch of lawn with an area of almost a thousand square meters, the grotesque reefs and rocks, nature's murals and beautiful fairytales that let your imagination soar. There is Bird Island that is packed with red-billed gulls in June, Snake Island and Wild Water Lily Island permeated with the fragrance of these flowers. It was here, too, that Zheng Chenggong trained his navy and where Mme. Chiang Kai-shek stayed when she visited Kuomintang soldiers stationed here. The place has even been selected as a national sea fishing base; it hosted fishing festivals in 2002 and 2004, drawing many fishing enthusiasts from Japan, Korea, Hong Kong and Taiwan.

The Nanji Island is divided into the Dasha'ao, the Sanpanwei and the Zhucaibaiyu scenic areas.

The large piece of natural lawn, the strange-shaped rocks, the thought-provoking natural murals and beautiful fishing villages are all at Sanpanwei

Island. This is the best spot on the Nanji Island from which to view the sunrise.

The island lawn is a magical thing; it looks like a man-made creation — as if meticulously cut and trimmed. It is green all year round and grasses are so densely rooted that it's hard to pull them out. It is strewn with rocks of various size looking just like grazing cattle or sheep.

There are two screen-like stones acclaimed as natural murals; the one on the left looks like a landscape painting — some people even see a meandering Great Wall in it; the right-hand stone seems to have life-like images of children, loving couples, fish and shrimp.... Close by is a rock 5.5 meters tall and 4 meters in diameter, and many more nearby whose shapes resemble those of animals and objects. Each one has an interesting myth attached.

Asking myself what particular aspect of the Nanji Island's beauty most impresses people, I realized that it was the beauty of natural mystery.

The sand is clean and soft; the seawater is so transparent that you can see as far as five meters below water. This is the wide and ideally situated Dasha'ao Beach, 800 meters wide and 600 meters long. The most attractive place on the Nanji Island, it boasts a unique kind of soft fine sand known as "shell sand," unique in China and very rare anywhere.

Number *6*

# Miaodao Islands
## *Immortal Hills in the Sea*

The Miaodao Islands lie between the Shandong and Liaodong peninsulas in north China, at the confluence of the Yellow Sea and Bohai Sea. The islands, including 32 islands and 25 reefs in the Bohai Straits, have a land area of 56 square kilometers and a coastline of 146.41 kilometers. They fall under the jurisdiction of Changdao County.

These bedrock islands were formed by the breaking and sinking of the earth's crust, producing grotesque terrain and varied topographies. Each island has its own charms. Wanniao (Ten Thousand Birds) Island is a bird sanctuary where migratory birds break their long journeys. The Greater and Lesser Zhushan (Bamboo Hill) islands get their name from their many bamboos, bringing with them a touch of southern China. Lesser Heishan Island is populated by over 10,000 highly poisonous vipers. Tuoji Island is a world of rocks in a dazzling variety of shapes.

The islands were settled over 10,000 years ago. Their long and colorful history and culture have produced a rich cultural atmosphere and historical relics in abundance.

# Number 7

# Putuoshan Island

## *Buddhist Realm between Sea and Sky*

Consisting of 1,339 islands and reefs, the Zhoushan Archipelago in the East China Sea is China's largest offshore island group, accounting for some 20 per cent of all the islands in China. A seaward extension of the Tiantai Mountains in east Zhejiang Province, the mountain chain was submerged about 8,000-10,000 years ago as a result of rising sea levels, creating what we now call the Zhoushan Islands. Ages of pounding and erosion by waves have left the islands with many caves. In both number and quality, Zhoushan's sandy beaches rank among China's best.

Putuoshan is the largest island in the Zhoushan Archipelago and Buddhism took root here in the ninth century, the late Tang Dynasty (618-907). Later, in the Song Dynasty (960-1279), it was dedicated to Guanyin, the Buddhist Goddess of Mercy, and became the world's largest site for the

worship of the bodhisattva. Long recognized as one of China's four sacred mountains of Buddhism, it attracts an endless stream of pilgrims. At its height, there were three major Buddhist temples, 88 nunneries and 128 shelters. The 19th day of the second, sixth and ninth months of the lunar calendar are three major Buddhist festivals, when the faithful congregate here to worship.

The island is a scenic resort too, with over a dozen sites of strange-looking rocks, dark caves, thick woods, ancient trees and sandy beaches. Whilst the West Lake in Hangzhou is reputed as the best combination of hill and lake scenery, Putuoshan Island has the best combination of hill and sea views.

Number *8*

# Dayushan Island
## *Epitome of Hills, Lakes, Grass and Sea*

Dayushan Island is part of the Fuyao Group off Fuding in Fujian Province. The island, 7.7 kilometers from east to west and 2.76 kilometers from north to south, has an area of 21.5 square kilometers and a coastline of 31.97 kilometers. The island has 36 bays large and small, and 20 hills of varying heights.

Fujian's highest island, it reaches 541.4 meters above sea level. At 400 meters above sea level, there are two natural lakes, about 1,000 meters apart. The larger of the two, at 60 hectares, is big enough for sailing; the other is about a fifth this size. Fed by their own springs, the lakes never run dry and their clear waters are sweet-tasting. The surrounding hill slopes are quite gentle, with occasional patches of reed plants. The green hills, blue waters and rocks together present a charming picture. There are tracts of grassland too, covering 600 hectares in total. These features give the island the name "magic island in the East China Sea."

# Linjin and Nanding Islands
## *Precious Legacy*

Off southeast Fujian Province, in the Zhangzhou City coastal volcano scenic area, lie two magic volcanic islands — Linjin and Nanding. Though small — one 0.16 square kilometer and the other 0.07 square kilometer — they are both testimony to the movement of the earth. Studies by Chinese and foreign experts have confirmed that the islands represent the most complete and best preserved ancient volcanic geological resource — a great rarity.

The two islands were produced by repeated volcanic eruptions during the Miocene Epoch, thus their basalt rock scenery (right page), ancient volcanic craters (above), sea-eroded lava rocks, huge volcanic necks, basalt cones, terraces, cliffs and caves are of great research value in the study of geological structures, ancient volcanoes, ancient geology, earthquakes and earth structure. Then there are the remains of ancient forests buried for 8,000 years, and fabulous sandy beaches. In 2001, this place became one of China's first batch of geological parks and the only marine volcanic park.

Number *10*

# Hailing Island
*Silver Beach in the South China Sea*

Hailing Island lies south of Yangjiang City in Guangdong Province and, with an area of 107.8 square kilometers and a coastline of 123.5 kilometers, is Guangdong's second largest island. At its center is a land basin and there are two townships, Hailing and Zhapo.

Zhapo's Dajiaohuan-Mawei Beach is a provincial Class-A sea beach, its wide, flat sands facing the sea on one side and screened by hills on the other three.

Gentle waves and breezes in the bay, coupled with fog on either side make it an enchanting spot. Of Guangdong's 14 scenic areas, this is the only area named after that of the sand beach.

The south bay has a 9,250-meter-long beach, known as the "ten-*li* silver beach," where clear waters caress soft sand. The pure sand beach, blue seawaters and stretch of green woodland set each other off to perfection, resulting in the accolade "God's masterpiece." □

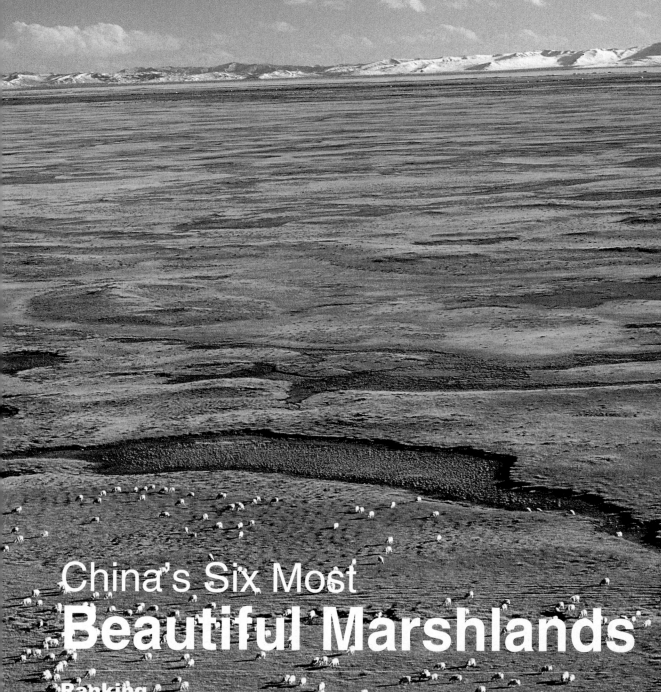

# China's Six Most
# Beautiful Marshlands

**Ranking**

1. Rogye Marshland

                       (Northern Sichuan and Southern Gansu)

2. Bayanbulak Marshland                        (Xinjiang)

3. Sanjiang Plain Marshland                (Heilongjiang)

4. The Yellow River Delta Marshland      (Shandong)

5. Zhalong Marshland                       (Heilongjiang)

6. Liaohe River Delta Marshland           (Liaoning)

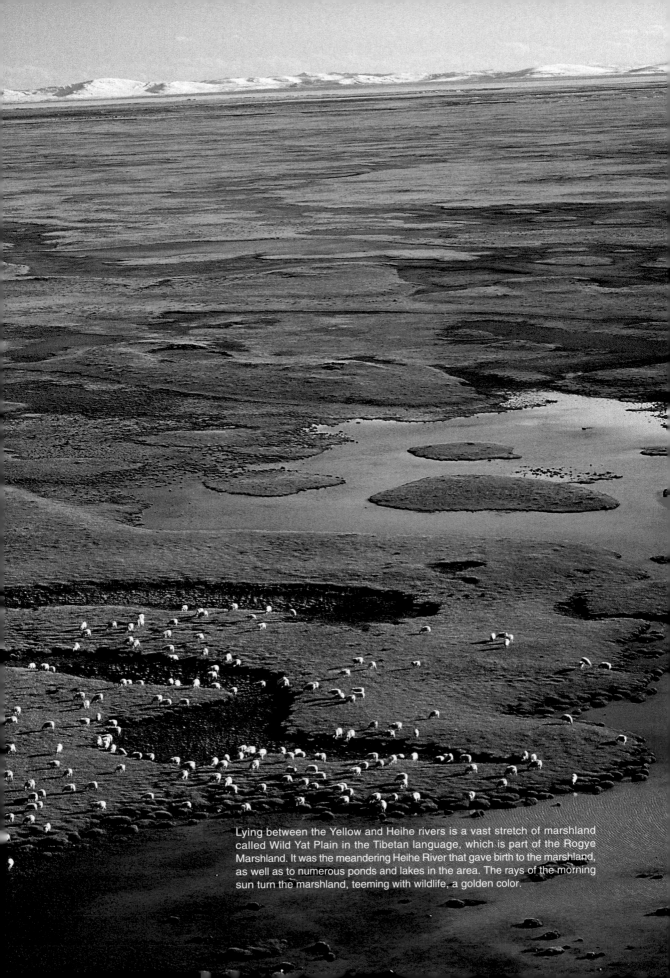

Lying between the Yellow and Heihe rivers is a vast stretch of marshland called Wild Yat Plain in the Tibetan language, which is part of the Rogye Marshland. It was the meandering Heihe River that gave birth to the marshland, as well as to numerous ponds and lakes in the area. The rays of the morning sun turn the marshland, teeming with wildlife, a golden color.

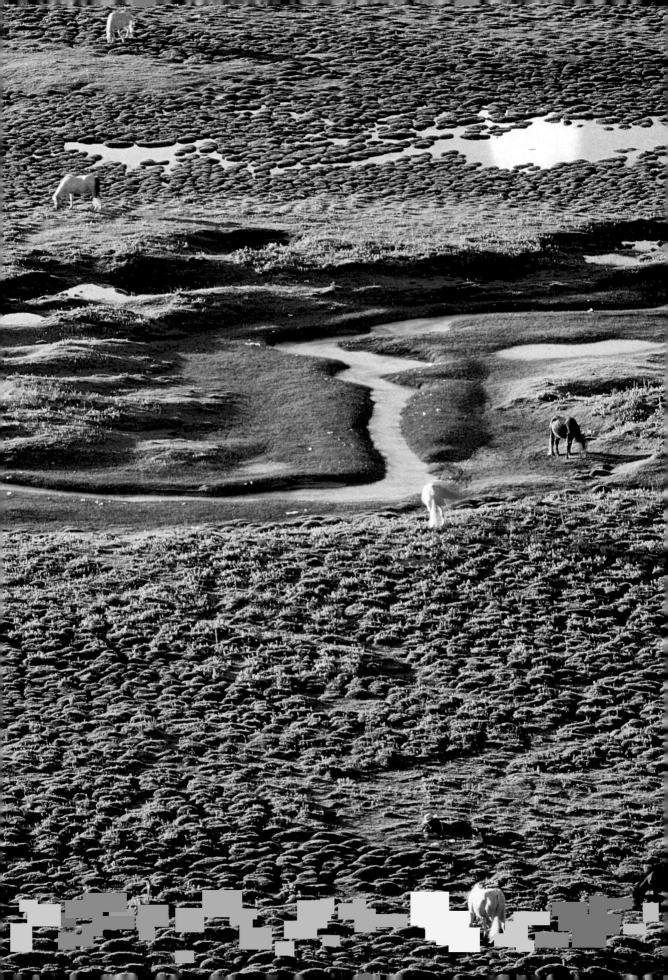

Number *1*

# Rogye Marshland
## *Jewel of the Plateau*

In the eastern part of the Qinghai-Tibet Plateau, 3,400 meters to 3,600 meters above sea level, lies what is acclaimed by international wetland protection experts to be "the world's largest, most primitive and best preserved wetland on plateau, without any human devastation — Rogye." Straddling Sichuan and Gansu provinces, and covering a total area of almost one million hectares, this wetland includes the Shamen, Rogye, Mandraktang, Sibcho and Garhe nature reserves. Typical of the wetland ecosystem in high and cold areas, it is a major base for preserving the fauna and flora systems and ecological diversity of the Tibetan-Himalayan area. It is home to some 900 black-headed gulls, birds under first-grade State protection and the only species that reproduce on highlands, spend summers here.

The Mandraktang Wetland plays an essential role in preserving the water system on the upper reaches of the Yellow River.

The First Bend of the Yellow River at Dangkhe looks tranquil and peaceful, silently gathering strength for its over-5,000-kilometer-long journey to the east.

Yaks provide meat, milk and fuel for the local Tibetan people.

Flower Lake in winter.

When winter approaches, the herdsmen
leave the grassland for milder pastures.

Number *2*

# Bayanbulak
## *Melted Miracle from the Tianshan Mountains*

In the Mongolian language Bayanbulak means "the source of fertility." This stretch of marshland in the bosom of the Tianshan Mountains is famous as the world's largest habitat for whooper swans. In this area of some 100,000 hectares, 2,300 to 3,100 meters above sea level, there is no clear distinction between the four seasons. Hundreds of thousands of other birds besides swans nest here in summer. Like silver ribbons, the winding Kaidu River and its tributaries float on this rich land of water and grass, with flocks of white sheep cropping the lush juicy grass. At dusk, the meandering ranges of the Tianshan Mountains crimsoned by the setting sun are blended in a harmonious whole with the Bayanbulak Marshland, also bathed in the golden touch of the evening glow.

A bird's eye view of Bayanbulak Marshland.

Bayanbulak Marshland is home to almost 200 species of plants. When the flowers bloom in the warmth of spring, the vast wetland is a sea of bright colors.

Bayanbulak Marshland has a cold climate, with a long winter and no summer to speak of. Snow-capped all the year round, the high mountains nearby are the source of water for the marshland. The sunshine seems purer and more dazzling over the white blanket of snow.

Each spring, the swans fly in wishbone formation from their winter homes in the remote south to Bayanbulak Marshland to nest. Because of their weight and inertia, it is common for these whooper swans to glide for 50-60 meters before landing.

Frolicking swans are dancing to the backdrop of this concerto of mountains, water and snow.

The vast Sanjiang Plain Marshland is thickly strewn with rivers and ponds.

China's Six Most Beautiful Marshlands

Number *3*

# Sanjiang Plain Marshland
*Lingering Magnificence*

The lowest plain in eastern Heilongjiang Province, the Sanjiang (Three-River) Plain embraces China's most concentrated and widely scattered marshlands. The plain came into being as a result of the alluvion of the Songhua, Heilong and Wusuli rivers. It has an elevation of only about 35 to 70 meters. Despite obvious signs of reclamation, its total wetland area is kept at about 1.04 million hectares. The plain is thickly strewn with wetlands of various types which undulate gently, and present richly colored wetland scenery, typical of the marshlands of northern China. The Sanjiang Plain Marshland is blessed with rich biological diversity, as it is home to 291 kinds of vertebrate animals and almost 500 species of higher plants. A number of nature reserves have been established there, among which the Honghe, Xingkai Lake and Sanjiang nature reserves have been put on the "Ramsar List of Wetlands of International Importance."

Lush plants grow widely on the Sanjiang Plain Marshland. The picture shows a banana plant and *monochoria korsakowii*, that grow in shallow ponds and lakes.

This low plain is China's largest fresh-water marshland, popularly known as the "Great Northern Wilderness." Walking through fields or marshes, and seeing oriental white storks, red-crowned cranes and other rare birds strutting at ease or flying freely between the green land and blue sky, I was often moved to tears by the perfect harmony of life and nature here, and from this I could feel the true beauty and tenderness of Mother Earth.

In March, the Sanjiang Plain Marshland is alive with waterfowls. Cranes, oriental white storks and whooper swans make the place their breeding ground, and some 100,000 to 150,000 wild geese and ducks use it as a resting place on their way to the north. Among them, bean geese and swan geese form the majority of the geese, and mallards form the largest group of ducks, followed by pintails, falcated ducks, greenwings, common pochards, tufted ducks and common goldeneyes.

In summer, the Honghe Nature Reserve is a world of water, with a bewildering number of ponds and rivers. Threading through the reed ponds in a boat, I could see pond lilies everywhere and riverbanks

(1) Water arums, a kind of perennial water plant, have flower-like green leaves and buds in the shape of horse's hoofs.

(2) The fruit of the broad-leaved cattail is called the spike of the cattail. The plant's slenderness, set off by the blue sky and green leaves, looks especially enchanting.

(3) Marshland with sedge clumps is a typical type of wetland on the Sanjiang Plain, and a unique marsh landscape. It is an oasis in summer, but in winter it looks as though there are myriads of lovely bulky penguins standing in the snow.

Marshland on the Sanjiang Plain makes an ideal herding ground.

covered with water plants. The water was lucid enough to see the bottom, with fish swimming merrily around and waterfowls chirping away.

In winter, the Sanjiang Plain Marshland puts on a completely different face. In March 2001, a snowstorm raged for two whole days. Braving the storm, and with a visibility of less than five meters, I hobbled along toward the wetland on the other side of Dalijia Lake, carrying my camera kit weighing 15 kilograms. It was a lonely

(1) There is a rich variety and large number of animals in the Sanjiang Plain Marshland. Tadpoles draw graceful arcs, and the cedar moss is clearly visible under the water.
(2) A grebe just out of the shell. Grebes look like ducks, but are smaller and have shorter wings. They often float on the water, and dive down into it to find food.
(3) White-naped cranes, under the State's second-grade protection, catch fish and insects in lakes and rivers.
(4) The endangered species of the Egretta eulophotes (Chinese egret) lives on fish which can be found in great abundance in the Sanjiang Plain Marshland. They build their nests and breed in trees and in reed ponds.

desolated islet covered with thick snow. The stream on the islet was also hidden beneath the snow, except for a narrow chink. Looking at the shrouded bushes, cotton-like snow and the winding river, I tried to find the best perspective for a picture. Turning around to change the lens, I found my camera box missing. A closer look showed that it was already covered with snow. I trudged through the knee-deep snow as I took pictures, unaware of how far I was walking. When I turned to look back at the way I had come, I found that my footprints had long been covered up by snow. My mobile phone and BP did not work in that area, and I was isolated from the human world. Having no sense of direction, I gritted my teeth and carried on, and after I don't know how long, I stepped onto firm ground on the other side when it was all dark.

## No Commanding Height on the Vast Wetland

On the Sanjiang Plain the green land stretches out to blend with the blue sky, making the ground a huge blanket. I could hardly find a higher point, for whenever I stood on a mass of tussocks, the surrounding area of a dozen square meters or so would sink with me. Scarcely had I got my camera set up and waited for the best light when the ground had sunk lower still. So I very often had to stand in waist-high or knee-high water to take pictures at level of the horizon.

In recent years, I have made a pilgrimage to the Sanjiang Plain Marshland every month. Once I fell into the marsh, and would have drowned if two local herdsmen had not happened to be passing, and pulled me out with a rope.

## The Homeward-Bound Chum Salmon

Among all the fish species in the Sanjiang Plain Marshland, chum salmon are the most special. They migrate from the Pacific Ocean to spawn in the Wusuli River in autumn. After their birth, they swim to the Pacific Ocean, staying within the area north of 350 north latitude in the Sea of Ochotsk. In the reproduction season, they return to the Maoniu Estuary of the Wusuli River of their birth. Every year around September 25 is the peak time of their return. Nothing can stop them from making their homeward trip, be it a riptide, dangerous shoal, waterfall or precipice. The water of the Maoniu Estuary is crystal-clear, and the sandy bottom lies less than one meter below the surface. Thus it is an ideal place for chum salmon to spawn, which they do only once, and then die shortly after. So their bodies can be found all over the riverbed and become nourishment for the waterfowls before their southbound flight. The fry also eat the dead fish, then float with the tide out into the Pacific Ocean.

Signs of reclamation are becoming more observable among the lakes and islets scattered all over the Sanjiang Plain.

# The Yellow River Delta Marshland

*A Land Created by the River*

The Yellow River Delta in modern times includes part of the Binzhou area and almost the whole of Dongying City in Shandong Province. With a great momentum, the Yellow River carries mud and sand along its way, and charges recklessly against its banks before emptying into the Bohai Sea, leaving behind it a newly created land — the world's youngest wetland ecosystem. Almost 300 kinds of birds make their homes here, a place called by officials of Wetlands International the "international airport for birds."

# Number *4*

This satellite photograph of the Yellow River Delta shows clearly how it is spreading toward the Bohai Sea. The mud and sand lines under the water are like blood vessels in the human body. One cannot but marvel at it after a closer look. The beauty of the Yellow River Delta lies right here.

China's Six Most Beautiful Marshlands

Number **5**

# Zhalong Marshland
*A Graceful World of Cranes*

The Zhalong Marshland is China's largest region where rare water birds, mostly large ones like cranes, are found. The lower reaches of the Wuyu'er River on the Songnen (Songhua and Nenjiang rivers) Plain provide water resources for the endless reed marshland, drawing tens of thousands of birds to rest and breed here. Possessing the largest number and variety of cranes in China, the Zhalong Marshland is also one of the places with the richest species of cranes in the world. Of the 15 kinds of cranes on earth, China has nine, and Zhalong has six, among which four are endangered worldwide. There are over 2,000 red-crowned cranes in the world, and Zhalong has more than 300.

(1)(3) Blessed with luxuriant reeds and an abundance of shrimps and fish, the Zhalong Nature Reserve has an excellent ecological environment for water birds, especially red-crowned cranes, to inhabit and breed. The red-crowned cranes have been referred to as "fairy cranes" since ancient times in China. Their elegant shapes form a graceful picture with the reed catkins.
(2) Frolicking red-crowned cranes only about a week old.

Covering an area of nearly 600,000 hectares, the Liaohe River Delta Marshland includes Panjin and Yingkou cities in Liaoning Province, where the Shuangtai Hekou Nature Reserve has been set up. This is a key habitat and a way station for migratory birds on their East Asia-Australia route. The endless stretch of its unique "red carpet," the world's second-largest reed marshes, and the wide variety of rare animals and birds, such as red-crowned cranes, black-beaked gulls and sounders' gulls, and spotted and common seals, are parts of a richly colorful wetland ecosystem. 

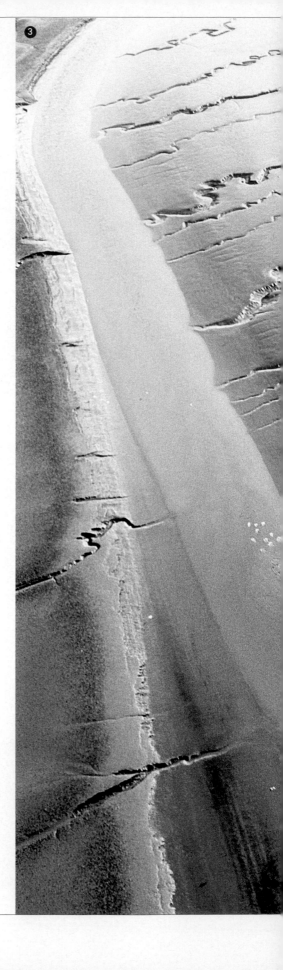

(1) A pair of snipes on a shoal.
(2) Here the endangered black-beaked gull has found a paradise for living and breeding.
(3) An aerial view shows a magnificent picture of a winding river heading for the sea through a vast expanse of red carpet.

China's Six Most Beautiful Marshlands

Number **6**

# Liaohe River Delta Marshland
## *"A Red Carpet"*

# China's Six Most
# Beautiful Grasslands

## Ranking

| | |
|---|---|
| 1. East Hulun Buir Grassland | (Inner Mongolia) |
| 2. Ili Grassland | (Xinjiang) |
| 3. Xilin Gol Grassland | (Inner Mongolia) |
| 4. West Sichuan Frigid Grassland | (Sichuan) |
| 5. Nagqu Frigid Grassland | (Tibet) |
| 6. Qilian Mountain Grassland | (Qinghai and Gansu) |

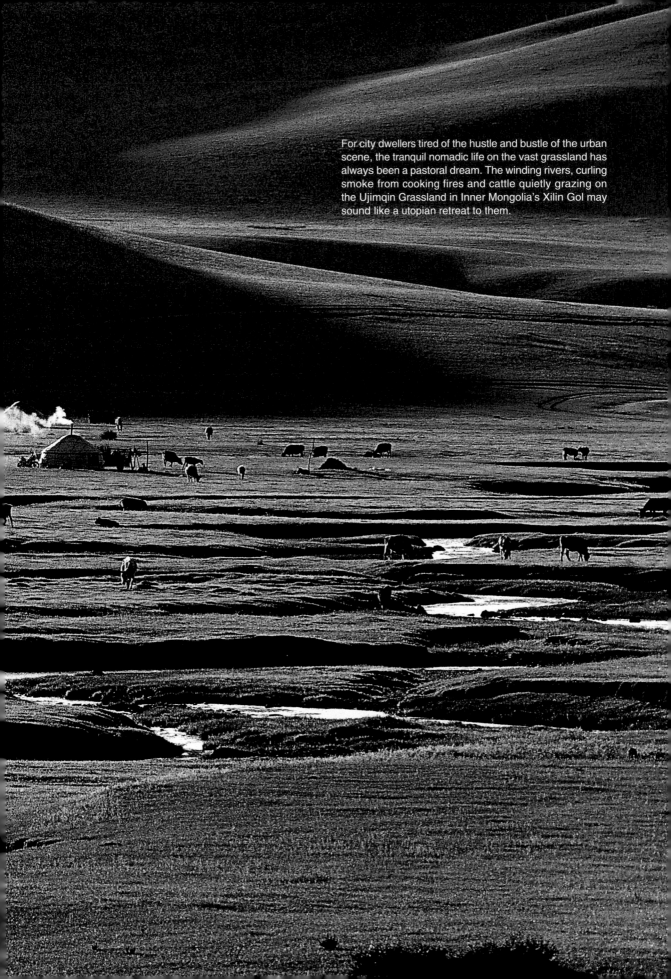

For city dwellers tired of the hustle and bustle of the urban scene, the tranquil nomadic life on the vast grassland has always been a pastoral dream. The winding rivers, curling smoke from cooking fires and cattle quietly grazing on the Ujimqin Grassland in Inner Mongolia's Xilin Gol may sound like a utopian retreat to them.

In summer, lush grass turns the land into a huge green carpet stretching under the high sky and white clouds. For the flocks and herds, it is the fattening season.

China's Six Most Beautiful Grasslands

Number *1*

# East Hulun Buir Grassland
*The Beauty of Harmony*

Standing on the vast Hulun Buir Grassland, you may feel somewhat puzzled at its boundlessness. The brocade-like clouds look so near — as if they were just a stone's throw away, giving you the impulse to catch them. Eagerly you jump up, and start to run. But you soon find that they are retreating at the same speed at which you are running toward them. A little disappointed, you stop and look around. Alas, in all directions you see the horizon in the distance. At that moment, you'll feel that, except for the sky and the earth, you are the only being in this borderless universe, and you can gallop freely like a horse without a bridle and grow vigorously like a tree.

Besides changing patterns of cloud clusters high above, this fertile land is also adorned with hundreds of silver chains and numerous pearls: The rivers and lakes originating from the Greater

Numerous winding rivers add softness and tenderness to the vast grassland, while bringing plenty of water and lush pastures to the nomads.

Xing'an Mountains that range across eastern Inner Mongolia and northern Heilongjiang. Rivers in Hulun Buir share one feature: they all dash down the mountains, but when they get to the flat terrain, they become mild and take their time meandering through the meadows.

The Mergel Gol River in Chen Barag Banner is said to have "the most bends on earth," but the Yimin River, which runs from Ewenki Banner into

Wrestling has been a traditional sport of the Mongols since at least the 13th century. At the Nadam fair, held once a year, the nomads compete in horse racing, wrestling and archery. The winners of these contests are renowned far and wide on the grasslands.

the city of Hailar, has even more bends. Looking down from an airplane, you'll see that the upper reaches of the Yimin River form a pattern of tortuous ribbons. The flat terrain enables the rivers to linger on as long as they wish, nurturing the land on both banks and supporting the numerous flocks and herds of Hulun Buir.

The Hulun Nur ("nur" means "lake" in Mongolian), on the Orxon Gol River, is the fifth-largest freshwater lake in China. Covering 2,339 square kilometers, the lake is also referred to by the Mongols as a "dalai (sea)." Also on the Orxon Gol River but upstream in the south is Buir Nur, the boundary lake between China and Mongolia. When spring comes, shoals of fish in the Buir Nur will swim downstream along the Orxon Gol River to lay their eggs in the Hulun Nur.

Between the two lakes is the Dalai Lake Nature Reserve. The abundant food and high reeds here have made the large marshes an ideal habitat for birds and an important stopping-off place on their migration route.

In spring, thousands of white swans hover in the sky here; in summer, flocks of cranes, egrets and storks gather; and in autumn, wild geese fly over in tight formations to their havens in the south.

The Ergun River in Chen Barag Banner flows north, forming part of the boundary between China and Russia. On the way, the 700-kilometer-long watercourse is joined by other smaller ones flowing across the Hulun Buir Grassland, and plunges through deep valleys and past precipitous cliffs in the Greater Xing'an Mountains, before joining the Heilong River and emptying into the sea.

Rich water resources have brought vitality and vigor to Hulun Buir, and more than 600 kinds of high grassland plants, including *aneurolepidium chinense*, *stipa baicalensis*, *stipa capillata* and *filifolium sibiricum*, make it one of the richest grasslands in the world. "The sky is blue, the land

The flourishing flowers are a particular attraction of the grassland. In July and August, the grasslands are covered with blue balloon flowers, white edelweiss and garden burnet — it is truly a feast for the eyes.

is vast, the cattle stand out when the grass bends in the wind" — this depiction of the prairie in an ancient folk song is still alive in Hulun Buir today.

Summer is the most spectacular season on the grassland: Green waves of grass wave in the wind, larks sing by the waters, and blue butterflies dance on the petals of the flowers, forming a peaceful and harmonious scene in which horses and sheep

The *leleche* (light wooden cart) is a traditional vehicle on the grassland. Since ancient times, these carts have carried the nomads from summer camps to winter pastures. The carts are equipped with awnings, water vats, cowhide bags and iron kettles. They are also used to store grain and meat.

graze serenely.

The birds fly over, leaving no trace of their passage in the sky; the grass thrives and withers every year, leaving no trace of change on the prairie. However, the legends about the prairie are alive in the memories of the local people. Hulun Buir, the cradle of the Mongols, was also a realm of the Xianbei people in the 4th-6th centuries. Ancient spearheads and the ruins of the fief of one brother of Genghis Khan, who founded the Yuan empire in the 13th century, all tell stories of war.

Today, also living on the grassland are the descendents of the Daur and Ewenki peoples, who used to hunt in the nearby forests, and Russian-Chinese families. The traditional ceremony of building *aobao* (cairns) and the Nadam fair held in Xin Barag Left Banner and Xin Barag Right Banner, and the summer carnival and winter Nadam fair held in the Ewenki Autonomous Banner are all grand events on the grassland. Wrestling matches, sled, horse and camel races, and dairy and lamb delicacies will feast both the eyes and stomachs of everybody.

Hulun Buir offers charming attractions all year round.

Extending 100 kilometers along the Tianshan Valley, the Tangbula Grassland is known for its 113 ravines. Tangbula is not a typical grassland: Rather than being flat and wide, it is like a long green corridor, with numerous spruce trees scattered in the thick grass.

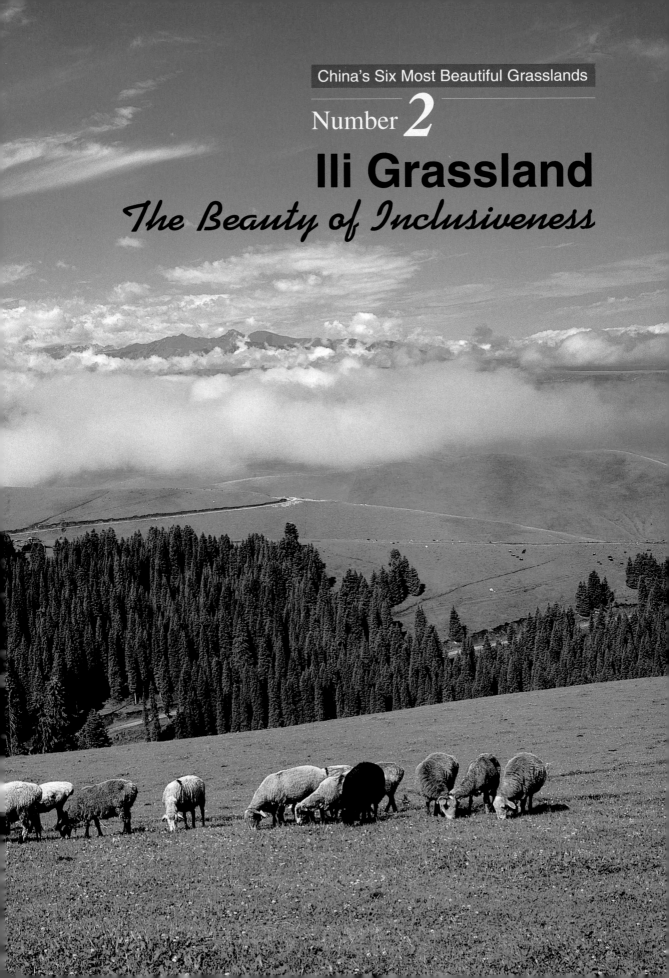

China's Six Most Beautiful Grasslands

Number **2**

# Ili Grassland
*The Beauty of Inclusiveness*

The Zhaosu Grassland, some 2,000-3,000 meters above sea level, is located on the lower slopes of the Tianshan range. With the surrounding majestic peaks, tall spruce trees, golden rape flowers, white yurts and galloping herds of horses, this grassland resembles a gorgeous painting.

The Ili Grassland lies in a fold of the Tianshan Mountains, one of the largest mountain ranges in Asia. Surrounded by ridges on three sides, it is open on the west to humid currents of air. Thanks to this moisture, a vertical division of grassland belts has been formed ranging through frigid meadows, montane meadows, montane meadow steppe, montane steppe, montane desert steppe, plain desert and river valley meadows.

The Ili Grassland boasts fertile soil and a mild, humid climate, with more rainfall in the mountains than in the river valley. The average annual temperature is 8-9 degrees centigrade, ideal for both pasturing and farming. Between the plain and the mountains are scattered barren desert, grassland, meadow, bush and forest areas. In winter, the herdsmen usually tend their cattle on the plain and in the desert; in spring they move to the mountain slopes; in summer, they go higher to the alpine meadows; and in autumn, they return to the lowlands.

While the Gobi occupies a vast area of southern Xinjiang, grasslands and forests are the main

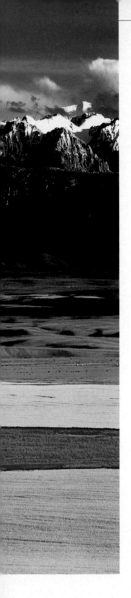

features of the landscape in the north. Ili is famous for the beauty of its mountains and rivers, woods and meadows.

Narat, Künes, Zhaosu and Tangbula are the four major grassland areas in Ili.

Unlike the grasslands in Inner Mongolia, their counterparts in Xinjiang are located at high altitudes, either on mountain plateaus or slopes, or at the foot of the mountains, neighboring large woods and deep vales.

Narat is at a relatively low altitude. Stretching along the Tianshan Valley, it occupies a strategic position in the western part of the Tianshan range, and is a key transportation link between northern and southern Xinjiang. It's said that when Genghis Khan and his troops were crossing the mountains from south to north, they got lost. Suddenly, the sun lit up the grassland ahead for them. Soldiers acclaimed, "Narat! Narat!" (Narat in Mongolian means the sun.) Hence, the grassland was later named "Narat."

In Narat, you'll be fascinated by the lush grass, full-blown wild flowers, and vigorous elms, spruces and poplar trees. The wide expanse of flat land is strewn with cottages and yurts, and flocks and herds graze there.

The 11-million-*mu* (15 *mu* = 1 hectare) Künes Grassland is located at an elevation of about 2,000 meters, and is surrounded by peaks and ridges of the Tianshan Mountains.

Like all the other grasslands in Xinjiang, those of Ili are companions to snow-capped mountains. They are home to horses and hawks, and are like beautiful picture scrolls hanging from the towering peaks.

The Kazak people are said to live on horseback. Rising at sunrise and returning at sunset, they live a simple but happy life on the Künes Grassland.

Number **3**
# Xilin Gol Grassland
*Breathtaking Vastness*

The Xilin River is the soul of the Xilin Gol Grassland. The meandering river is like a silver ribbon conjuring up visions of the remote past.

Volcano lava is witness to the enormous geological changes which have taken place on the Xilin Gol Grassland.

"Xilin Gol" means "river on the plateau" in the Mongolian language. This grassland covers more than 200,000 square kilometers on the Mongolian Plateau.

One summer, we set off from Baotou, a city by the Yellow River, bound for Xilin Gol Prefecture 800 kilometers away. Tramping over the Yinshan Mountains, we saw the great Xilin Gol Plateau extending before me as far as the eye could see. On the way, we passed Ulanqab in Siziwang Banner and the Sonid Grassland. When we were approaching Xilin Hot, the grass by the road grew greener, and we saw a number of gray cranes and hawks standing by ponds.

To the east and north of Xilin Hot, the Ujimqin Grassland stretches far away. The terrain is flat, with numerous rivers and small lakes. While the Xilin Gol Grassland is considered the best grassland in China and even Asia, Ujimqin is the

The Mongols ride their horses wherever they go: setting out to pasture, moving from one camp to another, visiting relatives and attending wedding ceremonies. To them, horse is a sacred animal which figures in all their special activities: mare's milk festival, lassoing competition and horse racing, to name but a few. On festive occasions, the herdsmen will put on their holiday best, sing melodious songs and play the *matouqin*, a stringed instrument with a horse-head decoration.

To children, the extensive grassland is a paradise, where they can run and play as they like.

best of Xilin Gol. Heading from West Ujimqin to East Ujimqin, we knew little about the direction, and it was only by following the telephone poles that we finally got to our destination at Uliastai. The vast grassland allured us so much that we stopped several times to measure the soft grass with our feet. As we gazed into the distance, we saw stretch after stretch of grass extending to the horizon, and clusters of white clouds sailing toward us.

The most beautiful place on the prairie is the bend on the Xilin River, the soul of the grassland. Originating in Chifeng, the 270-kilometer river winds like a *kadag* (or *hada*, a long piece of silk used as a greeting gift among the Mongolian and Tibetan peoples) near Xilin Hot, a stunning attraction to people from far and near.

The *Leleche* carts have big wheels made of birch or elm wood. The simple structure is easy to build and repair. The 50-kilogram cart can carry loads of up to 500 kilograms across grasslands, snow, marshes and deserts. The vehicle is especially suitable for carrying yurts and firewood.

In late summer and early autumn, horse races and carnivals are held on the grassland at Litang, during which there is a spectacular display of tents erected by herdsmen from far and near.

China's Six Most Beautiful Grasslands

Number *4*

# West Sichuan Frigid Grassland
## *The Beauty of Changes*

As we rounded a bend on Mount Jianziwan, the view ahead suddenly broadened, and there was the vast Bumyak Grassland. Going further, we found ourselves in the county seat of Litang, known to the locals as "the highest town of the world." This is where horse races and carnivals are held every August, when the sturdy Khampa Tibetan men and their beautiful women show off their skills.

The Bumyak Grassland, with an altitude of 3,800-4,500 meters, is the largest in the central Shaluli Range in the Hengduan Mountains. Winding through the grassland is the Litang River, with marshes and meadows scattered on the sides. From June to September, this land is dotted with flourishing flowers, the best season of the year. The flocks and herds add beauty and harmony to the huge scroll-like scene.

The Sichuan-Tibet highway extends 100 kilometers along the north of the grassland. While enjoying the pleasant scenery, we drove up 4,999-meter-high Mount Haizi. Standing on a mountain col and looking at the vast land, the dreamscape made us reluctant to leave.

At the foot of Mount Haizi is the Bachu River Valley, to the west of the Shaluli Range. The sharp drop of the terrain makes the river roar loudly and hides the highway behind woods.

Driving north some 20 kilometers from Tsola (formerly Yidun County), we arrived at the Tsophu Grassland.

The Tsophu Grassland is 3,800 meters above sea level. It offers a feast of beautiful scenery: blue sky, white clouds, towering peaks, temples and a lake among the woods, murmuring streams, grazing cattle, fluttering Buddhist sutra streamers and vapor curling from a hot spring.

The best of the Tsophu Grassland is the lake hidden among high grass and primitive forests. The erratic boulders scattered near the lake are relics of three ice ages. The Six-Word Mantra (om-ma-ni-bay-may-hon) carved on a huge rock are still clear despite erosion from the wind and rain. In the distance stands an old temple. An aged monk comes to feed the fish in the lake every day: an idyllic scene indeed!

While not as extensive as those in Inner Mongolia, the grasslands in western Sichuan have unique scenery featuring frigid meadows. Early summer is the golden season here. With rich plant resources, the grasslands offer ideal pasture for cattle.

# Number 5
# Nagqu Frigid Grassland
## *The Beauty of Sturdiness*

Nagqu is the name of a river in northern Tibet. Originating on the southern slope of the Thanglha Mountains, the river runs through Amdo, Nagqu, Biru, Sog and Baqen counties, where the land is vast, and low hills are interspersed with valleys. The abundant pastures and large numbers of cattle make up a grand plateau scene.

The best time to view this grassland is just after a summer shower, when the green land joins the blue sky in the far distance and the drooping white clouds float over the flocks and herds. As the tweeting of larks breaks the silence, hordes of Tibetan antelopes and kiang (wild ass) start a race on the pastureland, with their proud heads raised high.

The Nagqu Grassland, 4,200 meters above sea level in the Thanglha and Nyainqentanglha areas, is a typical frigid meadow grassland. On this vast no-man's land, there are numerous rivers and hot springs, and majestic icy peaks mirrored in the limpid lakes of Namtso and Serlingtso.

Nagqu is known for its vastness and iciness. The harsh natural conditions have also protected the grassland from human destruction, and maintained its overwhelming primitiveness, which often startles visitors.

The Nagqu area is mostly covered by wormwood. Only 3-5 centimeters high, the plant grows tenaciously in this cold land, with a well developed root system and a dense turf that covers the soil like a huge rug.

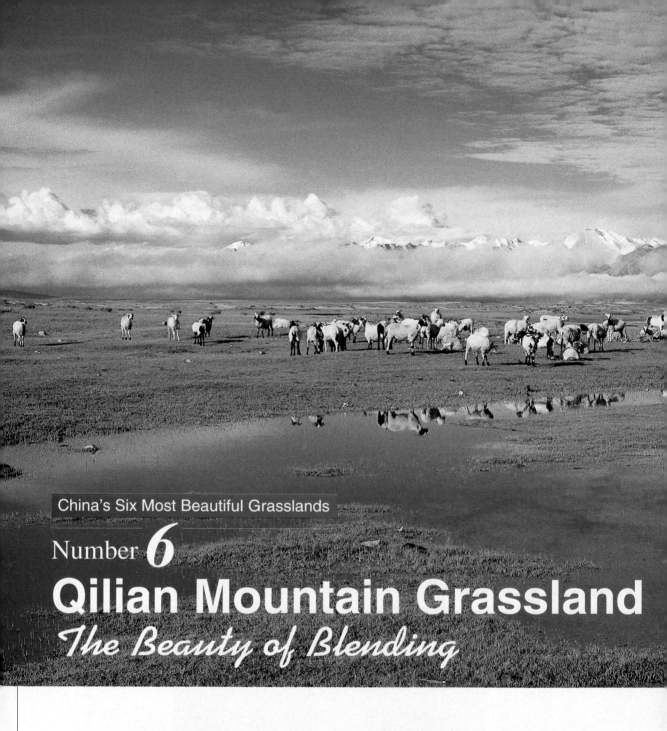

# Number 6
# Qilian Mountain Grassland
## *The Beauty of Blending*

About 570 million years ago, tremendous changes took place in northwest China. When the sea subsided, the Qilian Mountain Grassland arose.

"Qilian" is a term the ancient nomadic Hun living in north China used to refer to the "heavenly mountain." Today, the Uygur people,

the descendents of the Hun, still call Qilian the "heavenly mountain."

The grassland at the foot of the mountain has plenty of water and pasture. In ancient times, it was a grazing ground for the Hun chieftains and Mongolian nobles. Its distinct climate and good weather gained it the name of "golden lotus

The Damaying Grassland lies in the basin between Mount Qilian and Mount Nianzhi. In July and August, when the mountains are still covered with snow, the grassland is a brilliant green, and dotted with horses, cattle and sheep.

prairie" in the Tibetan epic *King Gesar*, and the Uygurs and the Mongols also call it "golden pasture."

To the east of this golden pasture is the Damaying Grassland at the foot of Mount Nianzhi. The slopes of the mountain are covered with dense forests and white caragana. Further to the east stretch the Xizhang and Dongzhang grasslands in the Sunan Uygur Autonomous County. When the yellow caragana flourishes in summer, the entire land puts on the color of sunshine, and the Uygur herdsmen rove about in this "golden sea" with their white and black yurts and their flocks of cattle. ▯

# China's Six Most
# Beautiful Show Caves
# Plus the Record-holders

## Ranking

1. Zhijin Cave             (Guizhou)
2. Furong Cave           (Chongqing)
3. Huanglong Cave       (Hunan)
4. Tenglong Cave         (Hubei)
5. Xueyu Cave            (Chongqing)
6. Benxi Water Cave     (Liaoning)

A huge stone curtain in the Furong (Lotus) Cave.

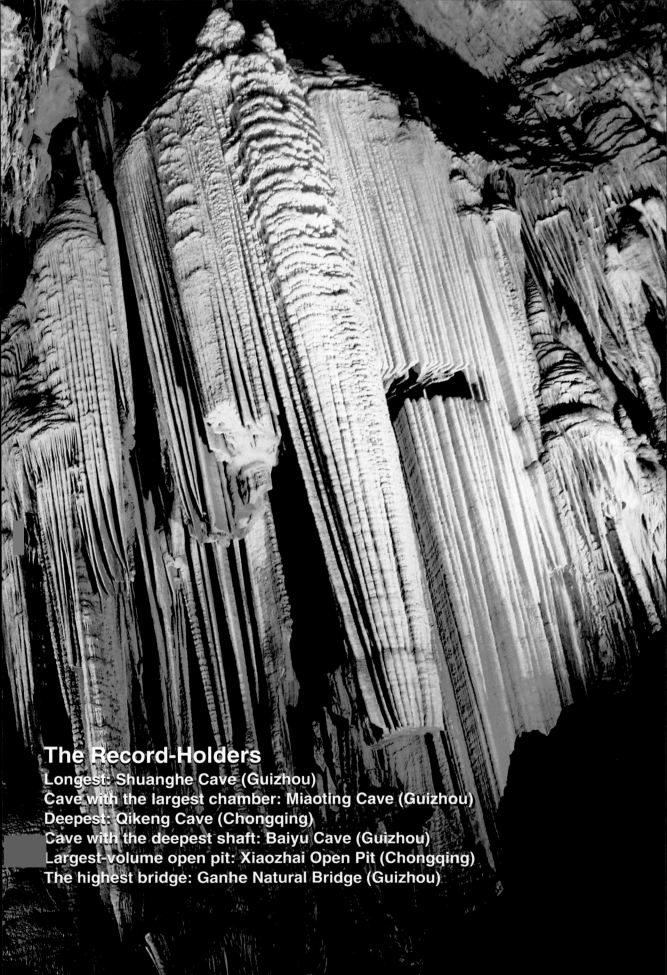

## The Record-Holders
Longest: Shuanghe Cave (Guizhou)
Cave with the largest chamber: Miaoting Cave (Guizhou)
Deepest: Qikeng Cave (Chongqing)
Cave with the deepest shaft: Baiyu Cave (Guizhou)
Largest-volume open pit: Xiaozhai Open Pit (Chongqing)
The highest bridge: Ganhe Natural Bridge (Guizhou)

**Highest Natural Bridge: Ganhe Natural Bridge, Guizhou Province**
The height of the arch of the Ganhe Natural Bridge in Jinpen Township, Shuicheng, Guizhou Province, is 121 meters, making it the highest natural bridge in China. Interestingly, running along the top of the bridge is an ancient highway which is still in use. So the Ganhe bridge can also be thought of as the highest natural highway bridge in the world.

**Deepest Cave Shaft: Baiyu Cave, Guizhou Province**
A shaft in speleological terms is defined as a pit down which a person can be directly lowered to the bottom with a rope — although the shaft may twist and turn. But a perpendicular shaft requires that the sky be visible during the whole process of lowering the person to the bottom. Based on this definition, the 424-meter-deep main shaft of Baiyu Cave in Panxian County, Guizhou Province, is the cave with the deepest perpendicular shaft in the world.

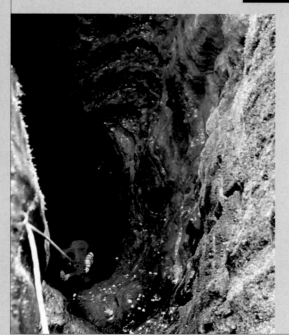

**Deepest Cave: Qikeng Cave, Chongqing**
Since the Furong (Lotus) Cave Complex was opened to the public in 1994, an international cave exploration team consisting of speleologists from China, the UK, the US, Germany and France has conducted large-scale scientific investigations, and so far has found 108 shafts in an area of 10 square kilometers. Among these shafts is the Qikeng (Gas Pit) Cave, which, 920 meters deep, is the deepest cave in China.

**The Largest-volume Open Pit: the Xiaozhai Open Pit at Fengjie, Chongqing**

Diameter, depth and volume are the three main measurements for judging the scale of an open pit. The Xiaozhai Open Pit at Fengjie in Chongqing Municipality is China's biggest open pit in volume terms, measuring 119 million cubic meters. So far it is still the biggest in the world.

**The Longest Cave: The Shuanghe Cave, Suiyang in Guizhou Province**

According to international convention, a cave's length can only be recognized after scientific investigation and measurement, so the holder of the title "China's longest cave" has changed many times. Previously it belonged to the Tenglong Cave with a total length of 52.8 kilometers, but from 2001 a caving team from the Fédération Française de Spéléologie started exploring and surveying caves around Wenquan Town in Suiyang County, Zunyi City in Guizhou Province, concluding that the Shuanghe Cave extended for 85.3 kilometers, making this the longest cave in China.

**The Cave with the Largest Chamber: The Miaoting Cave on the Gebi River, Ziyun, Guizhou Province**

Guizhou Province is a karst mountain region. With many caves and underground rivers, Ziyun County in Guizhou is known as "Place of Caves" and "Cave Classroom." Of all Chinese caves, the one with the largest chamber is named Miaoting Cave, located above the Gebi River in Ziyun. It has an area of 116,000 square meters, ranking second in the world. Taking a panoramic photograph of the cave has so far been impossible. This picture shows the clear and tranquil Gebi River.

# Number 1
# Zhijin Cave
## *The Dreamland*

China has the greatest concentration of karst topography of any nation in the world. It is so well endowed with caves across the country, it could well be called the "Kingdom of Caves." Now, nearly 400 caves have been developed as tourist attractions, accounting for half of the tourist caves in the world. That said, there is only one of them that enjoys four titles — "National Key Tourist Area," "National Geological Park," "A Top 40 Tourist Attraction," and "Museum of Karst." That one is the Zhijin Cave.

The cave is situated in the Bijie Prefecture of Guizhou, between the Liuchong and Sancha rivers, both of them sources of the Wujiang River. The first thing about the beauty of the Zhijin Cave is its colossal volume. Its entrance sits half way up a mountainside in the northeast of Zhijin County; it is bout 15 meters high, 20 meters wide, shaped like a tiger's mouth. But inside this ordinary entrance, lies a world of vastness.

At present, its confirmed length is 12.1 kilometers, consisting of four levels and five subsidiary caves, with a total floor area of 700,000 square meters — way bigger than Tian'anmen Square's 440,000 square meters. Its height normally ranges between 60 and 100 meters, but

There is a large and varied concentration of speleothems in the Zhijin Cave, many of them as superb as this one.

The Zhijin Cave is huge, unique and full of calcium carbonate deposits. The biggest of the 47 developed rooms, the Pervasive Cold Chamber, is a perfect example. It occupies an area of over 50,000 square meters, rich in calcium carbonate speleothems, including a precious, unique helmet-like stalagmite — Overlord's Helmet.

The Silvery-Rain Tree and the Overlord's Helmet that stand gracefully in the Pervasive Cold Chamber are the jewels of the Zhijin Cave. The 17-meter-tall "tree" is actually a stalagmite formed of petal-shaped forms. Research shows it takes about 150,000 years to form a stalagmite like this.

at its highest point of about 150 meters it is as tall as a 50-storey building. Furthermore, it cannot be traced how many collapses it took place over its long geological history to shape today's 12 splendid caverns and 47 rooms. Among the "rooms," there are five over 10,000 square meters in area; the biggest is called *Shiwan Dashan* (One Hundred Thousand Great Mountains). This is about 70,000 square meters in area — equivalent to 10 football pitches — but it is not open to tourists yet.

Zhijin Cave is not only large in scale but also rich in variety. The space formed by the roof and walls of the cave is sometimes conical, at other points arched, oblong, or square.... The 6.6-kilometer route open to visitors is in some parts deep and serene, other times it is lively and simple, as high as the night sky, or so low you could touch its roof; at times it is as wide as a boundless plain, at others as narrow as a valley path, as large as the firmament, as close as a canopy, as steep as a cliff or as flat as a field.

Unlike other caves which are normally rather empty, the Zhijin Cave is like God's treasure-house for keeping the world's most beautiful natural scenery. It has over than 40 kinds of speleothems, among them stalagmites, stelae, stone "pagodas," "drums," "shields," "flowers," helictites, and "beds." Nowhere else in the world has such a large variety or concentration of deposits. The Zhijin Cave stalagmites come in a great variety of amazing shapes — frozen mushrooms, flower petals, pine cones, pointed pagodas and helmets for example. The jewels in the crown are its two unique stalagmites, the Silvery-Rain Tree and the Overlord's Helmet.

Time contributes a lot to the beauty of the subterranean world. Scientists can deduce the relative climate, topography and environmental changes from speleothems. The Zhijin Cave is a

"There is no cave better than Zhijin." These words of the writer Feng Mu's are no exaggeration; it is a perfect combination of grandeur and grace, and when visitors stand here, they often feel it's a dream.

dry cave that lost its subterranean river long, long ago. Now people can only imagine what the river looked like. About 1.2 million years ago, the Zhijin Cave collapsed because of corrosion, erosion, scouring, seepage, and changes of flow volumes, eventually forming huge chambers. About 250,000 years ago, surface water no longer infiltrated into the cave and it became a dry cave, and gradually calcium carbonate speleothems began to take shape.

One intriguing thing was the discovery of a nearly 100-square-meter area of animal excrement and an one-meter-tall pile of hard thorns in a small branch cave on the second level of the Zhijin Cave. By isotope testing, experts have identified them as the remains of a group of extinct hedgehogs that liked cave living. Over 1,000 years ago, hedgehogs dwelt in this cave. They must have lived there for a long time to have left such "deep" remains.

The Xueyu (Snow Jade) Cave speleothems are predominantly "white as snow, delicate as jade." The Union of Speleology of the Geological Society of China established China's first cave observation station here.

# Number 2,5

# Furong Cave and Xueyu Cave

Near Jiangkou Town in Wulong County in Chongqing, halfway up the mountain, on the left bank of the Furong (Lotus) River, a branch of the Wujiang River there is a place called "Panjia Yan." This is the location of a "Vapor Cave" that gives off steam in winter and cool air in summer. All year round it is wreathed in mist, accompanied by a thundering sound. For centuries, creepy stories about this "Vapor Cave" have abounded and locals did not dare enter. In May 1993, several villagers braved to explore it with torches. One year after their first exploration, on May 1, 1994, this "Vapor Cave" was renamed the "Furong Cave" and was officially opened to tourists.

Entering Furong Cave for the first time, the first thing I saw was layer upon layer of silvery white stone curtains like clusters of clouds; below the stone curtains were tiers of stone "fields" and pillars like tall trees towering into the sky. What a beautiful scene... like a scroll painting. By a crystalline clear pool, calcites glittered under colorful lights; drooping down over the pond were two jade-like stalactites. This pool, one of the biggest and most beautiful speleothem pools, is called "Jasper Lake of Corals."

The opening of the Furong Cave was big news in Chongqing that year and immediately drew the attention of speleologists. Before it was opened, no one had found its natural entrance.

The Jasper Pool of Corals covering an area of 32 square meters, is the world's biggest speleothem pool in the world, 10 square meters larger than that of the Clamouse Cave in France.

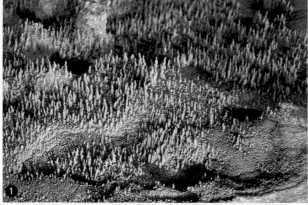

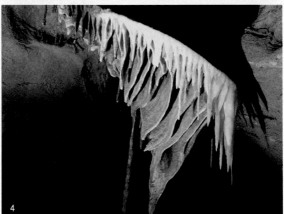

(1) Exquisite and rich in deposits, the Xueyu Cave has the largest-scale and most numerous pointed coral-shaped calcite crystal features.
(2) The world's biggest stone "flag" is about eight meters long.
(3) Delicate, transparent stone tubes and helictites
(4) Unique twin-color stone "shield"
(5) Snow-white stalactites

Later, an international cave exploration team carried out five large-scale scientific investigations over 108 days. They discovered a huge secret: that there were 108 perpendicular shafts within a 10-kilometer radius of the Furong Cave and that the Vapor Pit Cave, at 920 meters deep, was the deepest in China. And all of them were connected to the Furong Cave! They also found that the Furong Cave had more than 100 kinds of speleothems, a veritable cave science museum.

(6) Oulopholite is among the large variety of unique deposits in the Furong Cave.
(7) Flowstone dam and cave pearl
(8) Helictites shaped like reindeer antlers
(9) dog-tooth calcite crystal flowers

One day in 1997, during the Chinese New Year holiday, a retired official, Wang Chengyun, found a cave entrance near the Longhe Valley, 12 kilometers from Fengdu county seat. He immediately went home and invited some companions to explore it further. After two or more weeks' investigation, they discovered lots of white stalactites in the cave. They reported it to the local government and Professor Zhu Xuewen came to investigate it. Later, he gave a very high assessment of the cave's value in terms of tourism and of scientific research and named it Xueyu (Snow Jade) Cave. In the autumn of 2001, my friends in Fengdu invited me to visit the cave and Professor Zhu Xuewen volunteered his services as guide.

Torch in hand, I followed him into the Xueyu Cave. Everywhere I shone the torch was a staggeringly beautiful calcium deposit — a shimmering stone "flag," translucent and fine as a cicada's wings, snow-white stalagmites, a white and immaculate stone "shield" shaped like a penguin.... To me, caked in mud, their delicacy and purity was a reminder of teenage natural beauty.

In March 2005, when Professor Elery Hamilton-Smith, Chairman of the Special Cave Working Group of the International Union for

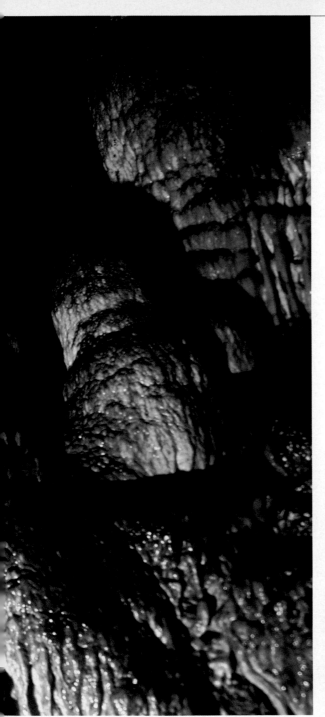

The stalagmite "Source of Life" with a total length of 120 centimeters and a perimeter of 124 centimeters, is one of the most famous points in the Furong Cave. Such stalagmites are extremely rare in the world.

Stone "shield" is a special form of speleothem. The "Snow-Jade Penguin" is a four-meter-tall snow-white stone "shield" — the "World King of Stone Shields." The lighting designer specially chose cold lighting to highlight and maintain its original color.

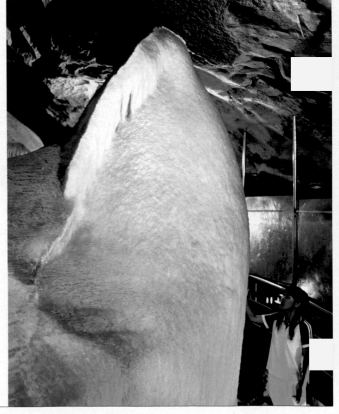

Conservation of Nature and Natural Resources (IUCN) visited the Xueyu Cave, he commented that of all ten thousand caves he had investigated, the Xueyu Cave was the most beautiful.

The Stone Field Chamber at Huanglong Cave, located at Suoxiyu Town in Zhangjiajie, Hunan Province.

Number *3*

# Huanglong Cave

The Huanglong (Yellow Dragon) Cave has many chambers and subterranean streams. The most fantastic of which are the Stone Fields Chamber and the Stalagmite Chamber. The stalagmite known as "Sacred Needle for Stabilizing the Sea" is unique in China. It is insured for a huge sum (although perhaps for publicity purposes) and is indeed a miracle of Zhangjiajie's subterranean world.

The Huanglong Cave is graceful, spectacular and has certain scientific research value. It has been sensibly developed and well protected.

The most amazing feature of the cave is its stalagmites. It is probably the greatest concentration of them in China.

The Benxi Water Cave is famed for its water scenery. Its underground river is over 3,000 meters long. With many twists and turns, it is named the "Nine-curve Silver River."

# Number *6*
# Benxi Water Cave

The Water Cave at Benxi in Liaoning Province has the longest boat passage of any show cave in China. The cave passage is wide, with fantastic views on both sides.

As a show cave with a subterranean river, the Benxi Water Cave is worthy of the title "Top Water Cave in North China." It is unique in the north of China.

The Tenglong Cave is grand and magnificent. It is the biggest of all the nearly 400 show caves in China. Looking inside from the entrance, you have a sense of its imeasurability.

# Number *4*
# Tenglong Cave

Before you even see the cave, you can hear it roaring. That's the Tenglong (Flying Dragon) Cave, located on the upper reaches of the Qingjiang River, on the outskirts of Lichuan City in Hubei Province. It first brings people a strong acoustic thrill. When I was two or three kilometers away from it, I could already hear a loud, insistent noise. At the entrance of the Tenglong Cave, the "400-kilometer winding Qingjiang River" suddenly drops, thus forming a waterfall some 50 meters wide and 30 meters high. Devoured by the "huge mouth" of the Tenglong Cave, the river meanders inside the cave for 16.8 kilometers, with a huge flow.

Of the some 400 show caves in China, the Tenglong Cave is amongst the largest, with a total length of 52.8 kilometers, second in length only to the Shuanghe Cave in Suiyang. Its entrance is 74 meters high and 64 meters wide. Inside, it reaches as high as 235 meters, with a total area of more than two million square meters, giving an average per capita living space of three square meters if Lichuan's 800,000 population decided to move in. The cave consists of five hills, 10 chambers and a dozen waterfalls.

Looking outside from within, the sky and stream seem smaller. It makes humans realize their own insignificance and the wonder of nature.

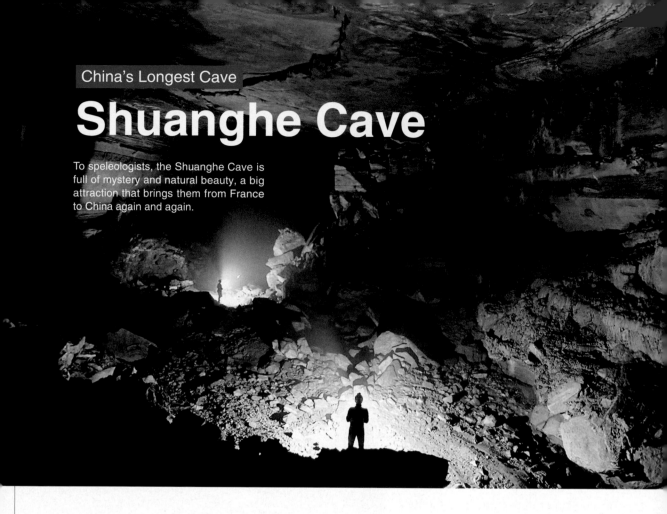

# Shuanghe Cave

To speleologists, the Shuanghe Cave is full of mystery and natural beauty, a big attraction that brings them from France to China again and again.

It was in the winter of 2001 that I came to Suiyang County and visited Shuanghe (Double-river) Cave for the first time.

The French cave exploration team I guided consisted of six speleologists, several of whom were world-record keepers on the depth of explored caves.

## Achievement Number 1: A 50-kilometer cave section mapped

It was raining when our car broke down on the way to Guihua. While we were waiting for help, I noticed there was a beautiful cave entrance not far away. Our tour guide told me, it was the Mahuang Cave and that a Japanese team had investigated it long time ago. It was not deep and not connected with other caves.

I need to explain here. A cave's life is, without exception, tied to that of a river. Shuanghe was originally a name for a surface river, so it was most appropriate to name the cave after the Shuanghe River that "gave birth" to it. The Shuanghe Cave has a complex cave system, and the Mahuang Cave, and some others mentioned later on, are all parts of this complex.

Going along a small lane, I entered the Mahuang Cave. To my surprise, the top of the cave had some marks of erosion, showing that it had been formed by water infiltration. And it had obviously been used by humans before; there were some big stones lined up to deter people from entering. We detoured around them and found some discarded cookers and traces of mining of saltpeter. I continued walking. The path was very pleasant; a gust of cool wind blew at me and water dripping from the roof of the cave left many long water trails. I walked a few hundred meters further on, as far down as the point reached by the Japanese team. Suddenly I had this feeling: the Mahuang Cave was actually really important and we should investigate it more deeply.

The next day, we went to the Hongzhaozi Cave — a typical water cave. At the entrance there are two waterfalls and the walls of the entrance have been washed to a shine. Because the temperature inside the cave is fairly high, the water evaporates and forms long-standing fog. Soon, we arrived at a shaft and we lowered ourselves into it. I found another passage half way down and we all went into it and continued walking. As we walked we could hear water somewhere. Then, turning a corner, we saw a tiny waterfall.

The Hongzhaozi Cave is a water cave where the water inside never dries, while the Mahuang Cave was created by the water that used to flow into it. Then where had the water in Mahuang Cave come from? And where does the water in the Hongzhaozi Cave go to? The Hongzhaozi Cave consists of three levels while the Mahuang Cave only has one passage. I guessed that the two caves must be connected.

The Shuanghe Cave is such complex and confusing place. At that time, we didn't know that it would be 85.3 kilometers long, the longest in China, the second longest in Asia and 20th longest in the world. All we had heard was that it was huge. One of the funs about speleology is that you can ask yourself questions, guess the answers and then go out and check them. But how could we measure such a huge cave? There was only one way, namely, section by section and solving the puzzle little by little.

So many questions put us into confusion, so we decided to stay in the cave for a while. After passing a huge, moist black rock, we reached a small cave within a cave — "Jiejie Hall." This is only 100 meters long and 25 meters wide, and doesn't look anything special. But it has seven exits. And it supplied the answers. The subterranean stream in

Of course, the Shuanghe Cave's beauty is hidden deep underground. Without special cave exploring skills, you cannot enjoy it.

the Hongzhaozi Cave flows all the way here and cool wind follows it here too.

Jiejie Hall was the "Aladdin's Magic Lamp" for our investigation and we reaped undreamed rewards. That year, we mapped a 50-kilometer section of the cave, including the entire Huangma Cave and the 18-kilometer Hongzhaozi Cave, Pixiao Cave, Tuanduiwo Water Cave, Shanlin Cave, Longtanzi Water Cave, and also located the entrance of the Shuanghe Cave subterranean stream.

This underground maze slowly revealed its mysteries to us.

### Achievement Number 2:
### China's Longest Cave Identified

Exploring the Shuanghe Cave was no easy matter. Sometimes, the floor was very muddy and slippery, and you could easily fall and get muddy all over; at places we had to go on all fours; at places, we would get stuck in narrow passages, unable to move forward or back; sometimes, we were up to our necks in cold water and practically had to swim to get across.

Despite the many difficulties encountered, we felt very satisfied. It is such a different cave — most

The Shanlin Cave being measured by the French Shuanghe Cave exploration team from the Fédération Française de Spéléologie. The team included several cave depth world-record keepers.

stalagmites had disappeared a long time ago.

We managed to climb up. We had thought ourselves the first to come here, but to our surprise, the ground bore prints of bare feet. These footprints seemed very old.

The spot was far away from the entrance, so I started thinking there might be another entrance, but on careful examination, my hypothesis was overturned. It's not unusual to see some footprints at the entrance of a cave, but the way to this place is not only long but also very complicated. So how did they get in? Perhaps there had been an entrance here previously that had perhaps vanished due to changes in the environment. I couldn't figure it out. I could only decide to leave these footprints as I had found them.

In the winter of 2003, we came to the Shuanghe River again, but with a team twice as large as last time. Among the team were experts on karst and cave species. There are many living species in the Shuanghe Cave, the most common of which is a kind of white tadpole. They merit further study by specialists. Apart from the usual speleological kit of

tunnel-type caves have only one entrance and one exit, but the Shuanghe Cave has over ten.

The Shuanghe Cave has some mysteries, too. Walking up from one exit of the Jiejie Hall, we found a small hall where there were traces that stalagmites had been stolen; if so it seems as if the theft took place in remote antiquity since the path up to the

"Safety First" is a first principle for all adventures, including cave exploration. The Shuanghe Cave team members prioritize safety and protection.

Like the Mahuang Cave, the deep Pixiao Cave is an important "communications hub" in the Shuanghe Cave system. This long passage leads to the beautiful Shigao Cave.

Going on inflatables into the Shuanghe Cave system is a delight. But if the passage is flooded, rubber boats don't work and exploration becomes difficult and for sure there will be no time to take pictures. So, every time we see the blue sky outside the cave, we feel excited.

ropes, boats, cables and electric drills, we also brought fishing tools to investigate aquatic life and colored dye to better verify the direction of the subterranean stream.

On our very first day of exploration, our truck again got stuck on the muddy road but, thank god, there were enough of us to push our way out. Finally we managed to reach our destination — Mahuang Cave. As soon as we got there, we carried out a simple test: we put some dye into the lowest reaches of the subterranean stream in the Mahuang Cave.

Over the days that followed, we kept our eyes peeled for any color change in the water of the Dayu Spring. Provided the dye appeared in the Dayu Spring, we could verify that water flow was what we had assumed. But we made a small mistake, using green dye, which is the color of most of China's rivers! As a result, when we saw it appearing, we could not be 100 per cent certain. Fortunately, we had installed some sensors, which told us the subterranean stream flows through under the riverbed of the Shuanghe River and comes out from

the Dayu Spring.

In 2003, our goal was to prove the Shuanghe Cave to be the longest cave in China. From a purely mathematical perspective, all we needed to do was to add together the lengths of all caves that were already known. The crucial problem was that the Pixiao Cave, Mahuang Cave and Tuanduiwo Water Cave and others, all developed in different geological ages. How did they connect with each other? We assumed the Longtanzi Water Cave's subterranean stream to be the upper reaches of the subterranean stream in the Tuanduiwo Water Cave. But this needed verification too.

The exploration packed in exciting challenges and unexpected surprises. One day when investigating the point where the Tuanduiwo Water Cave meets its branch cave the Shigao Cave, my partner and I tried measuring one section, but we seemed to be heading in the wrong direction. That night, after a heated debate, we mapped out all the caves that had been investigated and measured strictly according to direction and scale. Suddenly we discovered something new. The section that we had walked through in the wrong direction was right under the Darongdou Depression in the Tuanduiwo Water Cave.

Within the Shuanghe Cave Complex, Longtanzi Water Cave is the one with the greatest scenic value. The Japanese survey team had already measured it, but had not found any physical link between this and the Tuanduiwo Water Cave. Now, the other groups within our team had completed their tasks and found the connecting points between the Shanlin Cave, Hejia Cave and the Tuanduiwo Water Cave. So I divided the team members into two new groups, one starting from Longtanzi Water Cave and the other from Tuanduiwo Water Cave, arranging to rendezvous at regular intervals.

Nicolas and I started off from the Tuanduiwo Water Cave, heading against the current. At the beginning, the water course was wide and most of the time we could walk on the riverbank, jumping from rock to rock. But the further we went, the lower the ceiling became, until it was almost touching the ground.

In such circumstances, we could only go back and find another way. But there was no other way. If we wanted to go through, we had no alternative but to wade through the water. At the beginning, our heads were above water, but as we went on and turned a corner, there was just a narrow gap between the cave ceiling and the top of the water — so narrow I had to swim backstroke in order to breathe. Luckily, the ceiling gradually got higher. Ten or so meters on, I was completely out of the water.

On the riverbank, covered by black pebbles, I suddenly saw a brand new road sign! The group starting from Longtanzi Water Cave must have been here. Highly excited, I turned round and called out to Nicolas. Even more exciting was the fact that the person answering was not Nicolas!

It turned out that the group starting off from Longtanzi Water Cave had met the same barrier at almost the same time as us. They had concluded that it was not passable and had decided to turn back. But before getting too far, they had heard me shouting.

Nicolas soon caught up with me. The rest of the work was measuring and the equivalent of tourism. To our map of the Shuanghe Cave system, we added the link between the two water caves.

At the end of the 2003 expedition we came to these conclusions: the total length of Shuanghe Cave is 54 kilometers, surpassing the 52.8-kilometer length of the Tenglong Cave, therefore making it the longest cave in China. Furthermore, the Pixiao Cave, Dafeng Cave and Dadong Cave have a total length of 20 kilometers, but because we did not find their connecting points with the Shuanghe Cave, we excluded this length from the calculation.

## The Next Investigation Goal: 100 Kilometers

In 2004, our Shuanghe Cave exploration team had fewer members than the previous year and our first activity was in summer. Our goal was very simple: to find the connecting point between the Dafeng Cave and Pixiao Cave. To finish the work, we only needed to swim about 200 meters in our life vests.

In 2005, our task of discovering where the Pixiao Cave and the Shuanghe Cave converged was very complex one. The map shows that the entrance of the Pixiao Cave overlaps with the lowest reaches of the Shuanghe Cave, but there is an altitude difference of 180 meters between the two. Vertical investigation is always more difficult than horizontal investigation.

We tried starting from four sides of the Pixiao Cave. One time, we started with a chimney on the south side at the top end of the Pixiao Cave where we seemed to see a chink of light.

It was very hard to get into the chimney. As soon as we entered, we had to curl up so as to get

Apart from expert cavers, few people ever see the splendid scenery deep in the Shuanghe Cave. As a result, its ecology is well preserved.

into a second chimney, where water was flooding in from all directions. We got in deeper and deeper, clinging to the walls. Our urgent need was to find a small opening without water to block our way. Then I entered a small cave, at the end of which was a waterfall. With the help of my headlight, I guessed there was no more water behind the waterfall. So I passed through it, only to find another chimney. I didn't actually go to the bottom of the chimney, but I did see another waterfall at the bottom.

In speleology, we always avoid fighting against nature or waterfalls, because in the struggle between humans and water, the water will always win.

That was our 99th mission in Shuanghe. Later, we luckily found another longer route, avoiding the waterfall, and confirmed our assumption that one could get into the Pixiao Cave from there. But this was just one highlight in the process of looking for nexus points in this intricate network. Not until we did the 123rd investigation into Shuanghe did we complete the task.

Up to now, the meaured extent of the Shuanghe Cave is 85.3 kilometers long and with 27 entrances. At the same time, we found some more entrances, but because we could not confirm where they linked into the Shuanghe Cave system, we have a lot more work to do. We estimate that the total length of Shuanghe Cave might exceed 100 kilometers and become the longest in Asia (the longest explored and measured cave in Asia is in Malaysia, and has a total length of 109 kilometers). However, as the exploration continues, the work will get more and more difficult, so we need more and more free and capable explorers to dedicate themselves to this tough and expensive activity.

Cave exploration is not a profitable activity; its fascination lies in discovery. We shall continue in our exploratory endeavours. For one good reason — the Shuanghe Cave is worth the effort. ▢

The unique charm of Suzhou Old City after snow.

# China's Five Most
# Beautiful City Districts

## Ranking

1. Gulangyu                         (Fujian)
2. Suzhou Old City                  (Jiangsu)
3. Historic Center of Macao         (Macao)
4. Badaguan Scenic Area             (Shandong)
5. Shichahai                        (Beijing)

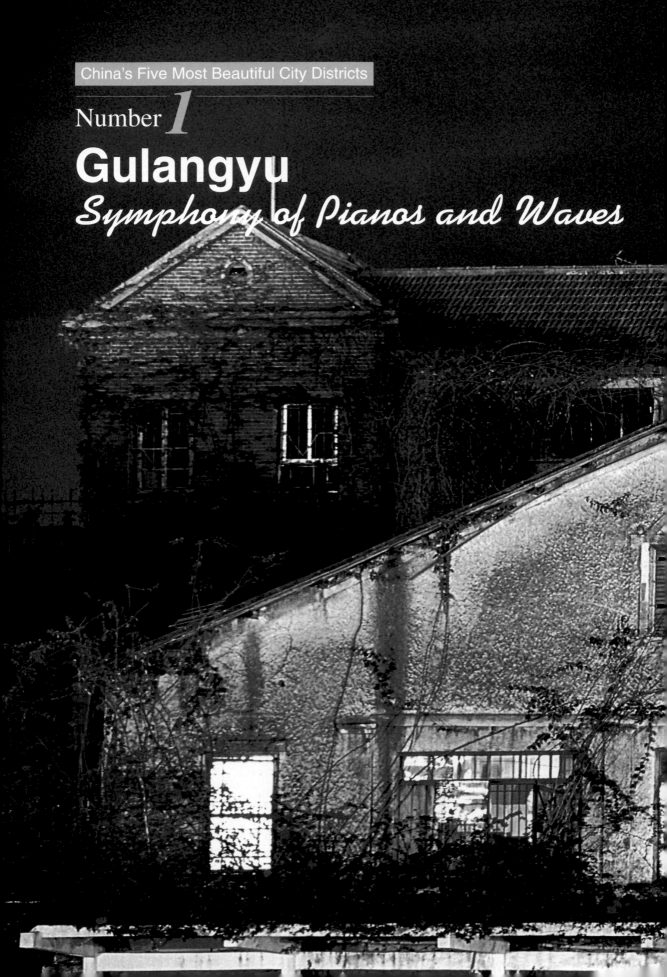

China's Five Most Beautiful City Districts

Number *1*

# Gulangyu

*Symphony of Pianos and Waves*

Many different architectural styles, both Chinese and foreign, are preserved at Gulangyu, Xiamen, known to many generations as the "Garden on the Sea." The islet has a population of some 20,000 music-loving people. With a rate of piano ownership among the highest in China, Gulangyu is also dubbed "Piano Islet."

Despite its small area of only 1.77 square kilometers, Gulangyu enjoys a great reputation. Separated from the downtown area of Xiamen by straits less than a kilometer wide, the islet is a scenic spot under the jurisdiction of Xiamen City, Fujian Province. Xiamen itself is a much bigger island and has been referred to as a peninsula since the building of a causeway in 1956. In recent years, a succession of cross-sea

the sandy shore, waves can no longer reach the Gulang Rock, but it is said that if you put your ear to the rock on a blustery night you can hear faint muffled drumbeats.

If it has not snowed for a long time, northern Chinese will long for snowy days. This is not sheer romanticism but born of their local environment. Similarly, southerners streaming with sweat in the intense heat will be anxious

Whether or not the day is windy, Gulangyu is always laced with waves. The famous poet Cai Qijiao compared it to a colorful many-decked ship, because the islet floats on the sea like a fantastic dreamland as if ready to head for the horizon at any moment.

bridges has been completed and these extend like tentacles in all directions. Seen from the air, Xiamen looks like a huge octopus or a brilliant sea anemone.

Most people mistakenly assume that Gulangyu (literally Drum Wave Islet) was named after the all-year-round drumming of waves; in fact, the name originated from the Gulang Rock in front of the Gulangyu Villa. In the past, on the incoming tide, the waves would hit on the rock on the reef beach, as if they were loudly beating a drum. With the seaward advance of

and yearn for a typhoon if there has been no news of one for some time.

Gulangyu is a completely pedestrianized area; even bikes are forbidden by law. The undulate asphalt roads spread out in all directions, turning the islet into a bewildering labyrinth.

Gulangyu has a resident population of about 20,000, but at weekends and holidays it can receive as many as 400,000 visits.

The islet has only one or two long avenues in the real sense of the word. The rest are meandering paths or confusing lanes, some narrower than others, but all tidy and clean. The few fallen leaves, flowers and fruits only enhance rather than detract from their idyllic appeal. In the stillness of the day, Lujiao Road in the former legation district, and Zhangzhou Road and Fuxing Road in the residential villa district, seem long and remote; at night, stretching far out into the dark, they look mysterious and unfathomable.

A network of mossy lanes threads between low buildings, single storey houses and grand black-tile mansions, comprising stone steps and brick paths, interlaced with asphalt roads. Some parts are wide enough for three women to walk back side by side from their morning exercise. The narrowest allows in just a palm-sized patch of sunshine, just enough for the lazy cats to bask in by the door.

Every footstep of every rare passerby is quite distinct; the sound of a leaf or two falling mingles with those steps in syncopation.

The old banyans stand slanting and the bougainvilleas' dense branches, tipped with brilliant flower balls, sweep down like long hair. Though there are no gorgeous "sprays of red apricot blossoms over-stretching the walls" as one ancient poet put it, there are loquats, longans, papayas, parambola and other fine southern plants, reaching over the high walls along the roads to delight the eye.

Gulangyu is best known for its wide variety of architecture. It is an overstatement to call it "a museum of world architecture" but it is an indisputable historical fact that the islet had a dozen or more consulates.

Among them are pure European-style villas. Although their vine-entangled portico columns and archways are now mottled and dilapidated, their exquisite lily carvings and magnificent classical Greek style can still be seen. The breeze gently sways the loose louver shutters, seeming to offer a glimpse of time back then... the fireplace, candlelight, fine porcelain, silver tableware and white satin dance shoes, carried away by the dance music on the phonograph....

There are the secluded grand residences of officials and of private citizens. In such mansions, the brass door knocker may be pitted and corroded, but it still sounds loud and true; in the inner red-brick-paved courtyard grow sweet-scented osmanthus, orchids and Chinese roses; water drips from eaves onto bluestone, worn and pitted over years and years. The long landscape scroll hung in the middle hall, the antique gold-traced celadon pot on the sandalwood table, even the shoulders of the old courtyard sweeper... all seem filmed with the dust of centuries, with the

Dressed up as angels, these little girls are real angels in the eyes of the people of Gulangyu.

Behind the exterior of every cool, deep old house, whether sumptuously adorned or simple, is concealed a true family history of overseas Chinese, who emigrated to Southeast Asia. Many such mansions lie long unnoticed, tucked away in the maze of paths and lanes. (right)

dust of history.

Hybrid Chinese-western style villas can also be found; in these the main body is Western, including a damp-proof basement with the last word in sanitary facilities, but the roofs have overhanging eaves and upswept corners, the door lintels are highly decorated, there are bow brackets and basket-shaped column capital. In the gardens, groups of fountains line up with rockeries and eight-sided pavilions. In the Bagualou (Eight Trigrams) Building, stylistic

elements from mosque, Greek temple, Roman church and classic Chinese architecture are combined; this now serves as the Xiamen Museum.

The names of those villas are really evocative. Just hearing names such as Yang's Garden (*Yangjiayuan*), Rich Old Woman's Building (*Panpolou*), Spring Grass Hall (*Chuncaotang*), Viewing the Sea Villa (*Guanhaibieshu*), Small Western European Building (*Xi'ouxiaozhu*), and Contentment Mountain Villa (*Yizushanzhuang*) conjures up a picture. The names indeed match the reality: every one of them, whether sumptuous or simple from the outside, contains a true family history of Chinese who emigrated to Southeast Asia. Many such grand old mansions, deep down in the paths and lanes, have remained hidden away for years.

Number *2*

# Suzhou Old City
*Antiquity in the Midst of Modernity*

The historic town of Suzhou City still stands on its original site, a rare phenomenon anywhere.

which had originally been part of private homes. Such classical gardens were actually the dream of a lifetime home to which the Chinese of old aspired.

I remember there were few tourists in the gardens back then, and all was very tranquil. The classical gardens were mixed shoulder to shoulder with common houses in the streets and lanes, so without guidance some were easily missed.

Suzhou is permeated right through with garden atmosphere. The famous gardens are few in number, but garden architecture has a solid popular foundation in Suzhou and you can find gardens large and small in the homes of ordinary folk  perhaps just a rockery or a tall and slender bamboo. The famous gardens grew out of Suzhou's cultural atmosphere and everyday customs; they are not transplanted products, the result of a pretended love of art.

Like an aristocratic family, a classical garden must have a history of at least a hundred years in order to be worthy of the name. The position of a grotesque rock or a water vat might change several times over a hundred years as the perspective, attitude and experience of the garden's owner changed over the course of his life, from innocence to sophistication, and back to naturalness.

The classical gardens of Suzhou are places where the heart finds ease. They are the perfect combination of ancient Chinese thought and life experience, of technique and economic strength. The saying "Up in Heaven there is paradise;

I first visited Suzhou in the summer of 1979. The city has thousands of years of history, so naturally appeared very old. This oldness gave me a sense of security; I felt I could trust its food like I trusted my old granny. And indeed I did enjoy many delicious things. I went to almost every classical garden open to the public, gardens

The classical gardens of Suzhou embody consummate landscape architecture skills. Little bridges and flowing streams, bushy trees and slim bamboos, grotesque rockeries and ornate buildings... everything about them represents the life ideals of ancient China and conveys the concept of "poetic dwelling" and what kind of world we should live in.

down here on earth we have Suzhou and Hangzhou" is not just words; it actually depicts the life ideal of ancient China. Like the temples of ancient Greece, the classical gardens of Suzhou are sacred shrines, and are the superb embodiment of Chinese thought. The greatness of Chinese thought lies in the unity of knowledge and action rather than in the abstract doctrinarism of pure metaphysics. It is a practical living world embodied in concrete situations. The gardens are among the highest manifestations of the philosophy of the oneness of man and nature. Conveying the most profound dimension of Chinese philosophy, they are good places for cultivating the mind and developing the character. At the same time, they are ideal places for easing the heart and living a peaceful life. Cultivating the mind and easing the heart is what essentially distinguishes Chinese from Western architecture.

The classical gardens of Suzhou demonstrate the concept of poetic dwelling. The poetry refers not only to little bridges and flowing streams, bushy trees and slim bamboos, grotesque rockeries and ornate buildings, nor simply to the arts of "borrowed views," but also indicates the fundamental meaning of human existence and what kind of world men want to live in. Modernists may be seduced by the process of modernization, but the real meaning of human life lies in ease of heart.

The classical gardens of Suzhou are the sacred shrines of Chinese culture. I describe those places, which were used simply for cultivating the mind and easing the heart, as such because they have transcended everyday life to become a cultural symbol and spiritual metaphor.

All of Suzhou City is one big garden, with little bridges and flowing streams, dwellings set off by green trees, combining to create a freehand ink painting.

The core of the Historic Center of Macao is the old city proper, where Chinese and Westerners coexisted in the past. It embraces more than a score of historic sites, many connected squares, such as the Senate Square and Cathedral Square, the A-Ma Temple and the Moorish Barracks. This area, basically preserved in its original state, boasts China's first Catholic church, its first Western-style theater, university and hospital. The picture shows Senate Square blazing with lights.

Number *3*

# Historic Center of Macao

## *Landing Point of Western Culture*

I take every friend that comes to Macao to visit the old city proper, namely the Historic Center of Macao. This area, recently listed as a World Heritage site, displays the history of Macao, and every brick and stone embodies the many changes packed into a fairly short history. This is harmonious Macao, where Chinese and Western

The Port Authority Building in the old Moorish Barracks by Barra Hill is a brick and stone building with both Arabic and Gothic features.

cultures have coexisted peacefully and given birth to a particular charming character, which is gentle, colorful, that puts visitors under its spell. Perhaps no other city in China gives one such a strong sense of harmonious combination of Chinese and Western cultures as Macao.

A combination of historical factors gradually turned Macao into a place where different cultures met and fused, and fostered its important role in the cultural coalescence between China and the West. That said, whilst praising this special cultural feature of Macao, let's not forget that this "cultural coalescence" was simply a byproduct of overseas expansion by Western nations. The decline of imperial China's status from being "the center of the world" to its sunset is clearly reflected in the mirror of Macao.

Strolling through the Historic Center of Macao is like crossing historical time and space. Stepping onto the Senate Square gives the feeling of walking over waves. Here, the paving stones, set out as waves, manifest the Portuguese fixation with the sea; it was the sea that drew them east, to achieve glory and fulfill their dreams. The splendors of the past have vanished like smoke, only the metal globe of the earth still stands at the center of the square. St. Paul's College was the first Western-style university of the Far East. "Men of outstanding wisdom," among them Matteo Ricci, Johann Adam Schall von Bell, and Ferdinand Verbiest, all set out from here to spread Christianity into China. But they failed in their mission to convert all the subjects of the Son of Heaven into lambs of God. The façade of St Paul's stands alone above the stone steps against the open sky. The A-Ma Temple attracts great throngs of worshippers. Endless devout believers come to offer incense and to pray for blessings. The temple is said to be the earliest building in Macao. When the first Portuguese came onto land here, they asked the name of the whole place. Thinking the foreigners meant the temple, the locals replied "Ma Kok," (which is how A-Ma Temple is pronounced in Cantonese) and the Portuguese transliterated this into "Macau." Macao also has other names, such as Haojing, Haojiang and Jinghai; Jinghai (Mirror Sea) is the most pleasant sounding in Chinese, conveying poetry and peace.

Possibly there's nowhere in the world as packed with churches as Macao; classicist, baroque, gothic and other architectural styles are all represented. The fine colors and poetic feeling of the beautiful churches of St Augustine and St Lawrence accentuate the religious serenity and solemnity of these places. Of Macao's many churches, the Rosary Church, in Renaissance architectural style, stands out as the most elegant. Like the name itself, its creamy yellow walls,

Wave paving on the Senate Square expressing the Portuguese love of the sea.

white cornices, green doors, windows and pediment exude the flavor and romance of southern Europe. From Penha Hill you can get a wonderful view of the sun, above a vast expanse of misty waters, slowly setting in the west and infinity of rosy clouds. You can lose yourself in the lush pinewoods of Guia Hill, listening to the wind and birdsong, imagining the mighty billows lashing at the shore below, and the first lighthouse in the South China Sea — a guide to vessels braving the wind and waves. Macao may be small, but this means that wherever you look there is something to see, a few steps in any direction will take you back into history.

In the parks, full of green trees and beautiful flowers, unhurried old folks play chess or enjoy the singing of their caged thrushes; gales of laughter ring out from carefree children at play; with the air of one with foreknowledge of everything, a fortune-teller sitting by the park gate points out to young people how to avoid mishaps and get onto the right path. The vibrancy of life and the lonely world of death are sometimes just a step apart. The lush green grass of the Christian cemetery keeps watch over the repose of the departed. Just beyond its walls are homes, restaurants and busy streets filled with the exuberance of life.

Macao is such an enchanting place that visitors forget to return home, charmed as they are by the tolerance and humanity of its cultural diversity, the poetry conveyed by its leisurely and easy life style, the simplicity and peace hidden behind the bright lights. In Macao, without having to dash hither and thither, you can really appreciate feeling free and relaxed, and be touched by the warmth of human relations here.

The photo shows Shaoguan Road in the Badaguan (Eight Great Passes) Scenic Area. The area originally consisted of eight roads including Shaoguan, Jiayuguan and Hanguguan, named after eight famous passes. These days there are 10 roads, crisscrossing to form a scenic area of several square kilometers.

China's Five Most Beautiful City Districts

## Number *4*

# Badaguan Scenic Area
## *Colonialist Scenic Legacy*

The Badaguan Scenic Area, where the roads are named after ancient Chinese passes, is a concentration of modern architectural heritage. Its buildings, with pleasing proportions and diverse styles, are in perfect harmony with the surrounding environment.

The Huashilou (Granite Mansion) is the most famous and the most representative villa in the Badaguan Scenic Area. Its architecture is of typical European castle style, integrated with certain Greek, Roman and Gothic features. Because of the materials used in its construction (granite and pebbles) the villa acquired the name Granite Mansion.

On October 12, 1898, the German Kaiser Wilhelm II formally named the Jiao'ao Concession downtown area as Qingdao, and went on to apply to Qingdao the late 19th century's most advanced European city planning concepts. The Badaguan villa area was a result of that city planning. Imbued with foreign flavor, Badaguan, this "museum of world architecture," encompasses nearly a hundred villas in different styles.

# Number 5

# Shichahai

*Fashion Close to the Seat of Power*

The 34 hectares of the Shichahai Lake integrates naturally into the surrounding street scene. Weeping willows along the bank and lotuses in the lake are special natural sights of Shichahai. (above)

The beauty of Shichahai lies in its unchanging ordinariness, simplicity and closeness to the common folk. For commoners living in Beijing, imperial capital for a thousand years, Shichahai was for many long years the only public space in the imperial city open to them. (right)

Nestling in a green valley, the Tibetan minority village at Rongchag in Sichuan Province is shielded by the mountains that guard its beauty.

# China's Six Most Beautiful Country Towns and Villages

## Ranking

1. Rongchag Tibetan Village (Sichuan)
2. Dayangjie Hani Village (Yunnan)
3. Tuwa Village at Kanas Lake (Xinjiang)
4. Zhaoxing Dong Village (Guizhou)
5. Wuyuan Village (Jiangxi)
6. Dayan Town (Yunnan)

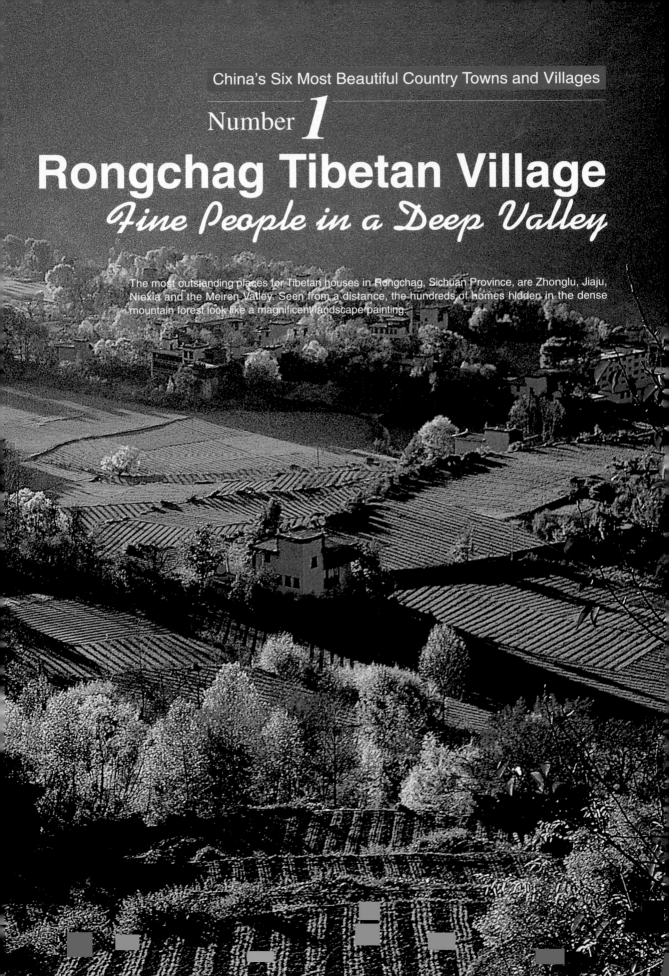

Number *1*

# Rongchag Tibetan Village
## *Fine People in a Deep Valley*

The most outstanding places for Tibetan houses in Rongchag, Sichuan Province, are Zhonglu, Jiaju, Niexia and the Meiren Valley. Seen from a distance, the hundreds of homes hidden in the dense mountain forest look like a magnificent landscape painting.

Rongchag Tibetan houses have L-shaped platforms on their second- and third-floor roofs, where grain is dried and the family can rest.

Rongchag County is located in Garze Tibet Autonomous Prefecture in the west of Sichuan Province. Five rivers merge here — the Greater and the Lesser Jinchuan, the Geshedra, the Donggu and the Dadu. The area is characterized by towering mountains, deep valleys and swift-flowing rivers. Scattered among the mountains below the snowline are Tibetan-inhabited villages such as Zhonglu, Pujiaoding, Dazhai, Jiaju and Badi with their own distinct architectural styles. The stepped-back red stone houses, shaded by many different kinds of tree, have a beauty beyond the ordinary. In front and behind the houses grow apple, pear and walnut trees, and in autumn there are just too many fruits to be harvested, so they simply fall to the ground. Sometimes, the sound of fruits dropping to the ground can be heard deep into the night. The villagers and nature live in great harmony here. Besides, there are many sites here in Rongchag that shed light on the mysterious past — including stone coffins dating from 5,000 years ago and, perhaps the best known, its ancient watchtowers.

Some contend that the people of Rongchag are descended from the royal family of the Western Xia (1038-1227). After their kingdom was destroyed by Genghis Khan, the surviving remnants of the royal family fled south across the Gannan Marshland and Hongyuan Grassland in Aba. One group settled in the Greater and Lesser Jinchuan river valleys, rebuilding the homeland of their dreams, shedding their noble sweat in this sunny land blessed by fine weather.

One morning, we walked east along the Lesser Jinchuan River to a place called Zhonglu. Most Tibetan villages were built near the top of the mountains, unlike Han Chinese villages that are usually located in the mountain valleys as close as possible to a water supply. This puzzled me. In a way, they had chosen the least convenient places to build their homes.

I saw women getting water from a river and then carrying the water jars home on their backs. The leather straps securing the water jars were crossed across the chest, cutting into their Tibetan robes and emphasizing their breasts. Bright beads of sweat rolled down their rosy red cheeks. Their legs were muscular and their delicately braided hair danced in the wind. Now and then, droplets of water would spill from their jars, these water beads like colorful butterflies. In the brightly painted houses, babies eagerly awaited their mother's return so that they could be fed. I even saw old women carrying heavy sand up the mountains, for building houses. The most important labor was not the building work itself, but the carrying of materials.

They were walking at such a pace that suddenly they were alongside us and just as quickly disappeared. Not much later, we met them again in the village; when we arrived there I discovered I knew nearly half the villagers already.

The Tibetan-style houses were scattered here and there, and cattle droppings could be seen on the dusty roads outside the wattle fence. Unlike in urban areas, here cattle dung in the streets was not considered dirty stuff, but rather a kind of

A typical Tibetan house in Rongchag has four stories. Domestic animals are kept at ground level. The second floor houses the kitchen and storage rooms. The third floor is reserved for bedrooms and the prayer room while the fourth floor serves as a watchtower.

The walls of Rongchag Tibetan houses are usually painted with typical Tibetan motifs.

display. Though the village roads were empty of people, the cattle droppings symbolized the village's vitality. The dung blended nicely with the land and looked rather clean in this context. Besides, the dung did not stink, rather it gave off a mixed sort of smell, combining animal droppings and plants.

Two lama monks in red robes walked towards us, carrying a large drum. They looked very young, and their shaven heads were showing signs of re-growth. I knew that a Buddhist ceremony was about to take place and so I asked them about it. The result was that they took us to the home of Yeshe Dorjie.

Though I had been to Tibet before, this was the first time I had ever been into a Tibetan family home, and so I was totally unprepared for their warm hospitality. Almost everyone smiled at us and I saw the glittering gold teeth of the old people. They received us with buttered tea and climbed the fruit trees in the courtyard to pick apples and pears and stuffed our backpacks with them. Only then did we realize the important decorative role of the red apples and yellow pears on the fruit trees across the mountains, just like festival

lanterns. Our host said that they had too much fruit for their own consumption, but that since the cost of transport would be more than the price it would fetch, so nobody wanted to send the fruit to market and it was left to rot on the ground. Lying there on the ground, there seemed to be a tie between the fallen fruit and the cattle dung — a relationship. In other words, everything in the mountains belongs to the same big clan.

A typical Tibetan house usually has a courtyard and four stories. The first level is for keeping domestic animals. The kitchen and storage rooms are located on the second floor. The third floor is reserved for bedrooms and a prayer room while the fourth floor is a watchtower. The area of the third and fourth floors successively reduces, giving space on the roofs of the second and third floors for L-shaped platforms where grain is dried and family members can rest. The structure of the lower part of the house is mud and stone, and the outside walls are painted white, or with stripes of white and primary rock colors. The upper part is a red-painted timber structure and the eaves are painted red on the upper part and black on the lower part. All the Tibetan houses looked more or less the same and so we often walked into the wrong house, but whichever house we entered, we were greeted with the same hospitality. This seems to be a cardinal rule in the village.

Every day when I sat down to write, I faced Mount Murdo, a huge snow-capped mountain, one of the most sacred mountains in the Gyarong region. On the far side of this mountain, "a journey of three days and nights," lies a mysterious lake, more beautiful than the famous Jiuzhaigou. But few people know this place as the road to it is very hard.

The watchtowers are military structures left behind by previous generations. They are generally between 20 and 30 meters high, and are a building form unique to Tibetan and Qiang

Zhonglu in Rongchag has the greatest concentration of watchtowers. In the cold wind, they seem very solitary; no one has conversed with them for ages. Their times seem so remote from today's modernity that they remain silent. Like time-proven heroes, they never boast of past glories.

ethnic groups; as a result they are widely distributed in areas inhabited by these minorities. But it is in Rongchag that the greatest concentration and variety of watchtowers can be found, providing examples of every architectural style. A careful visitor will not fail to detect history from the watchtowers.

The Shannan area in Tibet is said to be the birthplace of the watchtowers. Their construction went hand in hand with warfare, making Gyarong Tibetan area a key place for watchtowers. Most of the watchtowers in present day Rongchag are relics of campaigns fought along the greater and lesser Jinchuan rivers during the Qing Dynasty (1644-1911).

Watchtowers out in the wilds are usually village watchtowers, but the majority belong to individual households. As an integral part of the house, they witnessed the relationship between routine daily life and the life of heroes. In the history of Rongchag, life and warfare were one and the same. Between each individual household watchtower, a system of complex and responsive military defense works was formed; and when fighting broke out, the watchtowers gave the village settlements a new significance, turning them into imposing and impregnable strongholds.

There is a kind of harmony between the watchtowers and villages. They do not clash; the earth and stone watchtowers in tune with the fields combine perfectly, bringing into clearer relief the shifting relationship between war and peace.

Number *2*
# Dayangjie Hani Village
*Cooking Smoke Reflected in a Thousand Mirrors*

The misty Hani terraces are like a legendary fairyland

In the meandering Ailao Mountains, terraced fields cultivated by the Hani people lead up the mountainsides to reach the cloud seas, presenting a magnificent sight.

Standing on a high mountain above the east bank of the Honghe River, you will be swathed in the rolling magic cloud sea of the Ailao Mountains. In the brief gaps when the clouds disperse, you can see the Honghe River in the deep valley below, thin as a winding thread, weaving its way through the huge, naked-rock mountains.

Behind my back, a tape-recording was playing. Zhang Fa, a Hani priest, was singing a song related to the story of an ancient village god and his people that happened a long, long time ago. It seemed that with the singer's help, I was straddling the threshold between modern and ancient worlds, in contact with the ancient gods.

It was the fifth month of the Chinese lunar calendar, a time when the Hani people in the mountains had finished planting rice and were now welcoming the return of the God. The *peima* (Hani priest) is the busiest

person in the village at this time. When elders follow ancestral tradition by holding memorial ceremonies for the God who protects land, people, crops and livestock, the *peima* acts as an intermediary between the human and the divine; he uses long historical poems or short eulogies to call on and console owners of land, and sends best wishes both to the greening rice plants and to all the village households.

This place, in the heart of the Ailao Mountains, is called Dayangjie and is located in Honghe County, Yunnan Province. Its inhabitants are known as the Yeche, a branch of the Hani ethnic minority. The Ailao Mountains are an eastern spur of the Yunling Mountains, the watershed between the Hengduan Mountains in the west of Yunnan and the plateau in the east of the province. Moist warm air currents moving eastward from the Indian Ocean meet the barrier of the Ailao Mountains where they are transformed into abundant rain and fantastic cloud sea spectacles, moistening and nurturing the splendid terraces on the Ailao Mountains.

Yeche villagers, as with other branches of the Hani and the Yi minorities living in the Ailao Mountains, are usually located at mid-level on the mountain slopes. Higher up the mountain are forests and below are the terraced fields like stairways to Heaven, stretching from deep down in the river valleys up the mountain slopes to 2,000 meters and more above sea level. The terraces stretch their way, hugging the form of the mountainside, connecting several mountains together. The smallest terraces at the steepest spots are only about two square meters in area. Apart from the words of the *peima*'s songs, there are no written records to show when the Ailao Mountain terraces were first constructed. In any case, a project of this magnitude could not have been achieved in a day.

The rainy season was imminent, and the clouds massed in the Ailao Mountains were heavier with wetness. As the clouds moved lightly past, it was hard to tell if they were rain or fog. The fog had a taste to it — carrying the breath of all the trees, flowers and grasses in the forests. It carried sound with it too, of insects crawling among leaves, of little birds shaking their wings and of clear water dripping from ancient towering trees. One's vision, every human sense was mobilized in this dense fog. This was a place to move the soul.

Zhang Fa was still singing and the flames of the kitchen fire danced in his black eyes as he focused on one spot. I knew that the world he was seeing was from ancient history. Like the bards of the Homeric Age, Zhang Fa is, for the Yeche people, a priest, a singer, one who knows history, one with access to the divine. Through his songs, he tells the history of his people, his memories and his understanding of the world.

This was my experience in the Ailao Mountains many years ago. However, I did not have a real understanding of the content of Zhang Fa's songs until several months later. I made phonetic transcriptions of the tape recordings, invited Zhang Fa to Kunming and had the songs translated word by word by a Hani language expert. Once again the experience was moving and touching. This ethnic people that created these wonderful terraces have left mankind with more than just terraced fields and mushroom houses; they have also left their doctrine of respect for the land. Their teaching tells us that the world in the great mountain ranges is full of every kind of life. The God lives in the far off Heaven, while the *niha* (the Hani word for ghosts) roams the high thorny cliffs. Spirits who live between the God and the *niha* reside among the dense woods and streams of the deep shady valleys. The world of man is nothing more than just one part of this land, a land dominated by natural and supernatural forces. You know your own place in the world, and should also respect other lives including the gods, ghosts and spirits.

Hani homes are warm in winter and cool in summer. Because of their shape they are called "mushroom houses." Enchantingly beautiful groups of them dotted among the terraces look just like little mushrooms growing in the wild mountains.

Number **3**

# Tuwa Village at Kanas Lake
## *Sweet Home by Water*

Tuwa Village in autumn, as beautiful as an oil painting.

Over 1,400 Tuwa people live by the beautiful Kanas Lake. Before Kanas was opened to tourists, they lived in an almost isolated world. Some scholars believe the Tuwa to be the descendents of old, sick or disabled soldiers left behind by Genghis Khan when he led his troops west. The inhabitants customarily live in Mongolian yurts, but there are also a few timber houses in the village. Few tourists come to Tuwa in winter, when the snow-covered village appears like an ink painting.

China's Six Most Beautiful Country Towns and Villages

Number *4*

# Zhaoxing Dong Village
## *Homes Deep in the Clouds*

Zhaoxing Dong Village in Liping, Guizhou, is one of the largest Dong villages in southeast Guizhou. Known as No. 1 Dong Village in Liping, Zhaoxing has an area of 180,000 square meters, the over 800 households and more than 4,000 inhabitants. It lies in a basin surrounded by mountains and has one small river passing through. The serried stilted houses built on the hillside lay out in a pleasing configuration. They are all built of Chinese fir with blue tile roofs. The village has a theater stage, singing platforms and grain barns. Drum towers are the village's special feature. There are five of them here, looking like five lotus flowers scattered in five naturally formed villages called Ren, Yi, Li, Zhi and Xin — named after the five traditional virtues. (left)

The drum towers provide venues for the whole village to discuss and settle important matters, hold important festivals or entertainments such as singing and the playing wind instruments. A leather drum is placed in the drum tower. When there are important things to talk about, the drum is beaten by a respected villager to summon the villagers. There is a fire pit on the ground where a fire burns almost all year round.

# Number 5
# Wuyuan Village
## *A Sea of Golden Rape*

Wuyuan Village, in Jiangxi Province, stands against beautiful mountains and has a river running through it. It also has hundreds of ancient houses dating from the Ming (1368-1644) and Qing (1644-1911) dynasties, well laid out and displaying simple architectural elegance. These ancient Ming and Qing dynasty houses are typical of Anhui architectural tradition. The original shape of the village is well preserved, an accurate and complete reflection of its historical development. Spring is the most beautiful time in Wuyuan, when rape in front of the village comes into flower. The vast sea of golden rape, the white walls and black tiles create a lyrical picture of dazzling beauty.

Number *6*

# Dayan Town
## *Music and Thought*

The ancient city of Lijiang has a very special site. Here, every advantage of the natural environment is exploited to the full, making the town warm in winter and cool in summer, comfortable to live in. Its layout is special too — without enclosing walls or crossroads. Favorably situated, with mountains to its back and water alongside, the town enjoys a harmonious relationship between mankind and nature.

Is there any relationship between Dayan Town in Lijiang and deep thought? The small town, cooking smoke, brick and timber houses, gurgling creeks, bean-curd makers, copperware shops… there seems to be no traces of the history of thought. But in fact, thought in Dayan lies in its everyday life, something that exists but is not subjected to close scrutiny.

Dayan is a town of ordinary residents. People build it for living and life, not for leaving

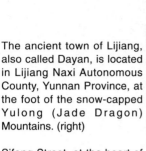

The ancient town of Lijiang, also called Dayan, is located in Lijiang Naxi Autonomous County, Yunnan Province, at the foot of the snow-capped Yulong (Jade Dragon) Mountains. (right)

Sifang Street, at the heart of the old town, symbolizes the ancient streets of Lijiang. (left page)

their names in history. Built for living, the town is warm, cordial, ordinary, equal and spontaneous.

The stone-paved streets shine glossy in the moonlight. The musty smell of mud and timber from the walls is closely linked with the earth. This town has experienced a hundred earthquakes.

You enter a deep courtyard, push open the doors and the bolts emit a squeaking sound. Some musicians have incorporated such sounds into their musical work. The sound evokes a sense of solemn ceremony. In fact, the Naxi are an ethnic group whose houses have no doors. Their homes are places for living. They live their world not behind closed doors, but out in the open. Dayan, therefore, is a town without walls, without barriers to keep it separate from the world. Its streets lead all the way to the corn fields, to the pine-clad hills, to the rivers....

The Naxi players of ancient music in Dayan are thought of as being able to communicate with the gods. They talk with the ancient gods, reporting to them on who is sick and who has just died, on disasters and bumper harvests, praying for forgiveness and happiness. On

enquiry I learned that they are teachers, tax collectors, cobblers, tailors, and leaders of a horse caravan...Their repertoire is not from well-recorded music pieces or from the national opera houses, but sitting among them are people like Bach.

Dayan is a living town. In his *Forgotten Kingdom*, Peter Goullart wrote: "Starting in distant villages early in the morning, the streams of farmers began to converge on Lijiang soon after ten o'clock, along the five main roads.... Shortly after noon the market was in full swing and was a boiling cauldron of humanity and animal. Towering Tibetans elbowed their way through the struggling masses. Boa villagers in their mushroom-shaped cloaks waved bunches of turnips. Chungchia tribesmen in their coarse hempen shirts and trousers, with peculiar little queues falling from their shaven heads, listlessly promenaded with lengths of narrow and rough hemp fabrics. Naxi women ran frantically after some wayward customers."

In 1994, I found that part of the scene described by Goullart still existed, but it seems now that all this happened a long, long time ago. 🗏

中国最美的地方

**主编出版:**《中国国家地理》杂志社
**出 品 人:** 李栓科

**发行推广:**
万信达文化传播国际有限公司
广州万信达文化传播有限公司

**印制:**
中华商务联合印刷(广东)有限公司
定价: 198元人民币
ISSN 1009-6337
CN11-4542/P

As a collection of China's natural and cultural heritage sites, this book displays China's wonderful lands and people. It is no exaggeration to say that it is a gift from China to the world.

—*Feng Jicai, writer, artist,*
*chairman of the China Society for the Study of Folk Literature and Arts*

This special book of *Chinese National Geography — Scenic Splendor of China* enables us to read the land as poetry.

—*Liu Xinwu, writer*

China boasts the most beautiful snow mountains and glaciers in the world but there were no aesthetic standards for them in traditional Chinese culture. This special book of *Chinese National Geography — Scenic Splendor of China* opens a new era for Chinese people's appreciation of snow mountains and glaciers.

—*Qin Dahe, member of the Chinese Academy of Sciences,*
*explorer, president of the China Meteorological Administration*

*Chinese National Geography* has done something nobody else has dared. Its editors have done an amazing job of picture selection, organization and acquisition. The book covers 114 most beautiful places in China. By any standards, it is a feast for the eyes.

—*Wang Jianjun, photographer*

Cherish our motherland.

—*Wang Meng, writer, former minister of culture*

*Scenic Splendor of China* displays the soul-stirring beauty of China. We should respect, love, and be a part of it, not allowing prideful human civilization to do it harm in any way.

—*Wang Shi, mountaineer, chairman of Vanke Group*

Since ancient times, we Chinese have regarded Heaven and Earth as the great beauty. Heaven and Earth comprise Nature — superbly crafted Nature. Today we have many female beauty contests, but *Chinese National Geography* has undertaken the creative and original task of selecting the best of China's beauties, to nudge man towards Nature and an appreciation of its majestic and beautiful landscapes. Armed with this outstandingly written and illustrated book, one can take a journey of the mind, or travel for real. In terms of sheer enjoyment and practical use, this is a good book!

—*Zhan Furui, president of the National Library of China*